T0326616

Qualitative Comparative Analysis

Qualitative Comparative Analysis

An Introduction to
Research Design and
Application

Patrick A. Mello

Georgetown University Press / Washington, DC

Library of Congress Cataloging-in-Publication Data

Names: Mello, Patrick A., author.
Title: Qualitative comparative analysis : an introduction to research design and application / Patrick A. Mello.
Description: Washington, DC : Georgetown University Press, 2021. | Includes bibliographical references and index.
Identifiers: LCCN 2021004429 | ISBN 9781647121440 (hardcover) | ISBN 9781647121457 (paperback) | ISBN 9781647121464 (ebook)
Subjects: LCSH: Social sciences—Research—Methodology. | Social sciences—Statistical methods.
Classification: LCC H62 .M38 2022 | DDC 300.72/1—dc23
LC record available at https://lccn.loc.gov/2021004429

22 21   9 8 7 6 5 4 3 2 First printing

Printed in the United States of America

Cover design by Martha Madrid
Interior design by BookComp, Inc.

For Tanja, Henry, and Mara

Contents

Boxes, Figures, and Tables

TABLES

Preface

As you begin this book, you may be asking what Qualitative Comparative Analysis (QCA) is all about, or what this method can do that other methods cannot. Or you may already know about QCA, but you are unsure whether you can make it work in your own research.

There is no silver-bullet method for all research inquiries in the social sciences. Yet QCA has several distinct strengths that set it apart as a method. Foremost is its ability to account for *causal complexity*. This means that cases are seen as configurations that entail various combinations of conditions (conjunctural causation). Causal complexity further acknowledges that outcomes can be reached through multiple, different pathways (equifinality). Conjunctural causation and equifinality both resonate with many of the social phenomena that we care about in the social sciences. At the same time, conjunctural causation calls into question the utility of exploring the net effect of individual variables without taking into account their interaction, whereas equifinality challenges the assumption that similar outcomes must be rooted in similar causes.

Another strength of QCA is the method's analytical protocol, which gives researchers the tools for *systematic comparison* across the included cases, while also taking into account the logically possible combinations that have not (yet) been instantiated empirically. The latter are so-called logical remainders, and QCA offers the tools to systematically address these and also to engage in *counterfactual reasoning* where plausible expectations about potential cases with certain characteristics exist.

Finally, QCA gives researchers generous *flexibility* in adapting the method to their own research needs. Surely, a certain number of comparable cases is required. But beyond that, the method can be applied in small-N settings of about 12 cases or it can be used for medium-N and large-N comparisons of dozens or hundreds of cases. This gives the researcher much more flexibility than with quantitative methods and allows for easier comparison of a large number of cases than other qualitative methods. Moreover, for the set-theoretic calibration, the method can equally draw on qualitative and quantitative data, and there are a variety of different approaches and variants to suit all kinds of research aims.

This book is designed for students and researchers in the social sciences. I am a political scientist with a focus on international relations. This may show in some of the examples that I am using, but I have also made an effort to draw on a broader repertoire of empirical applications. To foster this aim, I have asked a number of colleagues from sociology, law, public policy, environmental governance, political geography, political science, and international relations for reflections on their own QCA studies, based on their published work. I am grateful for their contributions, and hope that you will find the examples helpful when working on your own QCA applications.

Acknowledgments

This book emerged from working with QCA and teaching the method over a number of years in various contexts. When starting my PhD at Humboldt University in Berlin, Klaus Eder's research design course introduced me to Charles Ragin's *Fuzzy-Set Social Science*, even before I read his *The Comparative Method*. Looking back, I can see how these books had a formative influence on my PhD project, which later became *Democratic Participation in Armed Conflict*, and how they influenced my thinking about comparative methods. A series of QCA workshops followed, with Sigurd Vitols at HU Berlin; Claudius Wagemann at the Berlin Graduate School of Social Sciences (BGSS); with Benoît Rihoux and Carsten Schneider at the ECPR Summer School of Methods and Techniques in Ljubljana, where Ingo Rohlfing joined the course for a session on combining QCA and case studies; and eventually with Charles Ragin at the Institute for Qualitative and Multi-Method Research (IQMR) at Syracuse University. In parallel, I took courses on concept formation with Gary Goertz, also at IQMR in Syracuse, and on case study research methods by Andrew Bennett at the Oslo Summer School in Comparative Social Science Studies. I want to thank these teachers and mentors, without whom this book would not exist. I am also grateful for the opportunities provided to me by the BGSS and the funding of a PhD stipend by the German Research Foundation (DFG).

In 2013, Carsten Schneider asked whether I would like to join him as co-instructor for the QCA course at the ECPR Summer School, based on his *Set-Theoretic Methods for the Social Sciences*, coauthored with Claudius Wagemann. For the next four years, I taught the first week of the two-week long course, initially at the University of Ljubljana and later at Central European University in Budapest. I benefited enormously from this, including the many engaging discussions with our course participants, and I am grateful to Carsten for giving me the opportunity. During this time, the course was assisted by Priscilla Álamos-Concha and Ioana-Elena Oana, while Adrian Dușa joined in 2014 to introduce his QCA package for R. Thanks to Nena and Priscilla for their assistance with the course and to Adrian for his support in 2014 and for patiently answering all sorts of questions about the QCA package since then. Based on her work on the SetMethods package, Nena provided a first-rate introduction to R in the QCA course and this greatly enhanced my own transition to R, as I had previously worked mostly with the fs/QCA software. I also want to thank Eugène Horber who invited me to teach at the Swiss Summer School in Social Science Methods in Lugano, where I have been giving QCA courses since 2016.

Throughout my work on this book, I was fortunate to receive feedback from a number of colleagues—Gary Goertz, Benoît Rihoux, and Claude Rubinson—all of whom read the entire manuscript and wrote detailed comments on each chapter. I am grateful for their guidance, which greatly helped me in strengthening the manuscript. I also want to thank those who provided me with comments and suggestions on early drafts and individual chapters: Jan Dollbaum, Eva Thomann, and Francesco Veri. Their comments were well received and helped me improve the presentation of the material. I further thank the four anonymous reviewers that Georgetown University Press elicited during two full rounds of reviews and a review of my book proposal. Their constructive and critical comments encouraged me to undertake substantial revisions to strengthen the first version of the manuscript, and their perseverance and eye for detail made me go the extra mile in completing the final version of this book. I appreciate their professional ethos. I also want to express my gratitude to my editor, Donald Jacobs, for supporting this project from the initial stages and for shepherding the manuscript toward publication, as well as the people involved at Georgetown University Press for their assistance. All remaining errors are my own.

For fruitful exchanges about QCA and comparative methods in various contexts, I am grateful to Jonas Buche, Adrian Duşa, Manuel Fischer, Erik Fritzsche, John Gerring, Gary Goertz, Nina Guerín, Tim Haesebrouck, Christian Hagemann, Felix Hörisch, Tobias Ide, Matthias Koenig, Andreas Kruck, Hilde van Meegdenburg, Katharina Meissner, Johannes Meuer, Nena Oana, Falk Ostermann, Sofia Pagliarin, Charles Ragin, Benoît Rihoux, Ingo Rohlfing, Claude Rubinson, Christian Rupietta, Roel Rutten, Carsten Schneider, Andrea Schneiker, Markus Siewert, Eva Thomann, Barbara Vis, and Claudius Wagemann. Thanks to my student assistants, Teslin Augustine and Sarah Filippi-Field, for valuable research support during the completion of this book.

Thanks also to everyone who participated in my QCA courses and workshops in Ljubljana, Budapest, Lugano, Erfurt, Göttingen, and Lausanne. Teaching QCA to a variety of different audiences made me rethink my own approach to the method and prompted me to clarify many aspects. The feedback I received on early drafts of this book was tremendously helpful. Thanks also to Nina Guerín and Christian Hagemann as my co-conspirators of the informal QCA network at the Hochschule für Politik and the LMU in Munich.

Special thanks to everyone who contributed to this book with reflections on their own QCA studies. I am glad people shared my enthusiasm for the idea of having a look "behind the scaffolding" of published studies, and I am honored to have such a diverse group of contributors in this book: Matthew Andersson, Hilary Boudet, Maria Brockhaus, Pablo Castillo-Ortiz, Monica Di Gregorio, Alexander Gard-Murray, Leanne Giordono, Tim Haesebrouck, Sarah Harkness, Tobias Ide, Kaisa Korhonen-Kurki, Jenniver Sehring, and Marij Swinkels.

Finally, I want to express my gratitude to my family. My wife, Tanja, accompanied and supported me throughout the twists and turns of this book project. It would not have been possible without her. And our children, Henry and Mara, made us smile despite the challenges of homeschooling, closed down daycare, and two jobs to pursue. I dedicate this book to them.

1 • Qualitative Comparative Analysis in the Social Sciences

The causal relationships on which scholars now focus
are different from those posited two decades ago,
and many acknowledge forms of multicausality
that previous work ignored.

—PETER A. HALL

Social phenomena can rarely be attributed to individual causes. Instead, what social scientists observe is often the result of a combination of several factors. For instance, how to explain the global rise of populism? Depending on who you ask, different accounts are suggested. But many observers agree that important drivers are the socioeconomic effects of globalization and a general increase in uncertainty, which often boils down to questions of identity and meaning. To account for the electoral success of populist parties, either of these factors may need to be present. Moreover, multiple pathways may lead to the same outcome. Although the United States, Turkey, Bolivia, and Venezuela all saw the emergence of populist leaders, these countries' socioeconomic conditions are quite different, suggesting the existence of different trajectories toward populism. To complicate things further, the explanation for the positive outcome may not provide an explanation for the negative outcome. And though we may have empirically identified socioeconomic grievances as a cause of the electoral success of populist leaders, this does not allow us to say that the absence of such grievances means that populists will not be electorally successful.

Together, the concepts of conjunctural causation (combinations of conditions), equifinality (multiple pathways), and causal asymmetry (outcome and nonoutcome may require different explanations) constitute the core of *causal complexity*, a defining characteristic of Qualitative Comparative Analysis (QCA; Ragin 2008b; Rihoux and Ragin 2009; Schneider and Wagemann 2012). Drawing on set theory and the language of necessary and sufficient conditions, QCA is a case-based comparative research method that is ideally suited to capture causal complexity.

This chapter introduces readers to QCA, and to the approach to exploring it that is taken in this book. After a general overview on the method and the substantive research areas where it has been applied in the social sciences, I sketch the QCA research cycle that informs the book's chapter structure. This is followed by a brief history of the method and its development, a look into publication trends in various disciplines over the past decades, and a chapter-by-chapter discussion of the book's outline.

WHAT IS QUALITATIVE COMPARATIVE ANALYSIS?

Originated by Charles Ragin (1987) in his seminal book *The Comparative Method*, QCA was conceived as a case-based method for "comparing wholes as configurations of parts" (Ragin 1987, 84). Although there is undoubtedly more to QCA, this concise definition captures the essence of what the method is about. It is a comparative method that regards cases as combinations of conditions. The emphasis on cases and their complexities also reflects QCA's roots as a qualitative method. What is left out in this definition is that QCA compares cases to identify necessary and sufficient conditions for an outcome. This is done through a structured analytical procedure and a software-based algorithm—all of which are introduced in stepwise fashion in this book.

Throughout the past three decades, QCA has undergone a dynamic evolution. Although some of its early applications were still carried out by hand, where researchers manually filled out spreadsheets, the method nowadays draws on a reliable spectrum of software-based solutions that reflect a high level of methodological sophistication and refinement. Moreover, scholars have developed a broad repertoire of QCA variants to address specific needs and formulated sets of best practices to guide applied research.

The evolution of QCA went hand in hand with its spread across the social sciences, including the fields of sociology, political science, international relations, economics and management, public policy, political geography, legal studies, criminology, public health, evaluation studies, and many other areas of research.[1] Many early QCA applications were macrocomparative studies of welfare state formation in liberal democracies (e.g., Hicks, Misra, and Ng 1995). Nowadays there are applications at all levels of analysis. Besides the country level, studies have selected units of analysis ("cases"), such as regional parliaments (Buzogány and Häsing 2018), government cabinets (Vis 2010), national elections (Fernández-García and Luengo 2019), internet regulators (Ewert, Kaufmann, and Maggetti 2020), medical schools (Williams et al. 2018), project ventures (Bakker et al. 2011), communities (Kane et al. 2016), business firms (García-Castro, Aguilera, and Ariño 2013), civil society organizations (Durán Mogollón, Eisele, and Paschou 2020), peacekeeping missions (Gromes 2019), investment decisions (Berger, Wenzel, and Wohlgemuth 2018), and food safety inspectors (Thomann, Hupe, and Sager 2018).

Likewise, empirical studies have covered a wide range of substantive issue areas, including norm promotion (Schimmelfennig 2005), allocation of government ministries (Oppermann and Brummer 2020), compensation inequality (Greckhamer 2011), national convergence of EU law (Goanta and Siems 2019), stem cell regulation (Engeli and Rothmayr Allison 2013), sanctions effectiveness (Boogaerts and Drieskens 2020), authoritarian persistence (Grauvogel and von Soest 2014), labor market policies (Vis 2011), partisanship and policy change (Hörisch and Wurster 2019), environmental peacekeeping (Ide 2018), trade relations (Gansemans et al. 2017), postconflict democratization (Mross 2019), weight management interventions (Melendez-Torres et al. 2018), state collapse (Johais, Bayer, and Lambach 2020), democratic war involvement (Mello 2014), and the role of junior partners in coalition warfare (Schmitt 2018).

Methodology textbooks show that QCA has been widely acknowledged as a method that can have unique benefits for comparative research and multimethod research designs (Beach and Pedersen 2019; Blatter and Haverland 2012; Gerring 2012b, 2017, 2020; Goertz and Mahoney 2012; Moses and Knutsen 2019; Rihoux and Grimm 2006; Rohlfing 2012; Toshkov 2016). Unlike conventional statistical methods that focus on the "average effects of independent variables" (Mahoney 2010, 132), QCA explores the specific conditions under which outcomes of interest occur. Therefore, causal relationships are expressed in the set-theoretic terminology of *necessary and sufficient conditions*, a perspective that is "increasingly viewed as substantively important" in social science research (Collier et al. 2010a, 147). In a nutshell, necessity means that a condition is always present when the outcome occurs, whereas sufficiency indicates that whenever a condition appears, so does the outcome.

Although QCA has been recognized as a valuable addition to the social-scientific toolbox, the method's analytical protocol, available software, and standards required for peer-reviewed publications have gradually become more sophisticated. Clearly, these are welcome developments. But the methodological refinement has also created barriers for new users. For example, consider the R software environment, which has become the new standard for conducting QCA studies (Dușa 2019b; Oana, Schneider, and Thomann 2021).[2] Though R provides a powerful platform of boundless possibilities, it can also be forbidding and frustrating, even for people with a background in computational analysis.[3] This poses an even bigger hurdle for those without any prior knowledge of R, who are considering using QCA for a project. Others might be uncertain about whether QCA is a suitable method for their own research and the kind of data they have collected. Still others might have read a critique of QCA and are now unsure if the method can be fruitfully applied in their own project (critiques are discussed in chapter 9).

This book seeks to overcome such barriers and address conceivable concerns by providing a step-by-step introduction to QCA that emphasizes research design, practical application, and real-life examples from published studies. The book's online R Manual aims at new users who are not yet familiar with R (instructions are provided in the appendix). Beginners are taken through each step in the research process so that the method can swiftly be applied to individual projects. Experienced users will refresh their knowledge of QCA, learning about recent developments and new ways to apply the method, including up-to-date discussions of best practices. Both groups will profit from many illustrated examples from published studies, and a compendium of suggestions to improve QCA research design, the interpretation of findings, and the graphical presentation of results.

HOW TO USE THIS BOOK

This book provides a hands-on introduction to QCA. Because the chapters follow an ideal-typical research process, beginners should read the chapters in sequence. Experienced users who are interested in specific issues can directly move to the respective chapter or section, as highlighted in the table of contents and the index. Key terms are

Table 1.1   Overview of This Book's Infoboxes

Variant	Box	Field	Topic	Study
Multimethod QCA	2.1	Political geography	Environmental cooperation and peacemaking	Ide (2018)
Fuzzy-set QCA	2.2	Sociology	Biological attributions of mental illness	Andersson and Harkness (2018)
Fuzzy-set QCA	5.1	Political science	Leaders' economic beliefs	Swinkels (2020a)
Fuzzy-set QCA	5.2	Public policy	Climate change policy	Giordono, Boudet, and Gard-Murray (2020)
Multivalue QCA	8.1	Law	Judicial independence	Castillo-Ortiz (2017)
Two-step QCA	8.2	Environmental governance	Policies against deforestation	Brockhaus et al. (2017)
Crisp-set QCA, MDSO-MSDO	8.3	International relations	EU military operations	Haesebrouck (2017)

summarized in the book's glossary. The book is written for anyone interested in learning about QCA, how to use it properly, and how to make the most of their analytical findings. The book equally speaks to beginners, who may have heard about the method and want to understand its basics, as well as experienced users who are familiar with QCA but want to learn more about seizing its potential. There are no prerequisites, and the technical discussion is kept to a necessary minimum. To enable readers to engage in a seamless application of the QCA procedure, the R Manual provides a hands-on guide on how to install the software, how to prepare the data, and how to conduct the main analytical steps in R. This is complemented by an R script that users can customize for their own research needs.

A unique feature of this book is that the substantive chapters are complemented by seven infoboxes from authors of published QCA studies, who revisit their personal experiences with QCA and the decisions they faced when they conducted their study. The selected examples represent a diverse range of applications across the social sciences, including political science, sociology, law, public policy, environmental governance, political geography, and international relations. The infoboxes further draw on six different QCA variants and approaches, to document the full spectrum of empirical applications. The unique authors' perspectives allow readers a look "behind the scaffolding" of published studies, which rarely make such decisions explicit. Table 1.1 lists the contributions from various scholars found in this book, their QCA variant, field of study, and topic of application.

THE QCA RESEARCH CYCLE

The chapter outline of this book follows an ideal-typical QCA research cycle, as shown in figure 1.1. Typically, the starting point for a new project is the definition of a research problem, which is narrowed down to a focused research question in the next step. Potential answers for the research question are found in theory, whether as broad conjectures or formal hypotheses. The first stage is complete when theory is linked to empirical observations, in the form of cases and conditions selected for study. The issues that arise during this stage are discussed in chapter 2 on research design. The second stage begins with data gathering and the calibration of sets, to prepare for the QCA analysis. The foundation of set theory is provided in chapter 3. Chapter 4 considers causation and causal complexity, which equally inform the initial stages of research and the substantive interpretation of the findings. Calibration techniques and examples are introduced in chapter 5.

The core of the analytical procedure begins with the construction of the truth table and the analysis of necessary and sufficient conditions. Measures of fit, as a required background to make sense of the analytical results and to interpret empirical patterns are discussed in chapter 6, while the set-theoretic analysis as the core of QCA is the

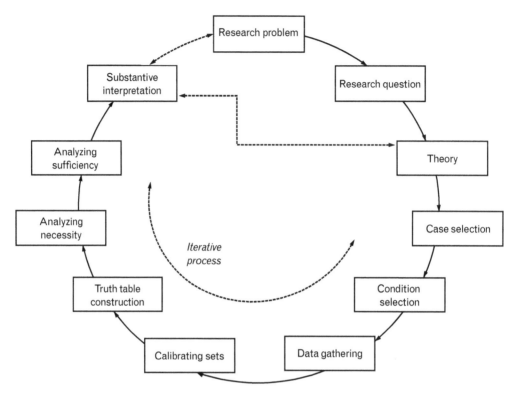

Figure 1.1   The QCA Research Cycle

topic of chapter 7. What remains is the substantive interpretation of the analytical results. It is important to underline that set-theoretic analysis is meant to be an *iterative process*—a "back-and-forth" between theory and evidence (Ragin 2000). Hence, initial results often lead to an adaptation of the theory, case selection, or other aspects of the research design, until a satisfactory explanatory model is found.

A BRIEF HISTORY OF QCA

At 30 years of age, QCA may still be considered a novel approach, at least when compared with statistical methods and historically informed case studies, each of which can trace their lineage to the eighteenth century (Moses and Knutsen 2019). Yet the method has undergone a substantial evolution since its inception by Charles Ragin in 1987. At its core, QCA is grounded in the algebra of George Boole, a nineteenth-century British mathematician and logician. Boolean algebra uses variables that occur in only two states: *true* (present) or *false* (absent). This conception proved central, for instance, to the development of electronic switching circuits, and Boolean algebra was soon widely used across the applied sciences (Whitesitt 2010). What is important for the aims of qualitative comparison is that Boolean algebra allows for set-theoretic operations, the construction of truth tables, and their minimization to derive solution terms—essential parts of QCA that are covered throughout this book.

Naturally, the Boolean use of binary categories meant that QCA was limited to working with *crisp sets*, where 1 indicated the presence of a condition and 0 indicated its absence. This drawback was overcome with the introduction of *fuzzy sets* (Ragin 2000), which allowed for graded set membership (any scores from 0 to 1). Fuzzy logic was developed by the mathematician Lotfi Zadeh (1965), who conceived of it as an extension of traditional set theory to tackle the problem of complex and imprecise concepts. Zadeh's work sparked a revolution in computer technology, which was narrated in the account by Daniel McNeill and Paul Freiberger (1993), and fuzzy sets have also made their way into the social sciences (Smithson and Verkuilen 2006), including linguistics (Lakoff 1973) and many other areas of application.

Another step in the refinement of QCA was the introduction of *measures of fit* to assess the strength of the empirical support for set-theoretic relationships of necessity and sufficiency (Ragin 2006b). The measure of set-theoretic *consistency* indicates the extent to which cases that share a specific combination of conditions also show the outcome of interest. In turn, set-theoretic *coverage* reflects "how much" a condition or combination of conditions accounts for the occurrence of the outcome. These measures introduced straightforward indicators to evaluate the analytical results of QCA, which are similar to the concepts of significance and strength in statistical analyses (Ragin 2008b, 45). Later, these were complemented by additional measures of fit, including *proportional reduction in inconsistency* (Mendel and Ragin 2011) and *relevance of necessity* (Schneider and Wagemann 2012). Chapter 6 develops these and additional metrics and illustrates them with empirical examples.

Evidently, the comparative logic of QCA was inspired by John Stuart Mill's well-known methods of scientific inquiry, which he put forth in *A System of Logic*, first published in 1843 (Mill 2006, book 3, chapter 8). His methods include the method of agreement and method of difference, as well as the lesser-known method of residues and method of concomitant variations. But Mill (2006, 388–406) also devised a joint method of agreement and difference. In some ways, QCA can be seen as a systematic application of the joint method, which Mill already regarded as an improvement over his more basic approaches (Mill 2006, 396).

However, it is important to note that QCA goes beyond Mill's methods in many respects. First, whereas Mill focused on individual variables to identify a single cause for an observed phenomenon, QCA explicitly considers equifinality and conjunctural causation. Second, Mill's methods cannot account for the phenomenon of limited diversity, but this is systematically addressed in QCA's truth table procedure, which identifies all logically possible combinations of conditions and enables researchers to deal with so-called logical remainders (combinations without empirical cases). Third, the advent of fuzzy sets meant that graded set membership became feasible and measures of fit gave researchers ways to assess the strength of set-theoretic relationships. Both features are missing from Mill's methods.[4] Finally, Boolean logic and minimization allow for a systematic comparative procedure and inferential analysis that is not found in Mill's methods.

Although crisp-set and fuzzy-set QCA are the method's most popular variants, there are also several extensions and approaches aimed to overcome specific limitations of QCA. For instance, *multivalue QCA* (Cronqvist 2019; Cronqvist and Berg-Schlosser 2009) allows for nominal variables that entail three or more categories. This can be helpful where explanatory conditions cannot easily be dichotomized without losing important information. For example, instead of distinguishing between "employed" and "unemployed," you may want to introduce further categories like "part-time employed" and so forth. Another variant is *temporal QCA* (Caren and Panofsky 2005; Hino 2009; Ragin and Strand 2008), which aims to overcome the static nature of QCA comparisons by introducing notions of time and sequence. This is done via an additional operator that distinguishes whether a condition occurred before another condition (see also Pagliarin and Gerrits 2020). *Two-step QCA* (Schneider and Wagemann 2006) was developed to tackle the problem of limited diversity and having too many conditions. The approach distinguishes between remote and proximate explanatory conditions and conducts consecutive truth table procedures instead of just one. Finally, *fuzzy-set ideal type analysis* (Kvist 2007) aims to understand the constitution of cases (rather than explaining an outcome), which are compared against preconceived ideal types rooted in theory. Chapter 8 introduces these and other QCA variants with examples from applied research.

One of the most dynamic areas in QCA's evolution is software development. Although the first version of what later became the fs/QCA software was already introduced in 1986 (Drass and Ragin 1986), it was soon complemented by a range of different programs and packages for various platforms. And though there is a healthy stream of published studies using the fs/QCA and Tosmana programs, the most advanced software for QCA nowadays is based on the R environment. Among other advantages, R is platform independent, which means that it can be used on any computer system. Unlike many commercial statistical programs, R is free of cost and open source. Most important, rather than a click-and-point software with predefined functions, R and its code can be tailored for individual purposes. This means that besides the QCA procedure, one can visualize the data and analytical results within R and complement the analysis with further computational tests as needed.[5] Finally, R code can easily be made available as a complementary file, which enhances transparency and replicability. The R Manual that complements this book provides a concise introduction to R, its functions, and relevant packages for QCA analyses (see the appendix).

Since its founding, QCA has also spurred an array of critiques. One of the reasons for this may be the method's *hybrid* nature as an approach with both qualitative and quantitative elements—which propels criticism from scholars trained in statistical methods, who usually work with hundreds or thousands of observations, as well as from those who conduct intensive studies on a handful of cases at most. Although not limited to a certain number of observations, QCA typically operates with 20 to 50 cases, which means that it is situated right between these camps. Chapter 9 reviews the criticism leveled against QCA and derives guidelines for how to respond to the arguments.

TRENDS IN QCA APPLICATIONS

The dynamic development of QCA is mirrored in the number of academic publications using this research method. Figure 1.2 displays the cumulative number of Web of Science journal articles between 1987 and 2020.[6] Growing slowly over the course of the 1990s, there has been an exponential increase in QCA studies since the late 2000s. The surge in QCA studies corresponds broadly to the publication of seminal textbooks that formalized the method and enhanced its widespread application, such as Ragin (2008b), Rihoux and Ragin (2009), and Schneider and Wagemann (2012).

As of 2020, the Social Sciences Citation Index (SSCI) of the Web of Science lists about 1,400 journal articles that referred to "qualitative comparative analysis" in one form or another. Although it should be noted that this number includes studies that use a broad understanding of the term or make only a passing reference to QCA, the complete number of empirical QCA applications and methodological articles is prone to be even higher because the SSCI covers only a part of all academic journals, and

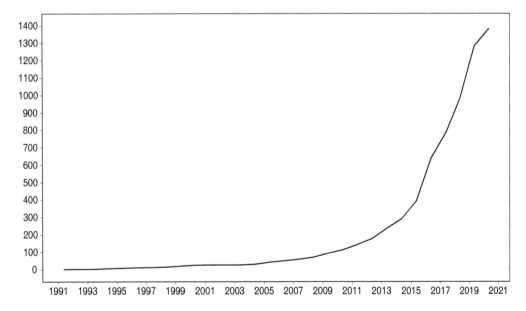

Figure 1.2   Cumulative Journal Articles on QCA, 1987–2020

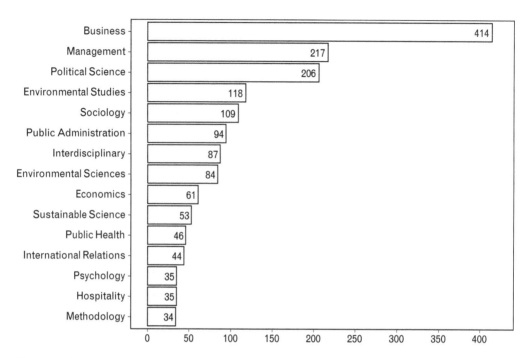

Figure 1.3   Journal Articles on QCA, 1987–2020, by Category

especially non-English publications are largely absent from its database. The growth of QCA also shows in the citation numbers for Ragin's (1987) *The Comparative Method*, which has accumulated about 10,800 citations on Google Scholar as of December 2020.

Which research fields of the social sciences contributed to this growth? Where is QCA most popular? Figure 1.3 differentiates the publication data from the Web of Science by research field for the top 15 categories in the SSCI. We can see that there are 10 substantive fields that each contain at least 50 articles on QCA in the years between 1987 and 2020. Business studies are out ahead, with 414 studies in the period. This is followed by the fields of management and political science, with more than 200 studies each; environmental studies and sociology, both with over 100 studies; and public administration, at just below that threshold. Overall, the Web of Science data differentiates more than a hundred different categories, with at least one study that mentions QCA (with an average of 20 and a median of 4 articles that refer to QCA).

To be sure, the Web of Science data do not differentiate by article length or publication output in a given field. Some fields have journals with a high volume of relatively short articles, which naturally drives up publication and citation numbers. Another caveat to the Web of Science data is that many journals are listed under more than one category, which leads to empirical overlap because the same journal article may be counted under several categories (on average, each of the 1,387 articles refers to 1.6 categories). However, these limitations notwithstanding, we can see that QCA as a method is recognized across the entire spectrum of the social sciences and firmly established in a broad number of research fields.

OUTLINE OF THE BOOK

This book comprises 10 chapters. Its outline follows a typical research process, which means that new users will benefit from reading the chapters in sequence. But readers can also use the table of contents and index to navigate among issues, based on their own interests and backgrounds. Two caveats are in order. The first concerns the use of methodological jargon. In this book, I aim to give a thorough but approachable introduction to QCA. Hence, to the extent feasible, I have limited the usage of technical terms and acronyms. However, a number of terms are essential for understanding what the method is about and how to apply it correctly. These terms are introduced throughout the book and are defined in the book's glossary.

The second caveat relates to chapter sequence. Introducing a method like QCA poses a chicken-and-egg problem. Before we can move to set-theoretic analysis, we need to lay the groundwork, but some of this may only appear useful once later chapters are read. Hence the book begins with three general chapters—on research design, set theory, and causation and causal complexity—but their implications may only be clear when all elements of the analytical procedure have been presented.

After this introductory chapter, chapter 2 opens with a guide to QCA *research design*, including the formulation of research questions, the different uses of QCA, and the selection of cases and conditions. The chapter closes with observations from a survey of recently published studies and recommendations for conducting multimethod research with QCA. Chapter 3, on *set theory*, lays out the distinctive characteristics of set-theoretic approaches. Starting with the distinction between crisp and fuzzy sets, the chapter introduces Boolean operations, formal notation, truth tables, and the concepts of necessary and sufficient conditions. The chapter concludes with a summary on how set relations can be identified in empirical data. Chapter 4 takes a step back to examine four major theories of *causation* in the philosophy of the social sciences. The second part of the chapter connects the discussion with an introduction to the concept of *causal complexity* and the prospects of *causal analysis* with QCA.

The subsequent three chapters develop the analytical core of the method. As a preliminary to set-theoretic analysis, chapter 5 discusses the *calibration* of crisp and fuzzy sets, including crucial differences in quantitative approaches to measurement. The chapter presents strategies to calibrate sets based on different kinds of qualitative and quantitative raw data, provides a guide to the mathematical transformation of raw data into calibrated scores, and introduces applied examples to underscore a range of different calibration approaches. Chapter 6 introduces *measures of fit*, which help to assess and interpret QCA results. Using empirical examples, the chapter explains how set-theoretic consistency and coverage are calculated and how the resulting scores should be interpreted. The chapter closes with discussions of additional measures of fit. Chapter 7 presents set-theoretic analysis, starting with the analysis of *necessary conditions*, proceeding to the construction of the *truth table*, and concluding with the Boolean *minimization* to derive *solution terms*. Using empirical examples, the chapter illustrates how researchers' decisions have an impact on solution terms and closes with a discussion of *counterfactual analysis* and the treatment of *logical remainders*.

Although the book's emphasis rests on crisp and fuzzy-set QCA as the most popular variants, chapter 8 introduces QCA *variants*—namely, multivalue, temporal, and two-step QCA—as well as fuzzy-set ideal type analysis. The chapter discusses the advantages and requirements of each approach against the backdrop of empirical examples. Chapter 9 reviews the methodological debate on QCA's strengths and limitations, aiming to summarize the conversation for new users and to highlight how prior critiques have been addressed in the development of QCA. Chapter 10 summarizes the book's core points and derives guiding principles for good research practice. It also provides readers with directions for further developing their own applications. Conceived as a supplement, the appendix provides instructions for the online R Manual that summarizes the core R functions needed to conduct QCA, including reading and manipulating data, calibrating conditions, testing for necessary conditions, constructing a truth table, deriving solution terms, and visualizing results.

NOTES

Epigraph: Hall (2003, 383).

1. For a general overview of trends in applied QCA research, see Rihoux et al. (2013). For an introduction to QCA from an ethnographic and social movement perspective, see Kröger (2021). There are also reviews of QCA studies in specific fields, including comparative welfare state research (Emmenegger, Kvist, and Skaaning 2013), public policy (Hudson and Kühner 2013; Rihoux et al. 2011), public administration (Thomann and Ege 2020), sociology (Buche and Siewert 2015), business research (Wagemann, Buche, and Siewert 2016), public health (Palinkas, Mendson, and Hamilton 2019), entrepreneurship (Kraus, Ribeiro-Soriano, and Schüssler 2018), spatial planning (Verweij and Trell 2019), democratization (Møller and Skaaning 2019), and on the combination of QCA with statistical analyses (Meuer and Rupietta 2017).

2. As an indication of this, QCA summer school courses at the ECPR Summer School in Methods and Techniques, the ICPSR Summer Program in Quantitative Methods of Social Research, and the FORS Swiss Summer School in Social Science Methods now exclusively work with R and the packages "QCA" (Dușa 2019b) and "SetMethods" (Oana and Schneider 2018). The R software environment is freely available for all operating systems; see www.r-project.org/. The major alternatives to R include the "fs/QCA" (Ragin and Davey 2017) and "Tosmana" software (Cronqvist 2019). A comprehensive list of all available software, including further R packages, is maintained at the QCA community website: https://compasss.org/community/.

3. For a "survivor's guide" to R, see Gaubatz (2015).

4. To be fair, Mill's method of concomitant variations does allow for quantitative differences (Mill 2006, 403). For a discussion of Mill's methods in the context of modern quantitative approaches, see Sekhon (2008).

5. For example, the studies by Ide (2018) and Schneider and Makszin (2014) conduct statistical analyses before QCA, and Mello (2020) complements the set-theoretic analysis of necessity with statistical tests of association.

6. The database can be accessed at www.webofknowledge.com.

2 • Research Design

Research design ensures that the answers we provide are as
valid as possible and are discovered as efficiently as possible.
—DIMITER TOSHKOV

Questions of research design are central to any scientific endeavor. To find appropriate solutions to social-scientific problems, we first need to define our scope of inquiry and the concepts involved, and to lay out our theoretical expectations. Moreover, we need to specify which methods to use for the answers we seek to find.[1] Naturally, these general concerns equally apply for QCA studies, but there are additional points to consider. What kinds of *research questions* can be addressed with a set-theoretic approach? How should *theory* be formulated to gain most leverage from using QCA? How should *cases* and explanatory *conditions* be selected? Finally, can QCA be combined with other methods and how should such *multimethod* research be conducted? This chapter addresses these and several related questions in turn.

Despite the evident centrality of research design, this is often given less attention than matters of technical implementation and refinement at later stages in the research process. However, many of the challenges involved in conducting sensible research should arguably be addressed right at the outset of designing a study. For instance, a vexing issue for QCA is that the method conducts *static* comparisons. There is no formal place for time, sequencing, or process.[2] That said, nothing stops a researcher from incorporating these into the conceptualization of his or her conditions and outcome. Likewise, studies with a small or medium number of cases are at times criticized for overstating their conclusions (Lieberson 1991). Yet a proper definition of scope conditions and case selection criteria can equally help to strengthen the inferences drawn from such studies as to designate their limitations. Finally, a sensible interpretation of QCA solution terms can pose a challenge in itself, especially if theory was not formulated in set-theoretic terms. This can be averted by clearly spelling out observable implications and potential combinations of conditions derived from theory *before* the analytical part.

Present debates about research design typically take *Designing Social Inquiry* by Gary King, Robert Keohane, and Sydney Verba (1994) as a starting point. In their influential book, King and his colleagues proposed a common inferential framework for scientific inference in quantitative and qualitative research. This ambitious goal naturally provoked criticism from those who liked to point out that, apart from causal inference, qualitative research aims for "thick description and interpretation" (Caporaso 1995, 457), and that King and his colleagues "inappropriately view qualitative analysis almost exclusively through the optic of mainstream quantitative methods" (Brady and Collier 2004, xvi).[3] Be that as it may, one upside of the debate about the "qualitative/quantitative divide" is that it set in motion a process of renewed thinking about methods and methodology. The two editions of *Rethinking Social Inquiry* with their individual contributions (Brady and Collier 2004, 2010) and Charles Ragin's *Redesigning Social Inquiry* (2008b) are landmarks in this regard. The volume edited by Henry Brady and David Collier provided a thorough critique of mainstream statistical approaches, while also building bridges and acknowledging common ground between qualitative and quantitative researchers. In turn, Ragin highlighted that despite his critical stance toward the "conventional quantitative template," he did not want his book to be understood as a critique of *Designing Social Inquiry*, but as a "middle path between quantitative and qualitative social research" (Ragin 2008b, 1).

RESEARCH QUESTIONS

When working on a new scientific endeavor, one of the first tasks is to turn an idea for a research topic into a *researchable* project, which often goes in line with a research question. Among other suggestions, most scholars agree that research projects should strive to meet the twofold criteria of (1) real-world relevance, and (2) making a scientific contribution to the scholarly literature in a given academic field (King, Keohane, and Verba 1994; Schmitter 2008; Toshkov 2016).

But even once a topic has been defined, formulating the research question can be a tricky business. One pitfall is that questions can be too narrow or too specific, leaving little room for discovery or alternative explanations. For instance, based on a reading of relevant studies, you may ask whether there is a relationship between poverty and health issues. The advantage of such a research question is that it provides clear guidance for the analysis. There is no need to explore alternative factors. However, this setup may also be a straitjacket when you discover during your research that poverty is but one of several important factors that are related to health issues. Here, casting a wider net would have given your research more leverage. Relatedly, your research question may mention a specific case or several cases—again, this may be fine because it provides focus; but it might also put you in a corner where it becomes difficult to account for relevant phenomena that only occur in other cases. Certainly, these concerns apply to all areas of the social sciences. In this chapter, we set aside such general issues and take it as given that we identified a research topic that meets the criterion of real-world relevance and that connects with scholarly debates in our field. Now our task is to turn this into a feasible comparative research project.[4]

But what are research questions that can be answered with QCA? And how are these typically phrased? Based on a twofold differentiation by *focus* and *level*, four types of questions can be derived. Level differentiates between *case-specific* and *general* research questions. As the name implies, the former type asks about the circumstances of a specific case or several cases, whereas the latter asks a general question about relations between theoretical concepts without reference to specific cases. Focus separates *condition-centered* and *outcome-centered* research.[5] Inasmuch as the former seeks to understand the effect of a particular condition or combination of conditions (a *configuration*, in QCA terminology), the latter aims to find the causes for an outcome, whether in one particular case or for a class of cases. Naturally, these aims can overlap in empirical research projects. With QCA, we may at times be equally interested in accounting for puzzling cases and identifying cross-case patterns. Nonetheless, the twofold distinction helps to clarify the primary analytical aims of a project and to tailor the research design accordingly.

Another way to look at the differentiation between research questions is whether they arise primarily from puzzling empirics (case-specific level) or from theoretical considerations (general level). As for the first type, a researcher typically starts out from observing a case that presents an empirical puzzle. For example, why did British prime minister David Cameron initiate a referendum on leaving the European Union? Why was Italy affected so severely from the coronavirus pandemic? Why did social protests break out in Chile? All these cases contain puzzling aspects. The questions can be framed by these outcomes, but they could also be centered on conditions such as Cameron's leadership characteristics, Italy's health care system, or social inequality in Chile. By contrast, the second type of research questions focuses on theoretical concepts or the relationship between several concepts. Here, the aim may be to explain the occurrence of a relevant outcome, or to examine whether a condition or a configuration leads to the outcome. For instance, rather than asking about the cases of Italy and Chile, we may be interested in generalizing across countries, to find out which conditions led to countries' being more affected by the pandemic or which led to the outbreak of social protests. Similarly, we could compare leaders' personality traits and place these in relation to certain outcomes.

Figure 2.1 summarizes the typology of research questions along the *focus* and *level* dimensions. The example is based on Spanish prime minister José Luis Rodríguez Zapatero's 2004 decision to withdraw from the Iraq War coalition. The first question remains case-specific, but it focuses on the impact that the condition of leadership change might have had on the withdrawal decision. By contrast, the second question highlights the outcome, asking for an explanation for this specific case. Question

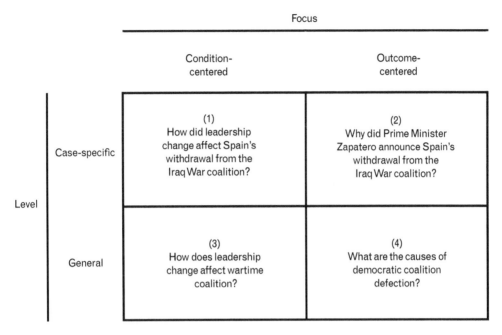

Figure 2.1 Typology of Research Questions

three moves the inquiry to the general level, probing the effect of a specific condition, whereas question four asks about the general causes for the outcome.

How does this look in practice? Here are some examples of research questions from published QCA studies in business and management, international relations, political science, and sociology:

1. "Under which conditions does spending on active labor market policies increase?" (Vis 2011, 229)
2. "Which policies promote the transition towards electric vehicles?" (Held and Gerrits 2019, 13)
3. "What explains the UN's selective response to humanitarian crises?" (Binder 2015, 712)
4. "How do the job attributes that comprise particular combinations of working conditions, or 'bundles,' interact to influence turnover decisions?" (Nelson 2017, 24)
5. "This raises the question if there are certain resources, or combinations thereof, that are necessary or sufficient conditions for civilians to employ control strategies successfully." (Kuehn et al. 2017, 425)

The first question, from Barbara Vis's study on welfare state reform, asks "under which conditions" the outcome occurs. This implies that there is more than a single condition to account for the outcome and that specific combinations may be important. The second example, from Tobias Held's and Lasse Gerrits's article on e-mobility, similarly asks broadly about policies that "promote" the outcome (the adoption of electric vehicles), the implication being that several feasible policies exist. The study by Martin Binder, on the United Nations' response (and nonresponse) to humanitarian crises, emphasizes an empirical observation ("The UN's selective response") and asks for an explanation for this puzzling finding. Research questions like this one can also be phrased generically along the lines of "why did X occur in [these cases], while it did not occur in [those cases]." The fourth example comes from Jennifer Nelson's article on the working conditions of schoolteachers. The study asks specifically about the interaction of "particular combinations of working conditions" that are expected to influence teachers' decisions on whether or not to leave a job. Finally, the article by David Kuehn and colleagues formulates an indirect research question about the occurrence of the outcome, framed in the language of necessary and sufficient conditions.

All these examples are suitable ways to formulate research questions in QCA contexts because they resonate with the method's core assumptions. As we can see, all of them are variations of *general outcome-centered* research questions, though examples 4 and 5 also highlight the condition side and causal complexity without referring to specific combinations. However, the prevalence of general outcome-centered questions should not be taken to rule out the other types (many examples can be found in the literature). Whenever there is a particularly prominent or puzzling case, a case-specific question may be a suitable starting point. It can also be complemented by a more general question about groups of cases. This can be a feasible strategy when a study aims to combine the QCA part with process tracing on a single case—for instance, to identify a causal mechanism.[6]

Finally, you may ask whether it is indeed needed to formulate a research question, because many authors do *not* explicitly mention these in publications. Clearly, this is a matter of personal style and convention in a given academic field. Yet, from a research design perspective, I recommend narrowing down each project to a research question, because even if this will not be explicitly mentioned in the eventual publication, it can serve to structure the analytical process.

USES OF QCA

QCA can be used for a variety of purposes, which may also differ by academic field and tradition. Yet four main uses of QCA can be distinguished, as summarized in figure 2.2.[7] The core difference is whether the method is applied for the aim of *description* or *explanation*. When used for descriptive purposes, the method can serve (1) to *summarize and identify patterns in the data*. This can be helpful to see which cases share certain characteristics or to describe the varieties under which an outcome occurs. For a handful of cases and, say, three conditions it may still be feasible to "eyeball" such patterns— but this swiftly becomes unwieldy as more cases and conditions are included. Here, the

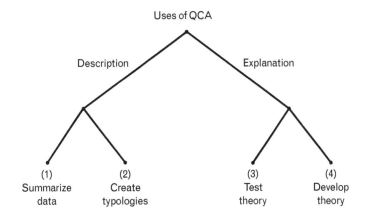

Figure 2.2   The Four Uses of QCA

truth table routine and its systematic comparison of logically possible configurations present a clear advantage over less-structured alternatives. This way of using QCA also resonates with more *inductive* approaches that seek to explore the data without fully specified theoretical expectations (Ragin and Rihoux 2004a, 6). Another descriptive function for which QCA can be used is the (2) *creation of typologies*. This relates to established traditions in qualitative research (Collier, Laporte, and Seawright 2008; Elman 2005; George and Bennett 2005, chap. 11) and it has been formalized as *fuzzy-set ideal type analysis* (Kvist 1999; 2007). Chapter 8 looks into this QCA variant and an applied example.

When QCA is used for explanatory purposes, this is typically done for (3) *testing theory*. In fact, an overwhelming majority of QCA studies broadly fall into this category.[8] What these studies have in common is that they formulate theoretical expectations about the relationship between conditions and outcomes. As we will see shortly, there are different ways to do this. Finally, a variant of the explanatory use of QCA is for (4) *developing theory*. Here, the emphasis is not on conducting tests of existing theory but to advance new theoretical arguments, often through the integration of various theoretical strands. That said, the categories of testing theory and developing theory are *not* mutually exclusive. Many applied settings contain elements of both, where established arguments from the literature are complemented by new theoretical elements to arrive at better explanatory accounts of the observed cases. Likewise, there are studies that would be better located on the descriptive side but that entail discussions of theoretical conjectures.

TESTING HYPOTHESES

When QCA is applied for the aim of *testing theory*, the most structured way of doing this is by *formulating hypotheses* and testing whether the theoretical expectations captured therein resonate with the empirical evidence (Amenta and Poulsen 1994, 29; Berg-Schlosser et al. 2009, 16). To be sure, this kind of usage rests on a broad conception of theory testing, where a hypothesis is understood merely as a "tentative answer to a research problem, expressed in the form of a clearly stated relation" (Frankfort-Nachmias and Nachmias 2008, 56). This differs from more formalized ways of statistical hypothesis testing, where the researcher formulates an experimental hypothesis and a null hypothesis and, ideally, proceeds to test these hypotheses on new data (Field, Miles, and Field 2012).[9] Clearly, the latter kind of hypothesis testing would not be sensible in a QCA context, where a "dialogue between theory and evidence" (Ragin 2014b, xxi) is expected, and where good practice entails "carefully crafting the data" (Schneider and Wagemann 2012, 296). This has led some to caution against set-theoretic hypothesis testing altogether (Schneider, Vis, and Koivu 2019, 7; Schneider and Wagemann 2012, 296).

At this stage, there is no consensus on the issue of hypothesis testing with QCA. Though I share some of the concerns raised about it—and I return to these at the end of this section—I believe that QCA applications *gain* inferential leverage from formulating their theoretical expectations in a clear-cut fashion. Certainly, this should not mimic deductive theory testing, as is common practice in statistics. Yet a clear explication of the *directionality* of each included condition and potential configurations enhances the interpretability of a QCA study because it allows an assessment of whether and how empirical results match theoretical expectations—and also what this might mean for some (yet) unobserved cases. That said, some requirements have to be met to do fruitful theory testing with QCA.

One prerequisite is that hypotheses must be framed in *set-theoretic terms*, meaning they use the language of necessary and sufficient conditions. Otherwise, there will be a mismatch between theory and methods. This can pose a problem when the research goal is to test established probabilistic hypotheses. Although a large body of work in the social sciences rests on a (sometimes implicit) understanding of necessary and sufficient causation, many hypotheses in the literature remain framed in probabilistic language, requiring prior *translation* on the part of the researcher who seeks to employ such hypotheses in a QCA study (Goertz 2003a, 2003b).[10] For example, *probabilistic* hypothesis 1, from international relations research on the "democratic peace," will be difficult to test with QCA.

Hypothesis 1: "The more democratic a country, the more peaceful its external relations"

How can we confirm or disconfirm such a statement as hypothesis 1 with QCA? We may expect that very democratic countries—consolidated democracies—are more peaceful than less democratic countries. But we do not know how many exceptions we can tolerate to still consider our expectation confirmed. Assuming that we have plenty of peaceful democracies, how many instances of consolidated democracies engaged in war would be needed to disconfirm the above hypothesis? Moreover, another question is whether the relationship expressed in the hypothesis also holds for small increases in a country's "democraticness." This question may arise, for instance, when an autocratic regime introduces democratic elements such as elections or a constitutional referendum. But we may doubt whether small-scale institutional changes also affect the country's peacefulness if the autocratic character of the regime remains untouched. In sum, probabilistic hypotheses require a *thorough clarification* of the underlying theoretical expectations to be used in set-theoretic contexts. On their own, probabilistic hypotheses are not helpful for QCA. Now consider hypothesis 2.

> Hypothesis 2: "Democratic political institutions are a sufficient condition for peaceful external relations"

We may doubt whether hypothesis 2 is empirically true—but clearly, testing it is a straightforward matter: the presence of the condition is expected to be sufficient for the outcome, which means that whenever we see the former, we should also observe the latter. Another point regarding hypotheses concerns *causal complexity*—the combination of conditions, alternate pathways toward an outcome, and causal asymmetry. Although authors habitually point out conjunctural causation and equifinality as particular strengths of the QCA approach, these are infrequently incorporated on a theoretical level. What would a configurational hypothesis look like? For instance, we could reformulate the previous statement as a configurational proposition in set-theoretic terms, expecting two conditions to be jointly sufficient for the outcome, as hypothesis 3.

> Hypothesis 3: "Democratic political institutions and societal norms of nonviolent conflict management are jointly sufficient for peaceful external relations"

Finally, expectations about INUS conditions can be used for the formulation of hypotheses. In some sense, INUS conditions present a *hedged* way of formulating theoretical expectations, because they do not require an advance specification of the condition(s) that are expected to combine with the suspected INUS condition. Still, INUS conditions entail a *directional expectation* about the respective condition, requiring a judgment on whether it is the presence or the absence that should lead to the outcome. Hypothesis 4 is an example from Barbara Vis's study on welfare state reform (Vis 2010, 138).[11]

> Hypothesis 4: "Rightist partisanship is an INUS condition for unpopular reform"

This leaves the question of whether formulating hypotheses can be reconciled with the back-and-forth between data and evidence that is characteristic of QCA. Surely, it would make no sense to first conduct a QCA and then formulate the resulting complex paths as "hypotheses" in the theory section. Hence, it often is sensible to begin with *modest* directional expectations (e.g., about INUS conditions) and to justify these expectations by referring to the existing literature on a topic. When this is done, the expected relationships can be examined in the set-theoretic analysis. This can either lead to theory confirmation or the discovery of combinations of conditions that help to reformulate and modify the existing theory. Indeed, as Ragin (2000, 58) states, if a modification is "part of an attempt to learn more about the world . . . and not part of an explicit program of theory testing, it is completely reasonable."

CASE SELECTION

An integral part of qualitative research design is the selection of cases. When thinking about case selection, several questions must be addressed: What are my cases? How can I distinguish positive from negative cases? How many cases shall I include? Should the cases be sampled from a population or comprise the entire universe of cases?[12] The next subsections address these questions in turn.[13]

What Is a Case?

Simply put, a case is a single row in the QCA data sheet. More substantively, a case may be defined as the *unit of analysis* or a "spatially delimited phenomenon (a unit) observed at a single point in time or over some period of time" (Gerring 2007a, 19). This means that a case can be anything in which we are interested, including a country, a government, an organization, a company, a village, a piece of legislation, or an individual. What is more, we can take into account *time* to separate our case (the unit) into several different subunits, if that helps our purposes. For instance, this can be done by looking at the same country over different years, or by examining an organization at different stages of its institutional development. Because of the implications for everything that follows, defining cases or units of observation should be among the first tasks in designing a QCA study.

That said, *revisiting* the case definition, and asking the essential question *what is this a case of?* (Ragin and Becker 1992), can also be a powerful tool to improve a study if problems occur during the analysis or the interpretation of the findings. For example, we may start with a comparative analysis of the 27 member states of the European Union, but later realize that we should differentiate between individual government cabinets, because of policy changes that occurred from one prime minister to another. Hence, we could revise our research design to include multiple different government cabinets per country, over a specified period. This would increase the total number of cases and would require new data gathering, calibration, and a reanalysis of our data.

The benefit of such a procedure is that it would make our analysis more fine-grained and would allow for the inclusion of additional conditions related to the adapted unit level—for instance, on the political partisanship of a government or the leadership traits of prime ministers.

Populations, Scope Conditions, and Samples

We can distinguish five ways for how cases can be selected for QCA. The first option is to select all the cases from (1) a *given population*. For example, we could include all 30 companies listed in the Dow Jones Industrial Average stock market index, the 27 member states of the European Union, or the 22 members of Boris Johnson's second cabinet. This approach means that once we have decided on a given population, case selection itself should be straightforward and unproblematic. Given populations have the benefit of *face validity* because they are not subject to a researcher's judgment about which cases to include. However, the caveat is that even supposedly "given" populations tend to change over time, and hence we must specify the period we seek to cover in our analysis. The Dow Jones Index for 1982 certainly looks different from the one for 2017, and the number of EU member states has changed considerably over the past two decades. Another downside of given populations is that these may contain *irrelevant cases*, to which we turn in the next subsection.

The second approach is similar, but further introduces (2) *scope conditions* to limit the selection of cases. Scope conditions are used to bring the range of cases in line with theory, because most social science theories are not meant to be universal but rather apply to a limited area of application.[14] This resonates with the conception of middle-range theory (Merton 1958). For instance, there may be theoretical reasons why we would want to consider only companies that have been listed in the Dow Jones for the past two decades—or why we prefer to restrict our analysis to EU member states with at least 5 million inhabitants. Finally, we might want to include only those members of Johnson's cabinet who supported the "Leave" campaign during the Brexit referendum in 2016. To take another example, studies that work with the Polity IV data on political regimes (Marshall, Gurr, and Jaggers 2019) typically introduce a threshold for the combined autocracy–democracy scale (which runs from −10 to +10), above which countries are included in the case selection. This may rest on the assumption that the theory is only valid for consolidated democracies, rather than defective democracies or hybrid systems. Here, a threshold of 7, for instance, may serve as a scope condition for the case selection where just those countries are included that meet or exceed this threshold. Finally, it should be noted that scope conditions can be combined with any of the other approaches to case selection, as in limiting a given population through a scope condition (Ragin 2000, chap. 2).

The third approach is to (3) *purposefully select* based on cases' value for the outcome. In the quantitative tradition, this is often seen as a violation of a core principle ("never select on the dependent variable"); but for qualitative research, this is a vital tool to focus on relevant cases.[15] For instance, imagine you want to study why some companies are more successful than others in implementing family-friendly working conditions. Your resources allow you to analyze not more than 20 companies, also because you plan to conduct interviews at each of these, but you have a population of *several hundred* companies that meet your criteria. Now the fourth approach would be taking (4) a *random sample* of 20 companies, but it may be that this sample of randomly drawn cases will contain none or only a handful of positive cases with successful implementation of family-friendly working conditions. It may also be that the random sample contains not a single typical case where the outcome and an expected causal mechanism are both present. This is why random sampling "is not necessarily a wise technique to use" for qualitative research with small to medium numbers of cases (King, Keohane, and Verba 1994, 125).

A more sensible approach for the chosen example would be to purposefully select 10 positive and 10 negative cases to compare their configurations of conditions and to identify difference makers between the two groups. As Ragin (2000, 59) notes, "researchers also may constitute a population of negative cases to compare with the positive cases." In our example, this would mean that we begin with a number of cases that show the phenomenon of interest and match this number with an equal number of cases that do not. Finally, a combined approach would be using a (5) *stratified sample* of cases. This means that the population is first divided into a number of meaningful subsets and from each of these subsets a random sample of cases is drawn in the second stage. Thereby, the population is effectively reduced, while retaining representativeness.[16] This approach works best with large-N data and it requires some prior information to use to divide the population into subsets of cases.

Most QCA studies base their case selection on *given populations*, *scope conditions*, or *purposeful selection*. These approaches also resonate with qualitative research methods. That said, I have further included *random sampling* and *stratified sampling* as quantitative approaches to case selection, and thus ones less often seen in QCA studies, because there are research settings where the advantages of sampling may outweigh the downsides to case selection. This may be, for instance, in sociological, medical, or business applications, where large-N data on individuals, patients, or companies are used. Table 2.1 summarizes the five approaches to case selection.

Positive, Negative, and Irrelevant Cases

When designing a study, we typically begin by thinking about *positive cases*. These are cases that have sparked our interest in a topic because they represent a new empirical phenomenon or because they contradict or resonate with our theories. At the early stage of research design, effort should be placed on conceptualizing the positive outcome and distinguishing it from neighboring concepts. Often, this entails a *back-and-forth*

Table 2.1   Case Selection Approaches

Approach	Characteristics	Strengths	Limitations
Given population	Predefined, given population of cases	High face validity	May contain irrelevant cases
Scope condition	Limits a theory's assumed scope of validity	Resonates with middle-range theorizing	Requires careful justification; may introduce bias
Purposeful selection	Selection on the outcome (and/or the nonoutcome)	Selection is guided by relevancy of cases	Requires careful justification; may introduce bias
Random sample	Random sampling from a population of cases	Representative sample, generalizable	May exclude important cases; requires large-N
Stratified sample	Random sampling among subsets of the population	Adequate representation of cases	Requires large-N and prior information on which to divide into subsets

between theory and cases as we discover that our outcome, as we conceptualized it, does not do justice to important cases (Ragin 2000, chap. 2). However, apart from the positive cases, for our research design we should also think about negative and irrelevant cases.

Upon first thought, *negative cases* may appear uncomplicated: these are cases that do *not* show the outcome. But for many concepts, it can be challenging to pin down what its nonoccurrence actually means. To take the example of Theda Skocpol's work (1979) on social revolutions, we may ask what it means to have a "nonsocial revolution" (Goertz and Mahoney 2006, 177). Similarly, what is the negation of "war involvement"? Is this involvement that is nonmilitary (as in political or humanitarian involvement), or does it refer to the absence of any kind of involvement? Often, the negation of a concept can entail a variety of meanings. For instance, "nondemocracy" might include monarchies, authoritarian states, and dictatorships. And the negation of a successful policy response to the coronavirus might include ill-suited measures, belated responses, and nonresponses. The bottom line is that QCA researchers are well advised to clarify their intended meaning of the nonoutcome and, more generally, to specify which criteria a case needs to fulfill in order to be considered inside or outside a set (see also chapter 5).

Another related category is *irrelevant cases*. As Ragin (2014b, xxvi) notes, given populations often comprise cases that are deemed "irrelevant," which can mean that cases are included that neither show the outcome nor hold meaningful values for the

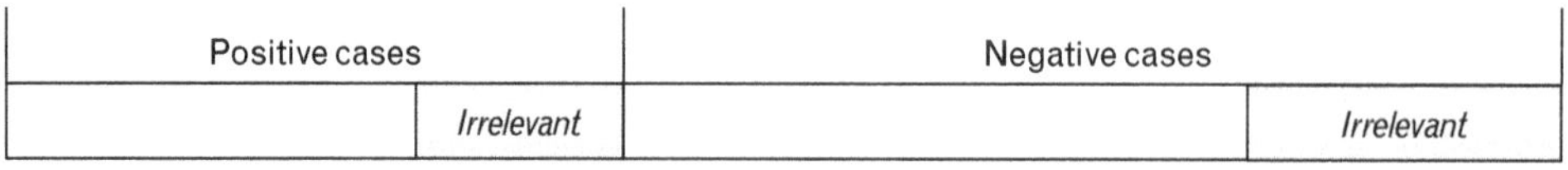

Positive cases		Negative cases	
	Irrelevant		*Irrelevant*

Figure 2.3   Positive, Negative, and Irrelevant Cases

explanatory conditions. For example, let us assume we want to study the conditions under which foreign aid is provided in humanitarian emergencies, based on the given population of the 193 United Nations member states. However, using this given population means that countries are included in the sample that may lack the economic and financial capacity to provide foreign aid in the first place. Hence, including such cases in our study would inflate the number of negative cases and may thus lead to flawed inferences based on conditions shared by the irrelevant negative cases. Irrelevant cases *partially* overlap with the set of "impossible cases," to use Gary Goertz's and James Mahoney's (2006) term. The lesson for case selection is that one should only include those cases where the outcome *could possibly happen* given what we know about the case. This implies that cases where the outcome is deemed impossible should be treated as "uninformative and hence irrelevant observations" (Goertz and Mahoney 2006, 179).

Figure 2.3 shows the relationship between positive, negative, and irrelevant cases. For many phenomena in which social scientists are interested, the size of the set of negative cases exceeds the set of positive cases, as indicated in the figure. Importantly, both positive and negative cases may entail irrelevant cases that should be excluded. These may be cases for which it would be impossible to show the outcome. Likewise, there might be cases that show the outcome; but given what we know about them, it would have been impossible for them to *not* show the outcome. For example, suppose you study why some countries abstained from implementing a certain EU policy at a given point in time. Now there might be a country that you would treat as a "positive" case because it did not implement the policy. However, closer inspection might show that the country experienced a constitutional crisis at the time and there was no functioning government to implement the policy. Hence, it might not be sensible to include this as a positive case of your outcome. Apart from cases where the outcome or the nonoutcome is impossible, the set of irrelevant cases can further entail those that are deemed substantively unimportant and that should thus be excluded from case selection. For example, suppose we wanted to study how various political factors make an impact upon parliamentary debates in consolidated democracies (the number of parties, their ideological positions, etc.). Now there might be a country that fulfills our criteria for case selection, because it meets a certain democracy threshold, but where parliament was dissolved during the observed time frame, owing to a constitutional crisis. Hence, we may consider this case irrelevant for substantive reasons. Ultimately, whether a case can be considered substantively unimportant depends on the research aims of a given study.

How Many Cases Are Needed?

There is no golden rule for how many cases *must* be included in a QCA study. Nor is there an upper limit for the inclusion of cases. That said, QCA works well with medium numbers, and this shows in the fact that in many academic fields the majority of published articles draw on a range of 15 to 30 cases, as reflected in the survey results discussed at the end of this chapter.[17]

More important than the absolute number of cases are two related indicators: (1) *the ratio between cases and conditions*, and (2) *the empirical distribution of cases across truth table rows*. The first indicator is relevant because the number of conditions determines the size of the truth table. With each condition that is added, there will be more logically possible combinations into which cases can fall. This means that, if this is repeatedly done, eventually there will be one row for each case (and many empty rows). The side effect is that *consistency*—a concept to be discussed in chapter 6—increases when conditions are added, but the resulting solutions may or may not be meaningful, because even random data may generate patterns of sufficient configurations when there are too few cases per condition (Marx and Duşa 2011).[18] Hence, because the truth table grows exponentially with each condition that one adds to a study, one should simultaneously increase the number of cases. This does not mean that the number of cases has to match the number of possible configurations, but we should keep in mind the size of the truth table when thinking about how many cases we want to include in our study.

As an orientation mark, I suggest using a ratio of *at least* four cases per condition, and higher ratios if five or more conditions are included because of the exponential growth of the truth table. This means that a standard QCA application with four or five conditions should entail at *minimum* 16 or 25 cases, respectively (see table 2.2). This recommendation broadly resonates with earlier efforts to formulate benchmarks for the inclusion of cases, as suggested by Axel Marx and Adrian Duşa (2011, 114), who ran simulations with crisp-set data (see also Marx 2006).

The second indicator, the empirical distribution of cases across truth table rows, reveals the *empirical scope* of the research design. This is often overlooked because discussions tend to focus on the absolute number of cases. Yet this may even be a more critical factor to consider, because studies can differ greatly in the extent to which the empirical cases are distributed among the logically possible combinations of conditions. Imagine that you have a research design with 16 cases and 3 conditions where the cases evenly fill out all the 8 logically possible rows with 2 cases per row. This would be a situation with a *complete* truth table without any logical remainders (and hence the solution terms that you would eventually derive from this would be identical, as is discussed in chapter 7). In another scenario, you might also have 16 cases and 3 conditions, but the cases cluster together in only 3 rows, leaving 5 logical remainders. This means that although you may have plenty of cases, there is little

Table 2.2   Cases, Conditions, and Truth Table Rows

Number of Conditions	Truth Table Rows	Suggested Minimum Number of Cases	Ratio of Cases per Condition
2	4	8	4
3	8	12	4
4	16	16	4
5	32	25	5
6	64	36	6
7	128	42	6
8	256	56	7

variation between them. This prompts questions about whether further cases should be added to reduce limited diversity and whether the selection and conceptualization of the conditions should be changed to achieve a more even distribution across the truth table rows.[19]

Now one may ask why the number of empty rows matters—why is it that we cannot simply work with the cases at hand, regardless of limited diversity and logical remainder rows? To be sure, the technical routine of QCA works even under extreme scenarios where, let's say, conditions outnumber cases. However, besides from the inferential problems mentioned above, looking at the *empirical scope* of a study can help us to identify problems at an early stage. When cases cluster in but a few rows, leaving many logical remainders, this suggests that there might be a *mismatch* between the explanatory model and the case selection. After all, there are simply no cases for many implied combinations of conditions. The apparent mismatch between the empirical variety and the logically possible variety, as in the above example, may result from the criteria that were applied for the selection of cases. If we had included a larger number of cases, then these might have filled more truth table rows. The mismatch might also result from our conceptualization of conditions. If conditions had drawn on different indicators, then the cases might have distributed more evenly. Even simpler, it might be that some of our conditions, though theoretically feasible, do not resonate with the empirics of our research design. Hence, revisiting and possibly replacing some conditions might be warranted.

Table 2.2 illustrates the relationship between the number of conditions and truth table rows, as well as the recommended minimum numbers of cases. The latter is based on a suggested ratio of cases per condition, starting with a minimum value of four cases per condition and increasing from five conditions upward. These recommended ratios are meant to provide *general advice* on how many cases should be included for a certain number of conditions—as this is one of the most frequent questions asked by new users of QCA.

The recommended ratio comes with the caveat that such thresholds should never be applied mechanically, nor can they replace individual judgment. In some research settings, one simply has to make do with a small number of cases. For instance, this can be because of the small size of a given population or for reasons of missing data. However, in both scenarios a researcher could still decide to focus on a smaller set of conditions and thereby limit the size of the truth table. From this perspective, there are always two possible adjustments to avoid a mismatch between conditions and cases: one can decide to either *increase* the number of cases or to *decrease* the number of conditions included.

CONDITION SELECTION

The selection of conditions is central to designing effective research with QCA. This selection compels us to balance opposing tendencies: On one hand, we often want to include as many conditions as possible, to provide a full account of the phenomenon we seek to explain. On the other hand, each added condition makes our analysis more complex and thus more difficult to interpret. Adding conditions increases the number of possible configurations (shown in the size of the truth table), and with it the scope of *limited diversity*, because there will be fewer empirical cases for each combination. Albert Einstein is reported to have said that "everything should be made as simple as possible, but not simpler" (Sessions 1950). In line with this adage, as QCA researchers, we may want to keep the number of conditions small, while allowing for enough complexity to investigate various configurations of relevant conditions.

Apart from balancing these two tendencies, QCA studies should always provide a careful *justification* for their selection of conditions. This serves to address a common response, because reviewers and audiences often rightfully ask why certain conditions were *not* included in a study (and how the results would have looked like if these had been included). To address such concerns, QCA studies should strive (1) to include all important conditions, or as many of these as feasible; and (2) to provide a thorough justification why these and not others were selected.

Plausible reasons why certain factors were not considered as conditions can be manifold: They can be due to a lack of available data (when there is no accessible information on some of the cases), because a considered factor does not vary across the observed cases (as when all cases hold similar or identical values on a condition), or owing to boundaries of the theoretical framework (which may specify certain kinds of factors but not others).

To reduce the number of conditions, we can also apply *scope conditions* by limiting the analysis to a certain domain or level. This is similar to the usage of scope conditions in case selection, as discussed above. For example, we may restrict our theoretical framework to the formal constitutional structures of democracies, hence excluding factors such as political culture or societal norms, both of which would be outside that scope. In another setting, we may restrict our analysis to a variety of personality traits among a group of entrepreneurs. This would rule out external factors, such as the socioeconomic environment that the respective businesses operate in. In both settings, these restrictions should be made explicit.

The number of conditions can also be reduced when there are several similar or related factors and including one of them suffices for our purposes. For instance, if our study already includes a condition "green party support" based on electoral votes for a green party, then we may not need another similar condition that reflects public preferences about green policy issues. If we do not want to lose information, we can also aggregate several related factors into index conditions or "macro-conditions" (Ragin and Fiss 2017, 75). This can be an effective way to take into account the various dimensions of higher-level concepts, such as "democracy" or "social equality." How this is done in practice is a matter of calibration, which we discuss in chapter 5. That said, regardless of which and how many conditions we eventually include in our study, there should be a discussion of *why* these were selected and, possibly, why certain other conditions were *not* considered.[20]

What is important to note in this context is that in QCA there are *no control variables*. This is another difference in relation to statistical methods, where control variables are frequently used to test for spuriousness (Frankfort-Nachmias and Nachmias 2008, 50). In statistics, this is done to ensure that an observed relation between an independent and a dependent variable is not caused by some third variable (the control variable). By contrast, all QCA conditions have the *same status* and are treated the same way throughout the analysis.[21] Therefore, it would make no sense for a QCA study to label some conditions as "controls" because all of them are part of the same analysis.

How to begin with the selection of conditions? Methodologists have suggested various ways of selecting and reducing the number of conditions used in QCA studies (Amenta and Poulsen 1994; Berg-Schlosser and De Meur 2009; Kahwati and Kane 2020; Schneider and Wagemann 2006). Although there are no firm rules on condition selection, and the context of a given study should always be kept in mind, we can still derive a few guidelines. First, as mentioned above, the *number of conditions should be kept as small as feasible*. The strengths of QCA show when the number of conditions is in the small to medium range (say three to five conditions). Working in that range allows the researcher to properly theorize the conditions and their expected relation to the outcome, and to discuss potential interaction between conditions. A small number of conditions is also helpful to focus on key aspects and to highlight individual paths in QCA solution terms. Yet this should not be taken to imply that more conditions cannot be managed— because there are examples of successful studies with more than five conditions—but larger numbers of conditions do pose particular challenges, and this should be kept in mind when designing a study.[22]

Table 2.3   Approaches for the Selection of Explanatory Conditions

Approach	Characteristics	Examples
Single-model approach	Stable set of conditions throughout the analysis	Boogaerts (2018), Pullum (2016), Vis (2011)
Integrated model	Stable set of conditions based on theoretical integration	Haesebrouck (2017), Mello (2012)
Exploratory models	Multiple models of conditions, used for explorative purposes	Avdagic (2010), Ahn and Lee (2012), Pinfari (2011)
Competing models	Multiple models of conditions, used to test rival theories	Hörisch (2013), Lilliefeldt (2012), Maat (2011)
Two-step approach	Remote and proximate conditions, sequential analyses	Brockhaus et al. (2017), Kirchherr, Ahrenshop, and Charles (2019)

Second, *conditions should be conceptualized in a way that resonates with causal complexity*. The identification of causal complexity is a particular strength of QCA. Hence, to make the most of QCA, studies should conceptualize their conditions in a way that builds on this strength of the method. This means that interacting elements and causal mechanisms should be conceptualized as separate conditions that can be analyzed empirically. The conditions should also allow for conjunctural causation and the existence of multiple pathways or recipes. Finally, *conditions should be conceptualized in a straightforward manner and not be too narrow*. The former ensures that it remains possible to interpret what it means when a case holds membership in a given condition, whereas the latter cautions that conditions should have broad applicability across cases. Because we can only accommodate a limited number of conditions, these should not be used to cover idiosyncrasies of specific cases (e.g., the particularities of an electoral system that can only be found in 3 out of 30 cases).

Empirically speaking, we can distinguish five approaches to the selection of conditions. These are summarized in table 2.3. The *single-model* approach applies a stable set of conditions throughout the analysis of the outcome and the nonoutcome. The conditions themselves are located at the same level or part of the same theory or theoretical framework. This may be the most commonly used approach among QCA studies. Examples include the articles by Andreas Boogaerts (2018), Amanda Pullum (2016), and Barbara Vis (2011). For instance, the study by Boogaerts (2018) aims to explain the European Union's use of sanctions during the Arab Spring. Because the study works with a relatively small number of only 13 cases, it constructs two *macro-conditions* that combine several indicators on the violent suppression of protests and material and security interests, in addition to two regular conditions, for a total of four conditions (Boogaerts 2018, 414). An advantage of the single-model approach lies in its simplicity: it is easy for readers to grasp which and how many conditions were used, and the results can be documented in a straightforward fashion.

The *integrated model* approach differs from the single-model approach only in the sense that conditions are explicitly drawn from different theories and integrated into a single, stable set of conditions. For example, for studies in international relations, some of the conditions may be derived from theories that are based on the level of the international system, whereas other conditions are rooted in the level of domestic politics (e.g., Haesebrouck 2017b and Mello 2020). Along those lines, Tim Haesebrouck (2017b) combines international factors with domestic constraints to provide an integrated model of burden sharing among NATO member states. The integrated approach works well with QCA because it often entails concrete expectations about the interaction between certain conditions, which can also be visualized.[23] The challenge is to provide a persuasive justification for the selection of conditions because the candidate pool of potential conditions tends to be larger than for studies with a single theoretical framework.

The other three approaches all entail several analytical steps. As the name implies, the *exploratory models* approach is based on several models of conditions, which are tested for their inferential value in terms of explaining the outcome. Typically, this approach is used when there is a broad but inconclusive literature on a topic (Ahn and Lee 2012; Avdagic 2010; Pinfari 2011). For instance, in her study of social pacts between governments, employers, and unions, Sabina Avdagic (2010, 643) sets out "to explore multiple models, each containing a modest number of conditions." Altogether, Avdagic derives 11 conditions from the political economy literature, but these are narrowed down to 5 conditions over the course of the analysis. The strength of this approach lies in its inclusiveness, as it covers all or nearly all potential conditions that are mentioned in the literature. But this comes at a cost, because the analytical steps are multiplied by the number of models, which poses challenges for the substantive interpretation and the documentation of the results.

The *competing models* approach works in similar fashion, but here the models are drawn from rival theories or schools of thought and are placed against each other in sequential analyses (Hörisch 2013; Lilliefeldt 2012; Maat 2011). For instance, Felix Hörisch (2013) derives conditions from the competing theories of partisan politics and varieties of capitalism, and Emelie Lilliefeldt (2012) draws on theories of social democracy and Protestantism, among others. Eelco Van der Maat (2011) pits different models based on theories of international relations against each other, including realism, neoliberal institutionalism, and domestic-level approaches. In his study, van der Maat conducts consecutive analyses of these models and also includes a combination of the latter two models. In his empirical analysis, the realist model emerges as the frame-work with the greatest explanatory power (highest consistency and coverage values). The competing models approach benefits from its comprehensiveness and its poten-tial to compare the empirical resonance of different theoretical accounts. Apart from the increased complexity, which it shares with the exploratory approach, an additional challenge lies in developing models that properly reflect the respective theories in an unbiased manner.

Finally, the *two-step approach*, developed by Carsten Schneider and Claudius Wagemann (2006) differentiates between remote and proximate conditions and runs sequential analyses to identify contexts under which certain configurations lead to the outcome. Using the two-step approach, Maria Brockhaus and colleagues (2017) analyze the implementation of environmental protection policies by distinguishing between institutional settings (conceived as remote conditions) and the policy arena (proximate conditions).[24] Similarly, Julian Kirchherr, Mats-Philip Ahrenshop, and Katrina Charles (2019) examine large dam projects and differentiate between struc-tural factors that are largely stable (remote conditions) for a single dam project and those that vary, like the project cycle and political stakeholders (proximate condi-tions). The two-step approach resonates with the way in which explanations are often formed in the social sciences. Typically, context factors may have a positive impact on the outcome (or they may be necessary conditions), but these may not in themselves provide sufficient explanations. Hence, there is a need to combine these with factors that are closer to the phenomenon that ought to be explained. As with some of the pre-vious approaches, the downside to this is increased complexity due to the sequential analytical steps (see chapter 8 for an example of the two-step approach).

What is the most suitable approach to selecting conditions? Evidently, there is no silver bullet for arriving at a sensible number of conditions. A core question is whether to work with one model of conditions or to include several models. The first two approaches apply the same model throughout, whereas the latter three approaches use sequential analyses with several models. Clearly, using multiple models allows more conditions to be included in the analysis. This can be helpful to test rival theories or to explore a broader number of theoretical conjectures based on comprehensive lit-erature reviews. The downside of a larger number of conditions and multiple models is that the analysis swiftly becomes unwieldy. For publications, particularly journal articles, this can pose a problem because there will be less space to discuss individual conditions and to explore the results. Ultimately, the decision of whether to use a single model or several models should be made in line with the research aims and the theoretical basis of a given study. If one is unsure about the inclusion of certain con-ditions, I suggest starting with a handful of the most important conditions and slowly increasing the complexity until a satisfactory explanatory model is found. Building up a study in an incremental and iterative manner, through a back-and-forth between theory and evidence, helps to identify patterns among the cases and relationships between the conditions, which can be further refined by adding conditions, cases, and successive analytical steps.

MULTIMETHOD RESEARCH DESIGNS

In many areas of the social sciences, multimethod research designs have become the *gold standard* for empirical studies. Publications and collaborative research projects show that there has been a virtual multimethod "boom" during the past decade as *nested analysis, mixed method*, and *multimethod* research strategies have gained considerable popularity (Beach 2020; Goertz 2017; Lieberman 2005, 2015; Seawright 2016).[25] This also applies to QCA, where a range of frameworks have been proposed on how to conduct multimethod research in set-theoretic contexts (Beach and Rohlfing 2018; Kahwati and Kane 2020; Meegdenburg and Mello forthcoming; Pattyn et al. 2020; Rihoux, Álamos-Concha, and Lobe 2021; Rohlfing and Schneider 2018; Schneider and Rohlfing 2013, 2019). Arguably, these trends are the result of both a broader recognition of the inherent limitations of social science methods as much as they are an acknowledgment of causal pluralism, which can be tapped into by using different inferential approaches (Anjum and Mumford 2018; Illari and Russo 2014).

But what are the advantages of multimethod research, and how can it be implemented with QCA? Before addressing these questions, it is vital to note that QCA, in itself, can be considered a multimethod approach, because it is based equally on the *qualitative* study of cases and *quantitative* analytical procedures (Rihoux et al. 2009). This requires intimate case knowledge, even though the level of detail will differ with the research aims and the number of cases in a given study. However, as Benoît Rihoux and Bojana Lobe (2009, 229) rightly highlight, "at virtually every step of the QCA procedure, there is a dialogue with the individual cases." Moreover, many set-theoretic studies draw on both qualitative and quantitative forms of data, as one of the characteristics of a mixed methods approach (Kahwati and Kane 2020, 12). As such, the outcome to be explained may rest on qualitative information that is gathered from interviews, official documents, media reports, and the like, whereas explanatory conditions may be based on preexisting quantitative data, such as economic or social indicators, or official statistics and other sources of numerical information. From this perspective, it may appear misguided to demand that QCA must *always* be combined with other methods, without taking into account the specific research context in which a study situates itself.[26]

That said, many scholars agree that the combination of several research methods holds potential because the inferential strengths of one method can be combined with those of another, and the blind spots of each may be overcome with a sound multimethod research design (Beach and Pedersen 2013; Blatter and Haverland 2012; Gerring 2012b; Goertz 2017; Seawright 2016).[27] As is explored in chapter 4, with its emphasis on causal pluralism, different methods are suitable for different kinds of causal explanations. For instance, though an intensive case study may provide us with a good grasp of a causal process at play in a single case, it would not necessarily allow us to engage in generalization to a larger number of cases. With QCA, we may be able to identify a cross-case pattern, but this might not suffice to uncover a causal mechanism. For that, we would need to examine whether the observable implications of our theory can be identified during the actual process as it evolves over time in a given case.

To be sure, there are different understandings of what multimethod research entails. One conception that is not considered here is the combination of large-N statistical analysis with case studies (Lieberman 2005, 2015; Seawright 2016) and, specifically, the combination of statistics and QCA (Meuer and Rupietta 2017).[28] In the context of set-theoretic methods, most work has focused on the combination of QCA as a method for *cross-case* analysis and process tracing as a method for *within-case* analysis, and, specifically, for the identification of causal mechanisms (Beach 2018; Beach, Pedersen, and Siewert 2019; Beach and Rohlfing 2018; Meegdenburg and Mello forthcoming; Pattyn et al. 2020; Rihoux, Álamos-Concha, and Lobe 2021; Rohlfing and Schneider 2018; Schneider and Rohlfing 2013, 2019). Though a detailed discussion of the suggested frameworks is beyond the scope of this section, four approaches can be distinguished, all of which focus on combining QCA and process tracing.

The first question when engaging in multimethod research with QCA and process tracing is whether to conduct the within-case analysis *before* or *after* the QCA part. Before QCA, the within-case analysis can serve, first, to *explore* potential conditions and to gain a better understanding of a prominent case. For this purpose, we would usually select a case that shows the outcome of interest, but we may not yet know how this case relates to the larger population of cases. Such an exploratory use of case studies can serve to identify relevant conditions and to build hypotheses (Rohlfing 2012, 11). In an ideal scenario, the exploration may even yield a mechanistic explanation of the outcome (Beach and Pedersen 2019, 9). A more formalized way of doing case studies before QCA is selecting a *typical case* based on a larger cross-case relationship. Clearly, this requires some kind of prior analysis to establish whether a case can be deemed typical, or representative of a population of cases (Gerring 2007a, 91–97). In a QCA context, it may be that a topic has been well researched, so that it is possible to identify a typical case based on existing studies in the field. Process tracing on this case would aim to identify a within-case relationship between a condition or configuration and the outcome, or to test a hypothesis about the presence of a condition or combination of conditions (Beach and Rohlfing 2018, 12). Both these uses of case studies may require some iterations on additional cases if the results are not conclusive, before one can proceed with the cross-case QCA part.

When intensive case studies are conducted after QCA, they can either serve to confirm theory or to modify and further develop the theoretical framework (Schneider and

Rohlfing 2013). For this usage, we can select a *typical case* from the QCA results, which is a case that holds membership in the solution term and the outcome. More precisely, we should select a *pathway case* (Gerring 2007a, 122). For the QCA context, a pathway case would be one that is uniquely covered by one of the solution paths. The alternative is to select a *deviant case*, defined as one that holds membership in the solution but that does not show the expected outcome.[29] Depending on the results, these case analyses may provide confirmatory evidence of causal mechanisms, but they may also identify shortcomings in the theoretical account, as in overlooked factors or unexpected effects, which may lead to a modification of the theory and a renewed cross-case case analysis with QCA. The general contours of the four basic approaches to combining QCA and process tracing are summarized in table 2.4. Boxes 2.1 and 2.2 provide examples of multimethod QCA in the context of environmental peacemaking (Ide 2018) and biological attributions of mental illness (Andersson and Harkness 2018).

Table 2.4   Combining QCA and Process Tracing

Research Phase	Process Tracing	Aims	Consequences
Before QCA	Exploratory process tracing	Identify relevant conditions	Follow-up with QCA (cross-case analysis)
	Process tracing on a typical case	Identify within-case relationship	
After QCA	Process tracing on a pathway case	Identify causal mechanism	Confirm theory
	Process tracing on a deviant case	Identify room for theory improvement	Modify theory

---

Box 2.1   Environmental Cooperation and Peacemaking Between States: A Multimethod Research Design Combining Statistical Analysis, QCA, and Case Studies

Tobias Ide, Murdoch University

Researchers have long speculated that environmental cooperation can facilitate peacemaking between states ("environmental peacemaking"), but little cross-case evidence on this hypothesis existed. In order to fill this gap, I

(continued)

Box 2.1 (*continued*)

employed QCA in the context of a multimethod research design (Ide 2018). Specifically, I aimed to study the links between cooperative environmental agreements (which might help to build trust or create interdependence) and the termination of international rivalries (by means of reconciliation).

In a first step, I employed odds ratio tests of all possible cases in the sample. These indicated a weak, yet significant link between the conclusion of an environmental agreement and rivalry termination. Based on the odds ratios and the existing literature, I concluded that environmental peacemaking is highly context dependent. It is here where QCA kicked in. I selected the 20 cases in the sample in which rival states signed a cooperative environmental agreement and identified the conditions distinguishing the 6 case of rivalry termination (in the five years after the agreement) from the 14 cases without this outcome. Results show that the combination of high environmental attention, political stability, and conservation cooperation is sufficient for environmental peacemaking.

In my view, the multimethod research design was key to convincing the reviewers. The total sample of cases (dyadic rivalries in the 1946–2010 period) would have been too large for the QCA. And starting the study outright with the 20 cases was infeasible as the key explanatory variable of the study (cooperative environmental agreements) would have shown no variation. So I decided to use statistical techniques in order to answer "whether" questions and QCA to answer "when" (or "in which context") questions.

Subsequent desk-based qualitative studies of the 6 positive cases significantly refined the QCA results. For example, they illustrated the causal links indicated by the QCA, but also qualified that environmental agreements catalyze, but do not initiate processes of reconciliation in rivalries (hence addressing "how" questions). Further on, the case studies identified one outcome not explained by the QCA as a false positive and uncovered an additional relevant causal condition: pre-existing, informal environmental cooperation.

So QCA shows considerable potential for application in multimethod research designs. But this is not always easy to do. Reviewers can be (and in my case in fact were) skeptical whether, for instance, it would be better to do one in-depth rather than three supposedly superficial analyses. Extensive references, a concise writing style and the preparation of informative online appendices can be helpful here. One should also keep in mind that reviewers are often more familiar with statistical and case studies approaches, and that QCA thus needs to be introduced more comprehensively than other parts of a multimethod design.

Box 2.2 When Do Biological Attributions of Mental Illness Reduce Stigma? Using Qualitative Comparative Analysis to Contextualize Attributions

Matthew A. Andersson, Baylor University; and Sarah K. Harkness, University of Iowa

In recent decades, lay and professional audiences alike have subscribed to a complex, biopsychosocial model of mental illness, which has come to supersede discrete biological, social, and psychological factors that may contribute to illness. In other words, most people usually endorse *several* intersecting beliefs surrounding the origins of mental illness—not just one or two beliefs. Beliefs about mental illness appear to be a setting where "theories do not contradict each other directly and thus do not really compete [as independent variables]" (Ragin 2008b, 179).

How can we better understand how stigmatization actually works? The answer, we suspected, had to do with taking a more contingent approach to analyzing stigma. Rather than treating beliefs as isolated entities, we sought to conceptualize beliefs as constellations or "causal stories" of mental illness, which are not reducible to the elements composing them. QCA is naturally suited to uncovering highly contingent pathways between conditions and outcomes.

For us, the most challenging part about designing the QCA study, beyond learning the logic and steps involved in fs (fuzzy-set) QCA, examining best practices for QCA (e.g., Schneider and Wagemann 2010), and implementing fsQCA with *fuzzy,* a user-written Stata package (Longest and Vaisey 2008), was supplying our readers with a compelling, concise explanation of the method. How does one get quantitative scientists, who are overwhelmingly regression-minded, to intuitively appreciate what QCA reveals once "variance explained" is removed from the analytic vocabulary? We settled on the key point that covariance- or clustering-based quantitative methods treat groups of variables and their relationships as "black boxes" from which it is very difficult if not impossible to know which variables are relevant to outcomes or under which conditions they become relevant. Then, to come full-circle in our paper, we used additional, regression-based analyses, to show how QCA-based solutions explained variation in stigma even net of the singular beliefs composing them.

Our experience through the peer-review process was a bit prolonged. We went through a rejection and even a rejected revise-and-resubmit. Reviewers saw promise in our approach but reasonably had a lot of thoughtful questions about what QCA involved and how to account for our key findings. These

(continued)

Box 2.2 (*continued*)

questions thankfully moved us toward a stronger paper that could communicate with a wider intellectual audience.

When it came to anchoring our paper in a concrete social problem, the turning point for us was realizing that QCA could illuminate the "biological turn" for how mental illness is viewed. Why, if "mental illness is a disease like any other," is public acceptance not increasing? To us, there seemed a basic oversight: just because biology has become a more common explanation doesn't mean that nonbiological explanations no longer are important to the public. And in fact, that is exactly what we found in our QCA study: biological and nonbiological beliefs work in tandem to structure the public's desire for social distance from those perceived as mentally ill.

A SURVEY OF EMPIRICAL APPLICATIONS

To give an idea of how current QCA research *practice* looks, as opposed to the general principles and recommendations discussed in the previous sections, this chapter closes with descriptive statistics from an original survey of 120 empirical studies. To begin with, this allows us to gauge the popularity of the different QCA variants, which are examined in more detail in chapter 8. More important, the survey sheds light on the number of cases and conditions used in applied studies from diverse academic fields in the social sciences, which we can contrast with the suggestions derived in earlier sections of this chapter.

For this survey, the Web of Science database was used to identify empirical QCA applications in six academic fields: business, political science, sociology, public administration, public health, and international relations. Although this sample is not exhaustive in scope, the selected fields cover a broad range of social science research and academic conventions. Moreover, the selection further includes research areas where the increase in QCA studies has been most dynamic (on publication trends, see chapter 1). Not surprisingly, publication practices vary in these fields, and the prevalence of QCA in them also differs. As mentioned at the outset of this book, some fields have hundreds of QCA studies that are listed in the Web of Science, whereas for others the method is less established, and the numbers are much smaller. There are also considerable differences in the lengths of the respective articles, ranging from concise treatments of 8 to 10 pages to comprehensive studies of more than 30 pages. Naturally, this also reflects in the level of detail that is given to the methodological documentation.

To identify *current* practice in QCA applications, the search was restricted to the 20 most recent journal articles from each discipline (as of May 20, 2020), making up a total sample of 120 empirical studies.[30] Emphasis was placed on *current* publications to assess present standards, rather than the evolution of QCA applications since the method's development in 1987. The sample was restricted to peer-reviewed journals that were listed in the Social Sciences Citation Index. To be included in the survey, studies had to have an empirical rather than a methodological focus and had to use QCA as their primary documented method. Journal classification was taken as an indicator of the article's disciplinary category. Because journals can belong to several categories, classification was done in accordance with the highest-ranking category for the respective journal.

Before proceeding, one caveat is in order: given the moderate sample size, I make no claims about the representativeness of the selected studies. It should also be noted that many well-respected journals are not included in the Social Sciences Citation Index, particularly non-English journals, which means that there is a systematic bias in the data.[31] That said, table 2.5 summarizes the survey results across the six disciplines. The left-hand columns show the absolute numbers of the major QCA variants (crisp-set, fuzzy-set, and multivalue QCA), whereas the right-hand columns show the median values for the number of cases, number of conditions, and the ratio of cases per condition for the observed studies.

What are the results of the survey? First, with regard to the QCA variants across the observed academic fields, it is apparent that fuzzy-set QCA has become the dominant variant. In business studies, it is virtually the *only* variant that is used, but it has outpaced the other variants in all the other fields as well. This is a surprising finding because it appears that the trend has *reversed* since the results of a comprehensive survey of 313 journal applications from 1984 to 2011, where Rihoux and others (2013) still found that crisp-set QCA was the most popular version of QCA, with fuzzy-set QCA following at some distance. To be sure, the data might look different if we were to look at a larger time span (e.g., from 2011 to 2020), and supposedly the share of crisp-set applications would then be larger. Moreover, of the 120 studies examined, only 4 used multivalue QCA (Cronqvist and Berg-Schlosser 2009), which shows that this variant has remained "rather marginal," as Rihoux and others (2013, 177) already noted in their survey.[32] Not included in the table is two-step QCA (Schneider and Wagemann 2006), because it is an approach that can be combined with any QCA variant. Out of the sample of 120 studies, 6 articles used the two-step approach, 2 each were in political science and sociology, and 1 each was in business and public administration.

The second finding concerns the number of cases and conditions among the surveyed studies. Here, it is interesting to note that across fields, with the exception of business studies, the median numbers of cases and conditions used in the analysis are fairly similar—in the range of 20 to 30 cases and about 6 conditions per study. Correspondingly, the ratio of cases per condition runs from 4.1 in public administration to 5.3 in political science and international relations. At the far end are business

Table 2.5 Survey of 120 QCA Studies

| Academic Field | N | QCA Variants | | | Median Values | | |
		Crisp-Set	Fuzzy-Set	Multivalue	Cases	Conditions	Cases/Conditions
Business	20	1	19	0	182	6	30.3
Sociology	20	5	15	0	30	5	4.2
International relations	20	4	13	3	26	5	5.3
Public health	20	5	14	1	25	6	4.7
Political science	20	5	14	1	22	6	5.3
Public administration	20	5	15	0	20	5	4.1
Sum/median	120	25	90	5	26	6	5

studies, with a median of 30.3 cases per condition. With these median values, the surveyed articles are *above* the recommended threshold of cases per conditions, as summarized in table 2.2 earlier in this chapter. However, it should be clear that these numbers refer to the *median* across the sampled studies, so individual studies diverge from these values. Finally, there is an evident break between the business field and the other academic disciplines, with the former being characterized by large-*N* fuzzy-set QCA with considerably more cases per study than commonly used in other areas of the social sciences.

NOTES

Epigraph: Toshkov (2016, 1).

1. For texts on general aspects of research design in the social sciences, see Blatter and Haverland (2012); Brady and Collier (2010); George and Bennett (2005); Gerring (2012b); Goertz and Mahoney (2012); Gschwend and Schimmelfennig (2007); King, Keohane, and Verba (1994); Ragin and Becker (1992); Rohlfing (2012); and Toshkov (2016). On QCA research design, see Thomann and Maggetti (2020).

2. Chapter 8 discusses some proposals made toward temporal QCA, as a formal way of including sequence in the analytical procedure.

3. For further contributions to this debate, see, among many others, Tarrow (1995), George and Bennett (2005), Rihoux and Grimm (2006), Ragin (2008b), Collier, Brady, and Seawright (2010a), Mahoney (2010), Goertz and Mahoney (2012), and Cooper et al. (2012). Some of the discussions have been continued in various issues of *Qualitative and Multi-Method Research* of the American Political Science Association.

4. Along with King, Keohane, and Verba (1994, chap. 1); Schmitter (2008); and Gerring (2012b, chap. 2), also see the helpful discussion of types of research and research questions by Toshkov (2016, chap. 2).

5. This draws on the distinction between x-centered and y-centered research that was established by Ganghof (2005).

6. In his book on multimethod research, Goertz (2017) discusses published examples of how QCA is used to explore causal mechanisms.

7. Cast at a more general level than other accounts, my taxonomy differs from those who include five or even six types of different uses of QCA (Berg-Schlosser et al. 2009, 15; Ragin and Rihoux 2004a, 6; Schneider and Wagemann 2010, 400). The distinguishing criterion for these is whether a study's primary aim is descriptive or explanatory. Apart from that, some suggested categories such as "summarizing data" and "checking coherence of data" appear virtually indistinguishable in applied settings.

8. Apart from a handful of exceptions, nearly all the 120 QCA applications surveyed for this chapter used the method to test theoretical expectations in one way or another. The results of the survey are presented in this chapter's final section.

9. On the history of statistical hypothesis testing, see Haig (2018, chap. 3).

10. Formal differences between these perspectives are examined by Thiem, Baumgartner, and Bol (2016).

11. Other examples for the use of INUS hypotheses include Ide (2015), Mello (2020), Oppermann and Brummer (2020), and Wurster and Hagemann (2018). On the concept, see chapter 2.

12. The terms "population" and "universe of cases" are used interchangeably (Seawright and Collier 2010, 357).

13. Case selection and case study methods have spawned an extensive literature; see Blatter and Haverland (2012); Eckstein (1975); George and Bennett (2005); Gerring (2004, 2007a); Goertz and Mahoney (2006); Levy (2008a); Ragin and Becker (1992); Rohlfing (2012); and Seawright and Gerring (2008).

14. For illustrated discussions of scope conditions, see Goertz and Mahoney (2006) and Goertz (2017). More generally, on constituting populations of cases, see Ragin (2000, chaps. 2 and 7; 2006a).

15. A discussion of sources of bias in case selection is provided by Geddes (2007, chap. 3). See also Van Evera (1997, 46).

16. For more general considerations of sampling, see Frankfort-Nachmias and Nachmias (2008, chap. 8) and Toshkov (2016, 130–34).

17. A clear exception are studies in business, management, and economics, which tend to have considerably higher numbers of cases (see the discussion of the survey results at the end of this section).

18. Consistency and other measures of fit are discussed in chapter 6. Here, it suffices to grasp the general logic of the relationship between cases and conditions.

19. There is no general answer to these questions. For some studies, it may be feasible to adapt the research design to increase the empirical scope, whereas others might be constrained by prior decisions.

20. On omitted variables in QCA, see Radaelli and Wagemann (2019).

21. The sole exception is two-step QCA, which rests on a theoretical distinction between "remote" and "proximate" conditions (Schneider and Wagemann 2006). Examples are discussed in chapter 8.

22. Notably, this is not a technical limitation, because the QCA package for R can include up to 18 conditions (Dușa 2019b, 202). However, for applied research, a study with 262,144 truth table rows would not be feasible or allow for a shallow analysis at best.

23. Goertz (2017, 46–49) discusses the integrated model of Mello (2012).

24. See also the separate infobox by Maria Brockhaus and colleagues, who share insights on the larger research project behind their QCA studies (Brockhaus et al. 2017).

25. Although these terms are at times used synonymously, they reflect different understandings of how methods and data from different sources ought to be combined. For this book, the term *multimethod research* is used, to designate the combination of QCA with case studies.

26. Along such lines, George and Bennett (2005, 163) argue that it is necessary to combine QCA with process tracing.

27. Others have suggested that combining methods holds no inherent advantages over the use of a single method (Ahmed and Sil 2009; Coppedge 2009; Kuehn and Rohlfing 2009).

28. Though less common, QCA has been combined with large-N statistical analyses (e.g., Ahn and Lee 2012; Ide 2018; Karlas 2012). In this chapter, see also the infobox by Tobias Ide, reflecting on his study on environmental peacekeeping (Ide 2018).

29. Schneider and Rohlfing (2013, 585) further denote cases that show the outcome without membership in the solution as "deviant cases for coverage." These are cases that call for a different explanation.

30. Thanks to Teslin Augustine for research assistance with the survey.

31. On the coverage of the Web of Science and alternative databases, see Gerring, Karcher, and Apfeld (2020).

32. For an example of mvQCA, see the infobox by Pablo Castillo-Ortiz on his study on judicial councils (Castillo Ortiz 2017). Also see the discussion in chapter 8.

3 • Set Theory

Qualitative research is often based, explicitly or implicitly,
on set theory and logic, and these mathematical tools must
be comprehended in their own right.

—GARY GOERTZ AND JAMES MAHONEY

QCA is a set-theoretic method. But what are *sets*, and how does a *set-theoretic* approach differ from other kinds of approaches? At the most basic level, a set can be defined as a group of elements that share certain characteristics. A set is a class of objects (Quine 1969). For George Lakoff and Rafael Núñez (2000), one way to see a set is as a "containerlike entity," and James Mahoney (2010, 7) describes sets as "boundaries that define zones of inclusion and exclusion." Given these understandings, it is apparent that there is a close affinity between sets and social science concepts. In fact, most social science theories are grounded in set theory, either explicitly by using the language of necessary and sufficient conditions, or implicitly by invoking the set-theoretic logic without expressly referring to necessity and sufficiency (Goertz and Mahoney 2012; Ragin 1987; Schneider and Wagemann 2012).[1]

This chapter lays out the set-theoretic foundations of QCA, including key terms and concepts on which later parts of the book will build. Starting with the distinctive elements of a set-theoretic approach as opposed to a statistical approach, the chapter introduces crisp and fuzzy sets, set operations, formal notation, and the functions of truth tables. The chapter closes with a discussion of necessary and sufficient conditions and the assessment of set relations.

Sets exist all across the social world. Social kinds of sets are concepts that we use to describe groups of objects with specific characteristics. For instance, we may seek to study democratic states or developed countries. Yet the referent concepts "democracy" and "development" are not objectively given but are created in the human mind. As social science concepts, they may be "essentially contested" (Gallie 1956), and their meaning may have changed over time. We know that "democracy" means something else today than 100 years ago, when it was not seen as an essential property of democracy to have universal voting rights. Likewise, a country's "development" was long understood narrowly in terms of the size of its economy, whereas measures like the United Nations' Human Development Index rest on a broader conception that includes education, standard of living, and life expectancy (United Nations 2018).

What distinguishes a set-theoretic approach from other approaches? To illustrate this, we can juxtapose the set-theoretic approach with a statistical approach to derive six key differences (Goertz and Mahoney 2012; Ragin 2014b, xxiii).[2] To begin with, the statistical approach seeks to explain the occurrence of a dependent variable (*explanandum*) with one or more independent variables (*explanans*). These variables are labeled using nouns, as in *height* or *partisanship*. For each of the included variables, the selected cases are then scored based on measurement through indicators. Studies following this approach typically seek to identify linear relationships, as in correlations between the independent variables and the dependent variable, summarized in a correlation matrix, with the aim of identifying the net effect of each independent variable on the dependent variable.

By contrast, the set-theoretic approach uses the terms *conditions* and *outcome* rather than independent variables and dependent variable. The different terminology serves to emphasize the *qualitative* and *case-oriented* nature of set-theoretic analysis, which requires careful concept formation before the actual set-theoretic analysis (Ragin 2014b, xxv).[3] For each of these, nouns and adjectives are used. Hence the set-theoretic approach would refer to *tall* people or *left* partisanship. Other differences concern the way data is generated and analyzed. The set-theoretic approach refers to set membership scores, which are bounded between 0 and 1, as the minimum and maximum values that can be assigned. By contrast, variable-oriented approaches typically work with unbounded numbers, and various kinds of numerical scales can be used. Whereas operations on sets follow the rules of Boolean algebra and set theory—which are introduced in this chapter—variables can be manipulated by applying the rules of linear algebra.[4]

Moreover, sets are *calibrated* toward a predefined point of reference—we could say that they are directed toward a qualitative state—and hence there is more information entailed in calibrated than in uncalibrated measures (Goertz 2020; Ragin 2008a, 2008b). This means that once we know which concept a set refers to, then we also know how to interpret a case's membership score in that set. For example, a person with a score of 1 in the set of *tall people* would be a tall person. Now consider a person with a *height* of 5 feet, 10 inches. Whether this person should be considered tall will depend on contextual information like the person's gender, country of origin, and whether the data are based on a historical or contemporary record.

Finally, the set-theoretic approach aims to identify causally complex set relations involving necessary and sufficient conditions. The data are summarized in the *truth table*, from which solution terms or *causal recipes* are derived (Ragin 2014b,

Table 3.1 Concepts in Statistical and Set-Theoretic Approaches

Differences by Approach	Set-Theoretic Approach	Statistical Approach
Phenomenon to be explained (explanandum)	Outcome	Dependent variable
Phenomena to explain (explanans)	Conditions	Independent variables
Numerical conversion of concepts / raw data	Calibration	Measurement
Relationships to be explored	Causal complexity	Linear relationships
Analytical device	Truth table	Correlation matrix
Results	Necessary and sufficient conditions	Net effects of individual variables

xxvii). Table 3.1 juxtaposes these differences between the set-theoretic and statistical approaches. The bottom line is that it is vital to use the *correct terminology* when referring to each, because the terms are *not* synonyms but rather reflect distinct understandings of empirical research.

CRISP SETS AND FUZZY SETS

QCA is grounded in the works of George Boole, a nineteenth-century British mathematician and logician whose *An Investigation of the Laws of Thought* (Boole 1854) established the foundation for what was later termed Boolean algebra. Boole's approach uses variables that occur in only two states: *true* (present) or *false* (absent). This conception proved central to the development of electronic switching circuits, and Boolean algebra was soon widely applied across the natural sciences (Whitesitt 2010) and also made inroads into the social sciences. Charles Ragin adopted these principles to develop a "Boolean approach" for comparative studies (Ragin et al. 1984), which later was labeled "Qualitative Comparative Analysis" (Ragin 1987). What is important for the aims of qualitative comparison is that Boolean algebra allowed for set-theoretic operations and the construction of truth tables—introduced in this chapter—as well as the minimization of truth tables to derive solution terms (discussed in chapter 7).

The Boolean use of binary categories meant that QCA was, in its original form, limited to working with *crisp sets*, where 1 indicated the presence of a condition and 0 indicated its absence. Such a distinction emphasizes *qualitative* differences. Either a case belongs to a given set or it does not. Yet this procedure entails a loss of nuance, because regardless of how clear-cut our information on a case is, we must code it as either 1 or 0, and no further distinctions can be made (Rihoux and De Meur 2009).

The drawback of crisp-set QCA was overcome with the introduction of *fuzzy sets* (Ragin 2000), which allowed for graded set membership, as any scores from 0 to 1 became possible. Fuzzy logic was developed by Lotfi Zadeh (1965) as an extension of traditional set theory to tackle the problem of complex and imprecise concepts. Zadeh's work sparked a revolution in computer technology (McNeill and Freiberger 1993), and fuzzy sets have also made their way into the social sciences (Smithson and Verkuilen 2006), including linguistics (Lakoff 1973) and many other areas of application.

Fuzzy-set QCA combines qualitative and quantitative dimensions. Based on substantive and theoretical knowledge of their topic, researchers establish three *empirical anchors* that determine whether a case is considered to be "fully in" a given set (reflected in a fuzzy score of 1), whether it is "fully out" of a given set (fuzzy score of 0), or whether it is "neither in nor out" of a given set (fuzzy score of 0.5). The latter is the crossover, or "point of maximum ambiguity," which means that based on the available evidence, it is not possible to say whether the case is inside or outside a respective set (Ragin 2000; 2008b; Ragin and Fiss 2017). The empirical anchors form the basis for the calibration procedure, which is covered in chapter 5.

Fuzzy sets clearly were a major step forward in the evolution of QCA. They allowed for fine-grained differentiation and—addressing concerns of some of the method's critics—showed that QCA did not need to be rooted in a deterministic understanding of causality. They also paved the way for *measures of fit* that enabled researchers to assess the quality and robustness of their analytical results (chapter 6). Measures of fit established benchmarks to distinguish "perfectly" necessary and/or sufficient conditions from "almost" necessary and/or sufficient conditions (those that do not meet a deterministic criterion of necessity or sufficiency), and to identify situations where there is no set-theoretic relationship. Finally, fuzzy sets eased the transformation of quantitative raw data into set membership values, through software-based procedures of calibration.

Irrespective of these advantages of fuzzy sets, it is important to note that Boolean logic still applies to fuzzy sets—cases are treated as either inside or outside a given set, and the differences in degree only indicate that they are *more or less* inside or outside those sets. The researcher still must determine a criterion for how to distinguish cases that are inside a set from those that are outside.

This challenge has been described as the Sorites Paradox, or the paradox of the heap (derived from the Greek word *sorós*). Imagine a heap of sand. Now we may assume that the heap comprises 1,000,000 grains of sand. Removing a single grain of sand will not change its character as a heap, because 999,999 grains of sand are still a heap of sand. And so it will be if another grain of sand is removed, and another, and so forth. Yet at some point we will be left with a few grains of sand that are clearly not a heap anymore.

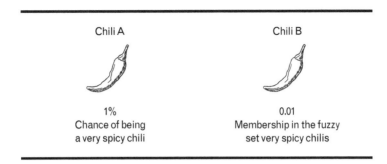

Figure 3.1   Probabilities and Fuzzy Sets

This prompts the question at which point the heap has turned into a *nonheap*—how many grains did we have to remove until the heap disappeared? To solve the paradox, we need to determine criteria to distinguish one state from the other. This is challenging for the heap of sand, because any firm numerical threshold will appear to be arbitrary. For social science concepts, it can also be difficult, but it is a helpful practice that lets us think about *difference makers* and the essential characteristics of our concepts.

A common misconception about fuzzy sets is that these somehow reflect probabilities. However, this is not the case. Let us take an example to illustrate the difference (figure 3.1). Suppose you have two red chilis of identical appearance. You have no other information but that the first chili has a 1 percent chance of being very spicy, whereas the second chili has a fuzzy score of 0.01 membership in the set *very spicy chilis*. You want to cook a nonspicy dish with mild chili as an ingredient. Which of these chilis would you choose? At first glance, it may appear that there is no difference between the two options. However, on closer look, it should become clear that for chili A, the odds are 1 out of 100 that you will pick a very spicy chili. For chili B, the information given is not a probability—you *know for your sure* that chili B is almost entirely outside the set of very spicy chilis—so this would be the better choice in the example. Fuzzy sets thus attribute a discrete score to a specific case and there is no uncertainty or probability involved.

SET OPERATIONS

Because QCA rests on Boolean algebra, we can use its rules for operations on sets to systematically assess the relationship between our outcome, conditions, and combinations of conditions. For our purposes, three operations from Boolean algebra are relevant.[5] The logical operator AND refers to the *intersection* or, to use the term from propositional logic, *conjunction*, between sets. The logical OR refers to the *union* or *disjunction* between sets, whereas the logical NOT describes the *negation* or *complement* of a set.

Table 3.2 Logical Operators and Notational Systems

Logical Operator	Boolean Algebra	Set Theory	Propositional Logic
AND	Multiplication: $A \cdot B$	Intersection: $A \cap B$	Conjunction: $A \wedge B$
OR	Addition: $A + B$	Union: $A \cup B$	Disjunction: $A \vee B$
NOT	Negation: $1 - A$	Complement: $\sim A$	Negation: $\neg A$

What can be confusing about QCA is that it draws on several different notational systems. Depending on a subfield's custom, it may be preferred to use symbols and terms from Boolean algebra, the logic of propositions, or formal set theory. Clearly, the existence of several different terms for the same set operations complicates things. In this book, an effort is made to keep formal notation to a minimum and to consistently use the same notation throughout. To enhance the translation of terms, table 3.2 summarizes the operators and notational forms that are commonly used, depending on whether the reference point is Boolean algebra, set theory, or propositional logic.[6]

How do set operations work in practice? The logical operators are best explained with examples. Table 3.3 gives hypothetical data for three cases, two crisp sets (labeled A and B), two fuzzy sets (C and D), and the results of calculations using the Boolean operators AND, OR, and NOT, in the six columns on the right-hand side of the table.

To begin, let us assume we are interested in cases that share two features. Only if both of these are present do we expect to see our outcome. In set-theoretic terms, the *intersection* between two sets is expressed as $A \cdot B$, where · stands for AND (not to be confused with the mathematical multiplication sign). Verbally, the intersection reads as "A AND B." For convenience, we may also omit the operator and simply write the letters for the respective sets next to each other. To calculate a case's set membership in the intersection, we take the *minimum* score across the sets, reflecting the weakest link or lowest common denominator between the respective sets. This means that cases 1 and 3 from table 3.3 both receive a score of 0 in the expression $A \cdot B$.

For example, we may be interested in calculating two cases' memberships in the intersection between the sets *populist leader* (P) and *supportive public* (S). The first case has fuzzy scores of 0.9 (P) and 0.3 (S), whereas the second case has fuzzy scores of 0.6 (P) and 0.7 (S). Based on the calculation rule, the cases thus hold respective fuzzy scores of 0.3 and 0.6 in the intersection $P \cdot S$. The set-theoretic intersection resonates

Table 3.3   Boolean Operations with Crisp and Fuzzy Sets

	Crisp Sets		Fuzzy Sets		Boolean AND		Boolean OR		Boolean NOT	
Case	A	B	C	D	A · B	C · D	A + B	C + D	~ A	~ C
1	1	0	0.9	0.3	0	0.3	1	0.9	0	0.1
2	1	1	0.7	0.8	1	0.7	1	0.8	0	0.3
3	0	0	0.2	0.4	0	0.2	0	0.4	1	0.8

with settings where several features all must be present and a high score in one condition cannot outweigh a low score in another.

We may also be interested in a situation where cases show at least one of two features, either of which we expect to lead to our outcome, but the cases may also show both features. The *union* between two sets is expressed as A + B, where + stands for OR. Verbally, the union thus reads as "A OR B." This operator is based on an *inclusive* conception of OR, as in "one or the other, or both." Again, this should not be confused with the mathematical operator for addition. Accordingly, a case's set membership in the expression A + B is the *maximum* score across the two sets.

It follows that case 1 and case 2 from table 3.3 get the same score for A + B, because each case has at least one set with a score of 1 and the maximum score determines the overall value. As an example, we may stipulate that governments that face either *constitutional restrictions* (C), *legislative veto players* (L), or both of these, will refrain from power abuses. The first case has fuzzy scores of 0.7 (C) and 0.3 (L), whereas the second one has fuzzy scores of 0.2 (C) and 0.7 (L). Despite these differences, based on the calculation rule, both these cases would receive fuzzy scores of 0.7 in the union C · L. The set-theoretic union reflects situations where there are multiple equivalent factors and either of them suffices for the outcome to occur.

The final set-theoretic operator refers to the *negation* of a set. Once we know that a case holds membership in a set, we can also calculate its membership in the *non*-set, or the negation of the set. Formally, this is calculated as 1 − A. Here, the minus sign actually refers to the mathematical operator for subtraction. The last two columns of table 3.3 show the values for non-A and non-C. Note that due to the bounded nature of set values, the scores for a condition and its negation will always add up to 1. For instance, case 1 has a fuzzy-set membership of 0.9 in C and a fuzzy-set membership of 0.1 in ~C, which add up to 1. For example, Germany may hold a fuzzy score of 0.2 in the set *high unemployment*, which means that it has a fuzzy score of 0.8 in the set *not*–high unemployment (1 − 0.2). When working with the negation of a set, it is vital to clarify the conceptual basis of the first set before interpreting scores in the negation of this

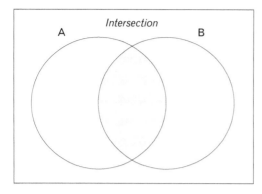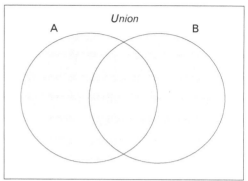

Figure 3.2   Intersection and Union of Two Sets

set. Some concepts may be symmetrical, but many are asymmetric. We return to this aspect in chapter 5.

Set-theoretic operations and relationships between crisp sets can be effectively visualized with Venn and Euler diagrams (Goertz and Mahoney 2012; Mahoney and Sweet Vanderpoel 2015; Quine 1982; Rubinson 2019; Schneider and Wagemann 2012). In *Venn diagrams*, overlapping circles inside a rectangle depict all logically possible intersections between the respective sets. This distinguishes them from *Euler diagrams*, which show only the empirically existing intersections (Shin 1994). Both types of diagrams can be helpful to illustrate set relations. The next figures show the previously discussed Boolean operations in simple settings with just two sets. Clearly, one could add further circles for additional sets, which can be a useful heuristic device when thinking about the relationship among explanatory conditions in a given QCA model. Venn diagrams are also useful to visualize the configurations of truth table rows, discussed in the next section, because the number of areas inside the rectangle always matches the number of logically possible configurations in a given QCA model (Dușa 2019, 263). The left panel of figure 3.2 shows the intersection of sets A and B (logical operator AND), whereas the right panel displays their union (logical operator OR).

Apart from the Boolean operators, there are two particular kinds of sets, which can become important in set-theoretic operations (Schneider and Wagemann 2012, 48–49). As its name implies, the *empty set* has no elements. It is designated by the symbol ∅, and it will result from the intersection of a set with its complement (or negation). This is so because a case cannot at the same time be a member of a given set and its negation, as illustrated in figure 3.4. Every case in the figure must be either a member of A or of ~A, because it cannot hold membership in both. Formally, this is expressed as $A \cdot {\sim}A = \emptyset$. This rule applies to crisp sets. With fuzzy sets, a case can have

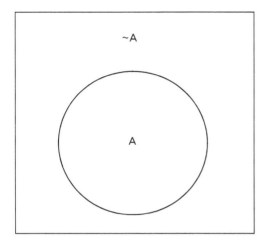

Figure 3.3   Set A and Its Complement

partial membership in a set and its negation, yet it can never have scores greater than 0.5 in both of these (Schneider and Wagemann 2012, 49). By contrast, the *universal set* is the set of all elements. As such, every other set is a subset of the universal set, designated by U (Smithson and Verkuilen 2006, 5). In figure 3.3, the universal set describes everything that is inside the square box, which is the set A and its complement ~A. Formally, this is expressed as A + ~A = U.

TRUTH TABLES

A central analytical tool for QCA is the *truth table*. The analytical procedure will be discussed in detail in chapter 7, but for now it suffices to introduce the key features of truth tables and to describe how they differ from a common data spreadsheet.

The truth table shows the number of logically possible combinations of conditions included in a study. The term stems from formal logic, where truth values for propositions are listed in table form (McCawley 1993; Tomassi 1999). To be sure, there is no sort of "higher truth" involved in truth tables! Each row in the truth table refers to a specific combination of conditions (a *configuration*). The number of rows equals the total number of possible configurations. The formula for this is 2^k, where k is the number of conditions included. This means that for 2 conditions, there will be 4 rows; 3 conditions will result in 8 rows; 4 conditions will yield 16 rows; and so forth. Individual cases are assigned to the row where they hold the highest membership score (Ragin 1987, chap. 6).

Table 3.4 shows a simple example with just two conditions, an outcome, and 10 hypothetical cases that are distributed across the rows of the truth table. We can

Table 3.4   A Simple Truth Table

Conditions		Outcome	Number of
A	B	Y	Cases
1	1	1	5
1	0	1	3
0	1	0	2
0	0	?	–

see from the table that three rows are populated with cases, whereas one row contains no cases. Hence, there is a question mark in the outcome column, indicating that there is no empirical foundation on which to decide whether the respective configuration should be associated with the presence or the absence of the outcome. With more conditions, truth tables become exponentially larger and the likelihood increases that cases will not fill all the logically possible combinations. This is the issue of *limited diversity*, which is addressed in chapter 2 in the context of the selection of cases and conditions, and to which we will return when discussing the treatment of logical remainders in chapter 7.

We can also see that the combinations represented by the top two rows of table 3.4 are associated with a positive outcome, whereas row three is associated with a negative outcome. Based on the empirical cases, we can say that $A \cdot B$ (row 1) and $A \cdot {\sim}B$ (row 2) lead to the outcome Y. This kind of information forms the basis for the *truth table analysis*, where a minimization algorithm will be applied (via software) to reduce the Boolean expressions and gain more parsimonious solution terms for the explanation of the outcome.

From a conceptual point of view, once fuzzy sets are introduced, we can conceive of the truth table as a multidimensional "attribute space" (Lazarsfeld 1937, 138), which circumscribes an area with as many dimensions as the number of fuzzy sets that are entailed in the analysis. Based on their fuzzy set membership scores, cases can be located at distinct points within the attribute space (Ragin 2000, chap. 7). This is shown in figure 3.4 for an analysis with three fuzzy sets. The key point is that cases can be anywhere inside the attribute space, whereas ideal types—with full membership or full nonmembership in the respective sets—are located in the corners of the attribute space (from 000 in the lower left corner to 111 in the upper right corner). This feature inspired the QCA variant of fuzzy-set ideal type analysis (Kvist 2007), where empirical cases are set in relation to preconceived ideal types (see chapter 8).

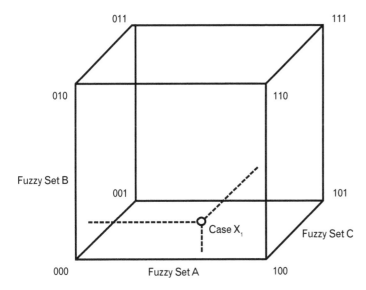

Figure 3.4 Truth Table as a Multidimensional Attribute Space

NECESSARY AND SUFFICIENT CONDITIONS

As a set-theoretic method, the analytical procedure of QCA aims at the identification of necessary and sufficient conditions.[7] For Gary Goertz and James Mahoney (2012, 12), the logic of necessity and sufficiency is what characterizes the heart of *qualitative* research.

A *necessary condition* means that the condition is always present when the outcome of interest occurs. Put differently, the outcome does not happen without the presence of the necessary condition. From a theoretical perspective, we can say that necessary conditions *explain failure* because they are a prerequisite for a phenomenon to occur.[8] For example, you may find that countries that experienced democratic breakdown always did so under conditions of economic crisis. This does not mean that an economic crisis causes a democratic breakdown in itself (because there may be other factors exacerbating that outcome), but whenever there has been a breakdown of democracy, it was preceded by an economic crisis.

A *sufficient condition* means that whenever the condition is present, the outcome occurs. For instance, a government change may be a sufficient condition for policy change. This does not mean that policy change can only occur after a government change (because there may be a variety of other factors that also lead to policy change), but for a certain population of cases it may be that whenever a new government has come to power, there has also been a subsequent policy change. Hence, we can say that sufficient conditions serve to *explain success*, as their presence always leads to the outcome.

By conventional notation, a necessary condition is indicated by a left-pointing arrow, directed from the outcome toward the condition that is necessary: A ← Y, whereas a sufficient condition is indicated by a right-pointing arrow, directed from the condition that is sufficient toward the outcome: B → Y (Rihoux and Ragin 2009; Rubinson 2019; Schneider and Wagemann 2012). It is important to note that this notation differs from a common understanding of causal arrows, where the arrow runs from cause to effect. With a necessary condition, the left-pointing arrow indicates a dependency or implication, as in "Y implies A" or "no Y without A."

Although the connection is often not made explicit, many social science theories are based on an understanding of necessary and sufficient causation (Goertz and Starr 2003; Ragin 1987). Here are some examples from studies in international relations, political science, and economics:

- "If not a necessary condition, nuclear deterrence may be interpreted as a *sufficient condition* for peace" (emphasis in the original) (Gleditsch 1995, 543).
- "The introduction of universal suffrage *led almost everywhere* (the United States excepted) to the development of Socialist parties" (emphasis added) (Duverger 1954, 66).
- "One cannot have the productivity of an industrial society with political anarchy. But while such a state is *a necessary condition* for realizing the gains from trade, it obviously is *not sufficient*" (emphasis added) (North 1984, 259).
- "Thus, international pressure was a *necessary condition* for these policy shifts. On the other hand, *without domestic resonance*, international forces *would not have sufficed* to produce the accord, no matter how balanced and intellectually persuasive the overall package" (emphasis added) (Putnam 1988, 430).
- "In the rationalist perspective, however, a community of basic political values and norms is *at best a necessary condition* of [EU] enlargement. . . . By contrast, in the sociological perspective, sharing a community of values and norms with outside states is *both necessary and sufficient* for their admission to the organization" (emphasis added) (Schimmelfennig 2001, 61).

What these five quotations illustrate—and many more examples could be given—is that authors frequently base their arguments on set-theoretic logic. The first quotation, from Nils Petter Gleditsch about nuclear deterrence, is straightforward in its mention of a condition that is sufficient but not necessary. The second quotation, from Maurice Duverger about electoral rules, differs from the first because it does not use the language of necessary and sufficient conditions. However, its essence is set-theoretic: universal suffrage is seen as an (almost) sufficient condition for the development of socialist parties. As such, Duverger's quotation is a typical example of the implicit usage of set-theoretic language. The third quotation, from Douglass North, turns the perspective by highlighting state institutions as a necessary condition for economic productivity. North also points out that though this condition is necessary, it is not sufficient to bring about the outcome. Similarly, Robert Putnam's quotation focuses on international pressure as a necessary condition for policy shifts. Interestingly, Putnam also argues in combinatorial ways, emphasizing that it needed international pressure *and* domestic resonance, which together form a sufficient condition for policy shifts. Finally, the quotation from Frank Schimmelfennig describes different expectations concerning necessity and sufficiency, based on competing theoretical perspectives. Whereas rationalist theory expects a weak necessary condition, social constructivism expects a condition that is necessary and sufficient.

ASSESSING SET RELATIONS

Now that we have defined necessary and sufficient conditions, what is missing is how we can identify these in empirical data. Chapter 6 introduces several metrics to calculate set relations, leading up to the set-theoretic analysis that is covered in chapter 7. For now, we examine three ways to *visualize* relations of necessity and sufficiency and to identify the respective data patterns. These include 2x2 tables (figure 3.5), Euler diagrams (figure 3.6), and X–Y plots or scatterplots (figure 3.7). The figures are grouped together to enhance their comparison.

An intuitive way to explore set-theoretic relationships for crisp-set data are 2x2 tables (Goertz and Mahoney 2012; Schneider and Wagemann 2012). Looking at the distribution of empirical cases across the four cells of a 2x2 table allows us to see whether there may be a set-theoretic relationship of necessity and/or sufficiency. Figure 3.5 shows separate 2x2 tables for relations of necessity and sufficiency. The left table identifies the cells that are relevant for a necessary condition. For necessary conditions, our focus rests on the presence of the outcome, indicated by the top row in the 2x2 table (the shaded area). If there are many cases that show the outcome and the condition (top right), and no cases that show the outcome but do not show the condition (top left),

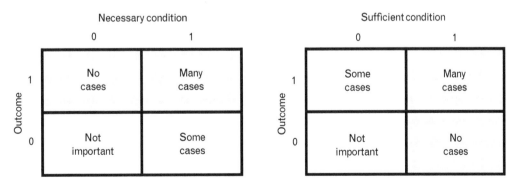

Figure 3.5   Necessary Condition and Sufficient Condition (2x2 Tables)

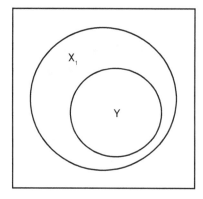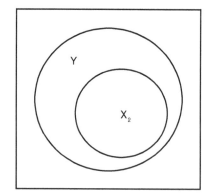

Figure 3.6   Necessary Condition and Sufficient Condition (Euler Diagrams)

then this suggests that we have identified a necessary condition. Note that cases without the outcome are not important for the analysis of necessary conditions, though it is fine if there are some cases where the condition occurs without the outcome (bottom right). This merely indicates that the condition is not also sufficient for the outcome.

For sufficient conditions, the procedure is similar, but inverted. The right table in Figure 3.5 shows the cells that are relevant for a sufficient condition. Here, we direct our attention to the presence of the condition, indicated by the right-hand column (shaded area). When there are many cases that show the condition and the outcome, and no cases that show the condition but do not show the outcome, then this designates a sufficient condition. Cases without the condition are not important for the analysis of sufficient conditions, but it is unproblematic if there are some cases that show the outcome, despite the absence of the condition, which simply means that the condition is not also necessary for the outcome.

These crisp-set relationships can also be visualized with a Euler diagram, as mentioned earlier in this chapter. Figure 3.6 displays perfect set relations of necessity (left panel) and sufficiency (right panel). In formal terms, a necessary condition is a *superset* of the outcome, which means that the circle for the condition X_1 fully encloses the outcome set Y. Hence, every case that holds membership in Y also holds membership in X_1. However, the reverse is not true, as can be seen from the dissimilar sizes of the circles, where many cases hold membership in the set X_1 but not in Y. There is also an area outside both sets, representing cases that hold neither membership in the condition nor the outcome.

The Euler diagram on the right side of figure 3.6 shows the relationship of sufficiency. Here the subset–superset relationship is inverted: a sufficient condition is a *subset* of the outcome, depicted in a circle for the condition X_2 that is fully enclosed by

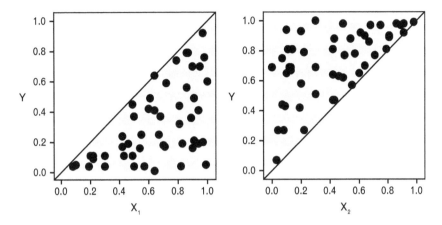

Figure 3.7   Necessary Condition and Sufficient Condition (X–Y Plots)

the outcome set Y. Every case that holds membership in X_2 also holds membership in Y. Yet this does not account for all instances of Y, because a large area is not covered by X_2 (but may be accounted for by other conditions).

So far, we have only looked at examples with binary data, where cases are either inside or outside a set. What about fuzzy sets? For these, neither X–Y plots nor Venn or Euler diagrams will work, because these visualizations cannot capture graded set membership. The best way to display fuzzy sets are X–Y plots, more generally referred to as *scatterplots*, which show the location of cases on a bivariate plot, with the condition on the x axis and the outcome on the y axis.

The left X–Y plot in figure 3.7 shows a data pattern for a perfectly necessary condition. We can see that all the empirical cases (shown with black dots) hold values for the outcome Y that are lower or equal to their respective values for the condition X_1. Hence, they reflect the expected set-theoretic relationship where the outcome Y is a *subset* of the condition X_1. This is highlighted by the diagonal line. The line separates cases with values that are equal to or higher for the outcome than for the condition $(Y \geq X_1)$ from those that are equal to or lower for the outcome than for the condition $(Y \leq X_1)$. Cases with equal values for the condition and the outcome are situated exactly on the diagonal line. Cases inside the lower gray triangle fulfill the criteria for perfect set relations of necessity.

For sufficient conditions, the situation is inverted. The right X–Y plot in figure 3.7 displays the pattern for a perfectly sufficient condition. All the empirical cases hold values for the outcome Y that are higher or equal to their respective values for the condition X_2, in line with the expected set-theoretic relationship where Y is a superset of the condition X_2. Hence, all the cases are located in the upper gray triangle, above the diagonal line.

NOTES

Epigraph: Goertz and Mahoney (2012, 17).

1. For an inventory of 150 necessary condition hypotheses, see Goertz (2003b).

2. This ideal/typical comparison should not imply that all statistical studies follow the described template.

3. An empirical illustration of the conceptualization of the outcome and explanatory conditions in QCA is provided by Mello (2017, 130–33).

4. However, set theory can be regarded as a "unifying theory for mathematics" (Cunningham 2016, ix).

5. For comprehensive treatments of Boolean algebra and set theory, see Quine (1969, 1982), Potter (2004), Whitesitt (2010), and Cunningham (2016).

6. Not listed here are two further operators that may be convenient depending on the theoretical context: The first is the *exclusive OR* (Hackett 2015, 2016), which describes membership in one or the other set, "but not both" as Hackett highlights (see also Quine 1982, 11–14). Another operator is the *set difference* between sets A and B, which is expressed as A \ B, or "A minus B" (Cunningham 2016, 4). For summaries of notational systems, see Quine (1982, part I), Smithson and Verkuilen (2006, 6), Whitesitt (2010, 4), Schneider and Wagemann (2012, 54), Cunningham (2016, 6), and Rubinson (2019, 4).

7. Although QCA can be used for different purposes, as discussed in chapter 2, many studies conduct some form of theory-guided analysis aimed at the identification of necessary and sufficient conditions (Mello 2013), which resonates with QCA's "orientation towards causal inference" (Wagemann 2017, 11). This topic is revisited in chapter 4.

8. Thanks to Gary Goertz for underlining this aspect.

4 • Causation and Causal Complexity

Embrace the messiness, the complexity: the real
rather than the ideal.

—RANI LILL ANJUM AND STEPHEN MUMFORD

Causation is a contested issue in the philosophy of social science. Having in mind the mantra *correlation is not causation*, many empirical researchers working in a positivist tradition decide to avoid using causal language, instead focusing on statistically identifiable empirical relationships (Pearl and Mackenzie 2018, 1–6). Likewise, constructivists and interpretivists, in their departure from positivist-empiricist assumptions, often also reject the use of causal language (Bevir and Blakely 2018, 35; Kurki 2008, 86). However, recent years have seen what could be termed a *renaissance* of causal thinking in the social sciences, with contributions from a variety of different perspectives (Anjum and Mumford 2018; Baumgartner 2009; Beach and Pedersen 2016; Bennett 2013; Collier, Brady, and Seawright 2010b; Gerring 2005; Guzzini 2017; Illari and Russo 2014; Jackson and Nexon 2013; Lebow 2014; Mahoney 2008; Morgan and Winship 2007; Pearl 2009; Peters 2020; Rohlfing 2012).

Against this backdrop, the first section of this chapter provides an overview of four major *theories of causation* in the philosophy of social science. This is followed by an introduction to the characteristic features of *causal complexity* as the core methodological assumption on which QCA rests. Together, these parts establish a foundation from which to assess current debates about *causal analysis*, as will be addressed in the final part of this chapter and picked up again in chapter 9, where some critical interventions are considered.

Before proceeding, one caveat is in order: although this chapter focuses on causation, this should not be taken to imply that QCA must be applied for causal inference. Clearly, the method can also be used fruitfully for *explorative* or *descriptive* purposes, as introduced in chapter 2, without striving for causal claims (Berg-Schlosser et al. 2009, 15; Thomann and Maggetti 2020, 10). Many empirical researchers would probably place their own set-theoretic applications rather in the area of explorative-descriptive work.[1] Nonetheless, causal language is frequently used by QCA proponents (Ragin 1987, 167; 2008, 125), and "causal analysis" is stated as an explicit aim of the method (Schneider and Wagemann 2012, 13).[2] Hence it is vital to clarify the basis on which causal claims can or cannot be made with QCA. This resonates with recent efforts at connecting empirical research methods with a coherent set of philosophical criteria (Haesebrouck and Thomann, forthcoming; Illari and Russo 2014; Rohlfing and Zuber 2019).

Relatedly, what is explicit or implicit in many accounts of causation and their related methods is their grounding in a *neopositivist* understanding of science, defined broadly as a perspective where human behavior is seen as governed by observable regularities that can be objectively assessed by the researcher. However, the prevalence of neopositivism in many fields should not deny the existence of alternative perspectives, like pragmatism, analytic eclecticism, interpretivism, or critical realism (Bevir and Blakely 2018; Jackson 2011; Kurki 2008; Sil and Katzenstein 2010). Clearly, a discussion of the intriguing ontological and epistemological questions raised by these perspectives is beyond the scope of this book (as in "what is the world made of" or "what can we know?")—the works just cited provide excellent treatments of these questions.

However, though it seems fair to say that QCA broadly resonates with neopositivist assumptions, I want to highlight that its methodology is open to other metatheoretical perspectives. In that light, it should be noted that *critical realism* has recently made some inroads into set-theoretic methods, and the number of studies that embrace a critical realist perspective continues to grow (Byrne 2009; Gerrits and Pagliarin 2020; Gerrits and Verweij 2014; Harvey 2009; Olsen 2014, 2010; Rutten 2019, 2020; Stevens 2020). At the most general level, critical realists share the ontological commitments that there is a reality that is independent of the mind of the researcher, that beliefs and knowledge are the product of social processes, and that it is possible to evaluate competing theories, despite inherent limitations (Bennett 2013, 465).[3]

THEORIES OF CAUSATION IN THE SOCIAL SCIENCES

We can distinguish four major conceptions of causation, emphasizing either *regularity*, *probability*, *counterfactuals*, or *mechanisms*.[4] Philosophers of social science are in dispute about which of these approaches to causation and their underlying theories should be given preference—subject matter that is complicated by the fact that "proponents sometimes treat them as competing or even contradictory" (Brady 2008, 218). Yet, for the purposes of *applied* social science, which is the perspective that motivates this book, each of these approaches can be valuable: they all "capture some aspect of causality" (Brady 2008, 218), and empirical research methods may identify multiple "symptoms of causes" that are rooted in different conceptions of causation (Anjum and Mumford 2018, 232). Finally, differences between the perspectives should not be overdrawn. On a closer look, it becomes apparent that they are not as mutually exclusive in their assumptions about causation as they are sometimes made up to be.[5]

Regularity

The *regularity approach* to causation is traditionally associated with the work of the eighteenth-century philosopher David Hume. Hence, as a shorthand, reference is often made to a "Humean" approach, even though modern variants may differ from what Hume had in mind. According to Hume's first definition of causation, we may conceive of a *cause* as "*an object, followed by another, and where all the objects, similar to the first, are followed by objects similar to the second*" (emphasis in the original) (Hume 2010, 146; orig. pub. 1772). Given this lean definition, two criteria must be met before we may say from a regularity perspective that "A caused B": A must precede B in time, and all objects of type A must be followed by objects of type B.[6] With this definition, Hume turned the relationship between correlation and causation on its head: rather than explaining covariance through reference to causation, Hume argued that the observation of regular co-occurrence explains causation (Mumford and Anjum 2013, 16), or at least that part of causation that is observable "in the world," without reference to metaphysics (Psillos 2009, 133).

Hume's definition also entails the distinction between singular and general causation. Humean regularity emphasizes *general causation*, also known as *type-level, regular,* or *generic* causation. This perspective seeks to arrive at causal claims by subsuming cases under a general law or regularity. Here, observations are not seen as singular cases (though they might be single cases) but as representations of classes of phenomena ("objects, similar to the first"). From this perspective, a relationship can be deemed causal only if cause and effect are observed repeatedly in a regular fashion. By contrast, *singular causation* seeks to derive causal claims from a singular case without assuming a larger, more general pattern. This is why it is also known as *token-level, actual,* or *single-case* causation (Illari and Russo 2014, 41–44; Pearl 2009, 309–10; Psillos 2009, 146–48). This distinction becomes important for instance in legal studies, where individual responsibility for a specific action needs to be shown rather than establishing a general claim or tendency.

The difference between general causation and singular causation can be illustrated with the findings from research on democracies and military coalitions. Some studies formulate general research questions, such as "what are the causes of democratic coalition defection?"; others formulate questions that focus on specific cases, such as "what caused Prime Minister José Zapatero to announce Spain's withdrawal from the Iraq War coalition on April 19 of 2004?" (on research questions, see chapter 2).[7] To answer these, different inferential strategies and causal evidence are needed. And though the former would resonate with a large-N statistical analysis based on aggregate data, the second research question requires an examination of the specific circumstances under which decision-making occurred in the respective case, which calls for small-N case studies and process tracing.[8]

Following in Hume's footsteps, most modern successors of the regularity approach seek to observe the joint and regular occurrence ("constant conjunction") of dependent and independent variables, measured in *statistical correlation* as the standardized form of covariance (Brady 2008, 219; Mumford and Anjum 2013, chap. 2). Moreover, proponents of regularity-based approaches aim for type-level generalization and the identification of nomological statements (Hempel and Oppenheim 1948).[9] Although the regularity understanding of causation has exercised a lasting influence on the development of the sciences, it has also received sustained criticism for its shortcomings, including the problems of common causes and "spurious," noncausal correlations (Moses and Knutsen 2019, chap. 2). Among postpositivists, "Humeanism" has turned into a foil against which to argue for alternative understandings of causation (Bevir and Blakely 2018; Jackson 2011; Kurki 2008). The limitations of Humean regularity, especially the problems that arise from multiple causes, led John Mackie to propose an alternative based on INUS conditions, which are defined as "an *insufficient* but *necessary* part of a condition, which is itself *unnecessary* but *sufficient* for the result" (emphasis in the original) (Mackie 1965, 245). Although Mackie's framework sheds light on configurational causation, and has resonated widely because of it, the INUS approach entails some limitations of its own (Brady 2008, 227–30; Pearl 2009, 313–16). We will return to these when discussing causal complexity in the next section.

Probability

The *probabilistic approach* to causation replaces the deterministic Humean notion of a constant conjunction between cause and effect with the conception of probabilistic dependency (Williamson 2009). Hence, rather than triggering an effect each time the cause is present, the occurrence of the cause merely *increases the likelihood* that the effect also occurs. This is useful in settings characterized by uncertainty. For instance, we may stipulate that the consumption of junk food will lead to health problems, but we do not know when that will happen, nor whether it will affect each and every junk food consumer (because regular exercise or an otherwise healthy lifestyle may outweigh the detrimental effect). However, based on existing studies, we may safely say that junk food consumption makes it *more likely* for a person to develop health problems at some stage in their life.[10]

In essence, "probability is the formal language of uncertainty" (Moore and Siegel 2013, 175). A primary distinction is made between *objective* and *subjective* probability. Whereas the former relates to factual knowledge (e.g., when you roll a six-sided die or flip a coin), the latter refers to beliefs and dispositions of individuals (as in someone's risk acceptance or their propensity to develop health problems). In formal terms, the conditional probability that event B occurs when event A has occurred is expressed as

$P(B|A)$. Based on a probabilistic understanding of causation, it can thus be said that "A causes B" if the conditional probability that B occurs when A has occurred is greater than the conditional probability that B occurs when not-A (¬A) has occurred (Selvin 2019, 2), which is expressed as $P(B|A) > P(B|¬A)$.[11]

The probabilistic approach to causation overcomes problems of the Humean regularity account. Most important, it tackles the issue of exceptional cases (e.g., black swan events), because it suffices to identify a general tendency without having to establish a deterministic relationship between the purported cause and effect. This is useful, because for many phenomena it is easy to think of at least one *deviant case* where the assumed relationship between cause and effect does not manifest itself. This is one of the reasons why probabilistic causation has become a mainstream approach in the social sciences and is sometimes equated with the scientific method, writ large (e.g., Slantchev, Alexandrova, and Gartzke 2005).[12]

That being said, there are at least three important limitations of the probability approach to causation. First, a probabilistic statement may not be of much help when the aim is to explain a *single case* or *specific cases* out of a larger population. To account for the decision-making of President Barack Obama before the military intervention in Libya in 2011, general statements about democracies and their conflict behavior can only get us that far. What would be more helpful are accounts of the political environment in which decisions were made and personal characteristics of the people involved. Relatedly, probabilistic methods often conceal *substantial heterogeneity* at the case level. Consider the long-standing debate about the "democratic peace" in international relations. Although the voluminous body of quantitative research has established a host of correlations between "democracy" and various indicators of conflict behavior (e.g., Brown, Miller, and Lynn-Jones 1996; Ray 2000; Russett and Oneal 2001), this kind of research typically neglects variance *within* the group of democracies, despite the fact that conflict involvement is limited to a minority of states.[13] Finally, probabilistic methods do not provide appropriate tests for *deterministic theories*. To continue with the example, some theoretical accounts suggest that democratic institutions impose structural constraints against certain kinds of conflict involvement. If taken seriously, then it follows that whenever such constraints are in place, a certain kind of conflict behavior should not merely become less likely but simply should not happen.[14]

Counterfactuals

As the name implies, the *counterfactual approach* to causation is based on thought experiments about what would have happened if the world had been different (Paul 2009). Interestingly, Hume complemented his first definition of "cause" with a counterfactual definition: "Or in other words, *where, if the first object had not been, the second never had existed*" (emphasis in the original) (Hume 2010, 146). Against this backdrop, Judea Pearl suspects that "Hume was not completely happy with the regularity account" and therefore provided an additional definition based on a different logic (Pearl 2009, 238). Be that as it may, to date, Hume has mostly been associated with the regularity account. Though early traces of counterfactual reasoning can also be found in the writings of Max Weber (1922), the modern counterfactual approach goes back to the work of the philosopher David Lewis (1973).[15] In essence, Lewis turns around the statement "A caused B" by formulating a counterfactual: "B would not have occurred without A." The counterfactual perspective conducts a "mental exercise" to assess the plausibility of possible alternative worlds (Pearl 2009, 238–40). For example, we may propose that "if kangaroos had no tails, they would topple over," to use Lewis's (1973, 1) own example. This means that in a possible world that is most similar to ours but where kangaroos are not gifted with tails, we would assume that they would fall over. In general terms, we can ask whether the outcome could occur without a specific condition.

The counterfactual approach to causation has equally inspired quantitative and formal work, as well as qualitative scholars. Among the former, counterfactuals have formed a starting point for the *potential outcomes model*, also known as the Neyman-Rubin model, which aims to identify the average causal effects of a "treatment" or manipulation when compared with a control group (Morgan and Winship 2007; Sekhon 2008; Woodward 2009). The potential outcome framework has become a standard tool for causal inference in quantitative social science (Imai 2017, chap. 2). Yet it should be noted that the potential outcomes model does not entail a counterfactual analysis at the level of individual cases, as highlighted by Goertz and Mahoney (2012, 117). This is the realm of qualitative case-based research, where counterfactual reasoning has an established pedigree. For example, Frank Harvey (2012) provides an exhaustive counterfactual analysis on the questions of what would have happened if Al Gore had won the contested election against George W. Bush in 2000.[16]

Among other benefits, the counterfactual approach to causation, unlike the regularity approach, does not require the observance of a constant conjunction between cause and effect in the sense of a universal law. According to Lewis (1973), causes are *difference makers*, and the counterfactual perspective allows analysts to explore the specific conditions under which the absence of a cause leads to the absence of an effect or outcome. Because of these advantages, variants and refinements of the counterfactual approach have received favorable treatment among methodologists (Brady 2008; King, Keohane, and Verba 1994; Rohlfing and Zuber 2019; Toshkov 2016). Nonetheless, proponents of the counterfactual approach are adamant about the fact that the "fundamental problem of causal inference" remains (Holland 1986, 947; Imai 2017, 47). Translated into a case-based perspective, this means that we can never observe the presence *and* the absence of a cause in the same case at the same time. Hence, despite all our efforts at rigorous research design, "we can never hope to know a causal effect for certain" (King, Keohane, and Verba 1994, 79). Apart from this general limitation on deriving causal inference from observational data, commentators have highlighted systemic interdependencies and dynamics that complicate and potentially undermine counterfactual reasoning (Jervis 1996), as well as psychological biases that may affect the construction of counterfactuals (Olson, Roese, and Deibert 1996).

Mechanisms

Finally, the *mechanism approach* to causation aims at opening the black box between cause and effect. The mechanistic perspective seeks to uncover the causal process or the interacting parts of a system that link a cause to an effect. For some, identifying a causal mechanism is considered the "gold standard for establishing and explaining causal connection" (Glennan 2009, 315). How does this differ from other approaches? Among other distinctions, regularity, probability, and counterfactual accounts have difficulties with *causal preemption*, which describes a situation where one cause happens just before another cause and thus preempts the latter—a situation that is also described as causal *overdetermination* (Mumford and Anjum 2013, 60). A widely used example in the philosophical literature helps to explain the challenge posed by causal preemption:

> A man takes a trek across a desert. His enemy puts a hole in his water can. Another enemy, not knowing the action of the first, puts poison in his water. Manipulations have certainly occurred, and the man dies on the trip. The enemy who punctured the water can thinks that she caused the man to die, and the enemy who added the poison thinks that he caused the man to die. In fact, the water dripping out of the can preempted the poisoning so that the poisoner is wrong. (Brady 2008, 241–42)

This setting poses a problem for regularity approaches because the constant conjunction between poisoned water and death (and, respectively, between a lack of water and death) do not help to discriminate between the *real cause* and the *preempted cause*. Similarly, probabilities may provide information about the average lethality of poisoned water and a lack of water, but this would not say much about the actual case at hand. The example also challenges counterfactual approaches, because the counterfactual "if the water had not been poisoned, the man would not have died" is *false* (because the man would still have died of thirst), just as the counterfactual "if the water can had not been punctured, the man would not have died" is *also false* (as the man would have died of poisoning). Apparently, because of their focus on the "effects of causes," counterfactuals cannot sufficiently explain why the effect happened (Brady 2008, 242). This is where mechanisms come in. To continue with the example, it would have required a close examination of the case at hand. For instance, an autopsy would have revealed that the water must have run out before a lethal quantity of the poison could have been consumed.[17]

How then are causal mechanisms defined? Matters are complicated by the fact that there is a *plethora* of different understandings of causal mechanisms in the social sciences (Elster 2015; Falleti and Lynch 2009; George and Bennett 2005; Gerring 2010; Goertz 2017; Goertz and Mahoney 2012; Hedström and Swedberg 1998; Machamer, Darden, and Craver 2000). Peter Hedström defines a causal mechanism as "a constellation of entities and activities that are organized such that they regularly bring about a particular type of outcome" (Hedström 2008, 321). A similar definition is offered by Peter Machamer, Lindley Darden, and Carl Craver (2000, 3), who define mechanisms as "entities and activities organized such that they are productive of regular changes from start or set-up to finish or termination conditions." The mention of "regularity" in both definitions may prompt the question whether mechanisms are truly distinct from a Humean regularity account. However, Machamer and colleagues underscore that explanation "is not merely to redescribe one regularity as a series of several," but rather that "explanation involves revealing the *productive* relation" (emphasis in the original) (Machamer, Darden, and Craver 2000, 21–22). These definitions highlight an understanding of causal mechanisms as a *generative process* where several elements interact to bring about an outcome. In this sense, the causal mechanism approach is closely related to *process tracing*, as a within-case method aimed at the identification of a causal link between a condition and an outcome (Beach and Pedersen 2013, 2019; Bennett and Checkel 2015; Blatter and Haverland 2012; Collier 2011; George and Bennett 2005; Rohlfing 2012).

As an aside, we should note that the study of mechanisms has some affinity with the metatheoretical perspective of *critical realism* (Bhaskar 2008; Kurki 2007), sometimes also referred to as *scientific realism* (Haig 2018; Wight 2007). However, philosophical realists hold different conceptions of mechanisms. Milja Kurki (2007) describes mechanisms concisely as "complexes of causes," a definition that is intended to be broad enough to cover multiple interpretations of the concept. Some process tracing methodologists have drawn a connection between their ideas about causal mechanisms and realist conceptions (Bennett 2013; George and Bennett 2005, 136).

Although the mechanism approach has distinct advantages, like other perspectives on causation, it is not without limitations. To begin with, there remains "substantial ambiguity" about what constitutes causal mechanisms (Jacobs 2016, 13), and its many different conceptions add to the challenges associated with the mechanism approach (Gerring 2007b). Moreover, a fundamental problem of causal mechanisms is that they are "ultimately unobservable" (George and Bennett 2005, 137; Toshkov 2016, 151).

This means that it is up to the researcher to provide a *substantive interpretation* that certain empirical observations can be regarded as evidence of a causal mechanism at work.[18] Although this is difficult enough in its own right, the task is complicated when theorizing explanations that entail multiple mechanisms.[19] Relatedly, at times it is not clear how a causal mechanism approach ought to be distinguished from a regularity perspective based on the observance of covariation. In practice, mechanism-based approaches typically introduce additional links in what is conceived as a causal process between a condition and an outcome. Critics might object that this simply means that instead of examining a single covariational relationship, several of these are linked together (Gerring 2010, 1516).

Irrespective of these limitations, the analysis of causal mechanisms via process tracing is considered to be one of the most fruitful methods to establish causal claims for individual cases (Bennett and Checkel 2015; Blatter and Haverland 2012; Collier 2011). There is also a natural affinity between QCA and process tracing, because their combination provides a way to integrate cross-case and within-case inferences in multimethod research designs, as mentioned in chapter 2 (Beach, Pedersen, and Siewert 2019; Beach and Rohlfing 2018; Meegdenburg and Mello, forthcoming; Schneider and Rohlfing 2013, 2019).

CAUSAL COMPLEXITY

The discussion in the first section of this chapter prompts the question: how does QCA relate to these perspectives on causation? The answer requires a short detour, because we need to take a look into the evolution of the method. When Charles Ragin developed QCA, it was meant to take a *holistic* perspective on cases and to examine "the combinatorial complexities of social causation" (Ragin 1987, 170). This was a conscious departure from so-called variable-oriented research that aimed for causal generalization and the identification of causal effects of single variables, without a deeper concern to understand or account for individual cases. QCA was devised to address settings that were characterized by "multiple conjunctural causation," involving various combinations of conditions that bring about an outcome (Ragin 1987, 26). Though the term *multiple conjunctural causation* remained in use (Berg-Schlosser et al. 2009, 8; Ragin 2000, 104), it has over time been replaced by the shorthand *causal complexity* as an umbrella concept that entails the specific methodological assumptions on which QCA rests (Ragin 2000, chap. 4; 2008b, 124; Schneider and Wagemann 2012, 78).[20] What are the defining features of causal complexity? Ragin (2008b, 124) offers this definition: "*Causal complexity* is defined as a situation in which a given outcome may follow from several different combinations of causal conditions—from different causal 'recipes.'"

Elaborating on this concise description, the concept of causal complexity entails three methodological assumptions that are constitutive for QCA: the first is *conjunctural causation*, which describes a setting where single conditions do not individually suffice to generate the phenomenon of interest but where specific combinations of conditions are *jointly sufficient* for the outcome. This is what John Stuart Mill described in *A System of Logic* (1843) as "chemical combination" and "conjunct action of causes" (Mill 2006, 370–71). As Mill elaborates, "Most of the uniformities to which the causes conformed when separate, cease altogether when they are conjoined; and we are not, at least in the present state of our knowledge, able to foresee what result will follow from any new combination, until we have tried the specific experiment."

What Mill emphasizes here resonates with a holistic perspective that sees *cases as configurations* rather than as collections of individual factors (Ragin 2000; Rihoux and Ragin 2009). The quotation also highlights that isolated effects may disappear when combinations are formed. This contrasts with a perspective where the aim rests on identifying the average effects of single variables (Mahoney 2010). When such a "net effect" perspective is adopted, a researcher may overlook patterns of conjunctural causation because no single variable may be able to account for the outcome. This is why QCA entails a systematic study of all logically possible combinations of conditions through the construction of the truth table and its subsequent minimization via Boolean logic (this part is developed in chapter 7).

The second methodological assumption entailed in causal complexity is *equifinality*, which relates to a setting where multiple paths made up of individual conditions or combinations of conditions independently lead to the same outcome. Although equifinality or "multiple causation" is ubiquitous among social and political phenomena, its methodological implications have long been neglected (Anjum and Mumford 2018, 54–56; George and Bennett 2005, 161–62; Ragin 1987, chap. 2).[21] Importantly, research designs that seek to reduce empirical phenomena to single causes will be weakened by the presence of equifinality in their data. As Alexander George and Andrew Bennett (2005, 161) stress, "Equifinality challenges and undermines the common assumption that similar outcomes in several cases must have a common cause that remains to be discovered."[22]

Instead, the analytical routine of QCA is designed to *reveal* rather than obscure equifinality, which is a fundamental asset of the method. In addition to the identification of alternative paths toward an outcome, QCA also allows researchers to determine the degree of equifinality and the empirical weight of the existing "paths" or "recipes." In some settings there may be several mutually exclusive combinations of conditions leading to the same outcome, each of them populated by numerous cases. In other situations, there may be a high degree of empirical overlap between different paths (indicating overdetermination), or the majority of cases may belong to just one of the solution paths.

Finally, the third methodological assumption in causal complexity is *causal asymmetry*, which means that a recipe for the outcome can usually not be mirrored symmetrically to explain the nonoutcome, but instead requires a separate analysis (Berg-Schlosser et al. 2009, 9; Schneider and Wagemann 2012, 81–83). By contrast, *causal symmetry* is characterized by a "fully reversible causal linkage," as stated by Stanley Lieberson (1985, 176).[23] Only under such circumstances should the presence or absence of the outcome respond in a symmetric manner to the presence or absence of certain conditions or conjunctions. However, many empirical research settings in the social sciences are instead characterized by causal asymmetry.

What does this mean in practice? The implication is that empirical applications of QCA should entail *separate analyses* for the outcome and the nonoutcome. Researchers should be cautious not to leap to inferences about the nonoutcome simply from examining the solution for the outcome (and vice versa). This may be tempting, but in most empirical settings the linkage between conditions and outcome will not be symmetric. There are different reasons why this may be the case in "real-life" settings, but the most important one is *limited diversity*, which simply means that some logical combinations of conditions are not filled with empirical cases, a point that we further explore in chapter 7.

Causal complexity and the meaning of its constituent concepts of conjunctural causation, equifinality, and causal asymmetry should become clearer with an illustration. In the previous chapter, the *truth table* was introduced as a central analytical device in QCA. Building on this, suppose we have a truth table with three conditions A, B, and C; an outcome Y; and seven cases, as shown in table 4.1. At this stage, we do not need to know about the details of the analytical procedure, but simply work with the elements discussed in the previous chapter on set theory.

Now our analysis may reveal that condition A is *individually sufficient*, whereas conditions B and C are *jointly sufficient* for the outcome Y. In formal terms, we write this as:

$$A + (B \cdot C) \rightarrow Y$$

This scenario is shown in panel A of figure 4.1. This means that we have a setting that brings together *equifinality*, because there is more than one path toward the outcome, indicated here by separate arrows directed at the outcome, as well as *conjunctural causation*, because conditions B and C are only sufficient for the outcome Y when both of them occur together, as indicated by their linkage.

Table 4.1   Causal Complexity: Truth Table Example

Row	Conditions			Outcome	Number of Cases
	A	B	C	Y	
1	1	1	1	1	1
2	1	1	0	1	1
3	1	0	1	1	1
4	0	1	1	1	1
5	1	0	0	1	1
6	0	0	1	0	1
7	0	0	0	0	1
8	0	1	0	?	–

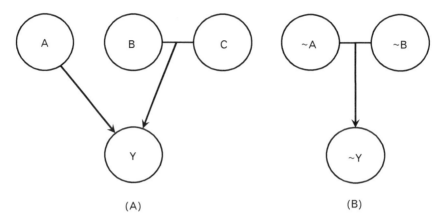

Figure 4.1 Causal Complexity: Graphical Representation

What about causal asymmetry? As we can see from panel B of figure 4.1, in this empirical setting with hypothetical data there is only a single path toward the nonoutcome ~Y, which entails the joint absence of A and B, written as such:

$$(\sim A \cdot \sim B) \rightarrow \sim Y$$

This is so because the underlying data for this example entails a single *logical remainder*, as in one logically possible combination without an empirical case. As we can see from table 4.1, each of the logically possible configurations in the truth table is represented by one respective case, except for the configuration in row 8 (indicated by a question mark in the outcome column). To keep matters simple, the solutions depicted in figure 4.1 treat the logical remainder as false. By comparison, if we had a fully specified truth table, with row 8 showing the nonoutcome, the solution for the outcome would remain the same and the solution for the nonoutcome would be as follows:

$$(\sim A \cdot \sim B) + (\sim A \cdot \sim C) \rightarrow \sim Y$$

In formal terms, the conditions B and C are "INUS" conditions, which means that each of them is "an *insufficient* but *necessary* part of a condition, which is itself *unnecessary* but *sufficient* for the result," to use the definition proposed by Mackie (1965, 245). INUS conditions are the nuts and bolts of QCA solutions, as we typically find combinations of two or more conditions that are individually insufficient but jointly sufficient for the outcome.[24] INUS conditions resonate with many theoretical frameworks in the social sciences, where multiple conditions can plausibly be conceived as elements in combinations that are jointly sufficient for the outcome, but where it is not possible to derive more specific expectations from theory, before the empirical analysis (see also chapter 2).

The logical complement to INUS conditions are "SUIN" conditions. James Mahoney, Erin Kimball, and Kendra Koivu (2009, 126) define these as "a *sufficient* but *unnecessary* part of a factor that is *insufficient* but *necessary* for an outcome." SUIN conditions can be considered "constitutive attributes" of a necessary condition. For example, the analysis may reveal that condition A is necessary for the outcome and there are two conditions F and G, each of which can bring about A. In this scenario, F and G would each be SUIN conditions.[25] SUIN conditions are interesting from a theoretical perspective, and sometimes they are also made part of the analytical routine, but most empirical applications do not explicitly conceptualize them.

CAUSAL ANALYSIS

The previous section introduced the methodological assumption of *causal complexity* that is central to QCA. What we have not discussed yet is how QCA relates to the different theories of causation. As a set-theoretic method, QCA is based on Boolean algebra and the logic of necessary and sufficient conditions (Goertz and Mahoney 2012; Mahoney 2008; Ragin 1987; Schneider and Wagemann 2012). However, though most introductions to set-theoretic and configurational comparative methods employ causal language of one form or another, explicit references to theories of causation are seldom made.

For instance, *Fuzzy-Set Social Science* (Ragin 2000) devotes an insightful chapter to causal complexity, but there is no further discussion of theories of causation in the social sciences. Likewise, the edited volume *Configurational Comparative Methods* (Rihoux and Ragin 2009) contains a chapter that spells out key assumptions of QCA (Berg-Schlosser et al. 2009), but these are not placed in the context of broader conceptions about causal relations in the philosophy of social science. Finally, though *Set-Theoretic Methods for the Social Sciences* (Schneider and Wagemann 2012) has become the standard textbook on QCA, it entails no part about how "causal analysis"—as one of the stated aims of QCA—relates to established theories of causation (Schneider and Wagemann 2012, 8; see also Oana, Schneider, and Thomann 2021). Arguably, these omissions have created some uncertainty about whether causal claims can be made and how these could be justified in QCA applications.

Against this backdrop, recent contributions have initiated a debate about the prerequisites of causal inference with set-theoretic methods, in the context of discussions about the accuracy of QCA solution terms (Baumgartner and Thiem 2020; Duşa 2019a; Haesebrouck 2019; Haesebrouck and Thomann, forthcoming; Schneider 2018). This section aims to give an overview of these exchanges and to connect them with the broader discussion about theories of causation introduced in the first section of this chapter. This ties in with considerations about QCA solution terms and counterfactual analysis, to be discussed in chapter 7, and the critical reception of QCA addressed in chapter 9. Here, rather than following the technical steps and detailed aspects of each individual contribution, emphasis is placed on the contours of the exchanges and their practical implications for applied QCA studies. I should mention at the outset that the current state of the scientific debate does not warrant a conclusive attribution of QCA to one of the existing theories of causation. However, some alternatives have been formulated, and we will certainly see future development in this area.

A first challenge to causal analysis with set-theoretic methods arises from the circumstance that set theory, in its origins, is a conceptual language of mathematics (Cunningham 2016; Whitesitt 2010). This suits the purpose of describing relationships between sets, including set membership in complex configurations of conditions, and the notions of necessity and sufficiency, which can be expressed in set-theoretic terms. However, to allow for *causal attribution*, set theory should be embedded in a theory of causation, and a theoretical rationale should be provided for how the cause brought about its effect.

Against this backdrop, it has been suggested that due to the deterministic logic that underpins necessity and sufficiency—namely, that a condition is either always present when the outcome is present (necessary condition) or that its presence always implies the simultaneous presence of the outcome (sufficient condition)—QCA is "best anchored in a regularity theory of causation," as suggested by Ingo Rohlfing and Christina Zuber (2019, 22), and that regularity theory is "the most obvious theory for underpinning QCA," as held by Tim Haesebrouck (2019, 2766). The studies by Rohlfing and Zuber and Haesebrouck both refer to the regularity account developed by Michael Baumgartner (2009, 2015). This resonates with the categorizations by Derek Beach and Rasmus Pedersen (2013, 28), who classify QCA as "regularity-deterministic," and Patrick Jackson (2011, 68–69), who sees the method as rooted in a "covariation definition of causality."

Undeniably, there is an affinity between QCA and regularity theory. To begin with, Ragin (1987) developed *The Comparative Method* on the basis of Mill's methods of agreement and difference, which also had a lasting influence on research approaches in comparative politics and other areas of the social sciences (Lijphart 1971; Przeworski and Teune 1970). To be sure, Mill's work was firmly rooted in a regularity understanding of causation (Psillos 2009, 139). However, with the inception of his new comparative approach, Ragin (1987) went beyond Mill's scientific methods, arguing that, among other deficiencies, these were "incapable of handling multiple and conjunctural causation." As shown in the previous section, these concepts form the very core of causal complexity, and they are among the key strengths of QCA. Adding to this, Mill's methods cannot accommodate degrees of set membership and empirical data fraught with limited diversity.

Another reason why QCA has been associated with a regularity understanding of causation lies in the frequent references to John Mackie and his work on INUS conditions.[26] INUS conditions embody both equifinality and conjunctural causation—as such, they can be seen as constitutive of causal complexity. Clearly, Mackie's conception of INUS conditions is a helpful *heuristic* to make sense of causal complexity. Yet this does not mean that QCA must be based on regularity theory. In fact, the INUS concept has been embraced by critical realists, among others (Kurki 2008, 56–57). In this light, it is revealing what Mackie (1980, iix) said about the reception of his theory of causation in the preface to *The Cement of the Universe*: "My position is in some respects intermediate between those of the best known rival schools of thought about causation—it has, understandably, been attacked both *for being too Humean* and *for not being Humean enough*" (emphasis added).

What this quotation indicates is that Mackie himself did not regard his theory of causation as a Humean regularity account in an orthodox sense. Indeed, Stathis Psillos (2009) suggests that Mackie "thought there is a lot more to causation than regularity," emphasizing instead, among other differences to the traditional Humean notion of regularity, a conception of "*complex* regularities" (emphasis in the original) (Psillos 2009, 150). Another difference from Hume is that Mackie (1965) is understood to have given *causal primacy to single cases*, whereas Hume deduced causal relationships from regularities observed across cases (Illari and Russo 2014, 44).

That being said, there are at least three additional criteria according to which QCA goes beyond Humean regularity theory. First, the deterministic assumption of "if A then *always* B" has been relaxed because the introduction of fuzzy sets and the calculation of set-theoretic measures of fit allow for imperfect set relations (Ragin 2000, 2006b).[27] This advancement recognized that social science data are inherently noisy, and even where a strong set-theoretic relationship is identified, individual cases may not match the general pattern (Wagemann and Schneider 2010, 389).

Second, limited diversity and the treatment of logical remainders are an integral part of QCA, but this rests on *counterfactual reasoning*—a topic on which we will elaborate in chapter 7. The scope of limited diversity varies, but nearly all empirical studies have to engage with situations where configurations of conditions are logically possible and of theoretical interest, but where simply no corresponding empirical cases exist. In such situations, QCA enables researchers to engage in thought experiments in a systematic fashion. Yet counterfactuals "do not sit easily with a regularity theory," as acknowledged by Rohlfing and Zuber (2019, 32), although they do not engage with the implications that this spells for their own argument about couching QCA in regularity theory.

Finally, causal asymmetry is a core element of QCA that does not square with regularity accounts of causation. According to Rohlfing and Zuber (2019, 14), positive evidence for a causal statement derived from regularity theory would be of the symmetrical kind: A is always followed by B, *and* non-A is always followed by non-B. Clearly, this is not what we would expect from a causal complexity perspective, where asymmetric explanations are common (Goertz and Mahoney 2012, 66), as illustrated in the example in the previous section.

To be clear, this should not be taken to imply that there are no ties between regularity theory and QCA. Nor should it be denied that the method owes a great deal to the works of Mill and Mackie, among others. But what I hope to have underlined is that the connection to regularity theory and the philosophical lineage are not as clear-cut as portrayed in some recent contributions (Haesebrouck 2019; Rohlfing and Zuber 2019). Just as QCA is neither a purely qualitative nor quantitative approach, it cannot be said that QCA is solely based on a regularity understanding of causation. Unlike regularity theory, QCA acknowledges (1) causal complexity, (2) incorporates counterfactual reasoning, (3) departs from a deterministic understanding of causal relations, and (4) places emphasis on the case-level rather than broad generalizations.

With what does this leave us? Of the four theories of causation that have been canvassed in this chapter, QCA shows some correspondence with regularity theory, while also showing affinity for a counterfactual perspective. The latter is examined more closely in chapter 7. Yet it is important to acknowledge that crucial elements of QCA are difficult to reconcile with a regularity perspective (as outlined above), and that counterfactuals only become relevant in the context of limited empirical diversity. The bottom line is that causal claims should generally be approached with caution when working with observational data. In itself, the identification of a set-theoretic relationship of necessity and/or sufficiency does not warrant a causal claim. What is of crucial importance is the *theoretical foundation* that endows meaning upon the identified set-theoretic relationship. In this light, research design and theory are crucial elements that help to circumscribe the explanatory scope and context of a given study. We will return to these aspects in chapters 7 and 9.

NOTES

Epigraph: Anjum and Mumford (2018, 253).

1. The inferential value of "mere description" is underlined forcefully by Gerring (2012a).

2. De Meur et al. (2009, 160–61) discuss causality in the context of what is seen as a "black box" problem, but their text does not provide criteria for the assessment of causal claims. A cautious perspective on "causal inference" with QCA is taken by Kahwati and Kane (2020, 10–12).

3. With regard to QCA, the critical realist perspective is most clearly expressed in the contributions to the *Sage Handbook of Case-Based Methods* (Byrne and Ragin 2009), where Ragin (2009b, 524) acknowledges in the concluding chapter that many of his ideas about case studies resonate with critical realism. However, a challenging aspect of critical realism is that conceptions of it vary widely and some of the more demanding ideas expressed appear difficult to put into practice in the context of comparative research designs (Bhaskar 2008; Kurki 2007; Wight 2007).

4. This is a concise summary of a voluminous literature. The *Oxford Handbook of Causation* (Beebee et al. 2009) discusses more than 10 different approaches to causality; Brady (2008) includes manipulation—but not probability-based approaches—and Rohlfing and Zuber (2019)

further distinguish between token- and type-level counterfactual approaches. See also Anjum and Mumford (2018), Beach and Pedersen (2013, chap. 3; 2019, chap. 1), Goertz and Mahoney (2012, part I), Illari and Russo (2014), Rohlfing (2012, chap. 2), and Toshkov (2016, chap. 6).

5. Among other overlaps, Hume's regularity definition of causation famously includes a "counterfactual companion" (Goertz and Mahoney 2012, 75; Pearl 2009, 238), some definitions of causal mechanisms entail reference to regularities or counterfactuals (Brady 2008, 243), and regularity accounts can be reconciled with probabilistic theories of causation (Mumford and Anjum 2013, 49; Psillos 2009, 154).

6. Notably, in the first edition of *An Enquiry Concerning Human Understanding* (1738), Hume further included the criterion of spatial and temporal contiguity between A and B, but this requirement was dropped from the second edition onward (Brady 2008, 226).

7. Related to this example, compare the general causation approach taken by Pilster et al. (2013) with the case-focused perspective taken by Massie (2016). A discussion of this literature is given by Mello (2020).

8. The seemingly simple distinction between singular and general causation has fostered some intricate philosophical problems (Baumgartner 2008; Pearl 2009; Psillos 2009). Methodologists in the social sciences typically take a pragmatic view that emphasizes the need for consistency between the research aims and the inferential strategy adopted within a research project (Beach and Pedersen 2019, 48; Rohlfing and Zuber 2019, 6–8).

9. In the social sciences, this lineage is also known as "naturalism" (Moses and Knutsen 2019). For a contemporary reassessment of regularity theories from a philosophical perspective, see Baumgartner (2008, 2013b).

10. Another important distinction, which is left aside here, concerns the question of whether the world itself is governed by stochastic processes or whether probability is the result of researchers' inconclusive evidence (Anjum and Mumford 2018, 157).

11. It might be premature to infer causality on this basis, because the data may be characterized by Simpson's Paradox, which applies to data where a statistical association for the entire population is *inverted* at the subpopulation level—e.g., when a group of people is subdivided by gender or age cohort (Pearl, Glymour, and Jewell 2016, 1–6). This problem can be addressed by specifying that A causes B when A increases the probability of B "in every situation which is *otherwise causally homogenous*" in regard to B (Cartwright 1979, 423).

12. Probability is also at the heart of Bayesian reasoning, which rests on the principle that beliefs about the probability that a theory is true should be updated when new evidence becomes available. In this sense, Bayesianism acknowledges that all scientific theories remain fraught with uncertainty (Anjum and Mumford 2018, 158–60; Bennett 2008).

13. For an elaboration on this point and arguments in favor of a set-theoretic perspective, see Mello (2014, 46–50).

14. In his critique of mainstream quantitative democratic peace research, Rosato (2003, 2005) points out a mismatch between theoretical claims, methods used, and empirical findings. The probabilistic view on the democratic peace is articulated by Slantchev, Alexandrova, and Gartzke (2005). More generally on determinism, see Mahoney (2003), Goertz (2005), Adcock (2007), and Beach and Pedersen (2019, chap. 1).

15. In his essay "Objectivity in Social Science and Social Policy," Weber (1922) ponders the question of what would have happened if Bismarck had not decided for war in 1866: "Was hätte

werden können, wenn z.B. Bismarck den Entschluß zum Kriege nicht gefunden hätte" (Weber 1922, 266).

16. In addition to case-based analyses (Fearon 1991; Lebow 2000; Levy 2008b; Tetlock and Belkin 1996), there is work on necessary condition counterfactuals (Goertz and Levy 2007; Goertz and Starr 2003b), and counterfactuals in the context of set-theoretic comparative approaches (Ragin and Sonnett 2005; Rohlfing and Schneider 2018).

17. For a more detailed narration of this example, see Brady (2008, 241–43).

18. A critique is given by Lieshout (2007).

19. For a discussion of several examples of mechanistic explanations, see Blatter and Haverland (2012, 123–34) and Rohlfing (2012, 33–40).

20. To be sure, the term *causal complexity* already appears in work by Ragin (1987, chap. 2), and has since been in continuous use (see, among others, Berg-Schlosser et al. 2009; George and Bennett 2005; Gerrits and Pagliarin 2020; Koivu and Kimball Damman 2015; Mahoney 2008; Ragin 2000; and Schneider and Wagemann 2012). For a discussion of multiple causality and causal complexity in the philosophy of science, see Anjum and Mumford (2018, 54–56).

21. See also Guzzini (2017) for an interpretivist perspective on equifinality and causal relations.

22. For a different perspective on equifinality, see King, Keohane, and Verba (1994, 87–98).

23. On the temporal aspect of causal asymmetry, see Psillos (2009, 153). Asymmetric hypotheses are assessed by Rosenberg, Knuppe, and Braumoeller (2017).

24. On INUS conditions and the "multiplicity of causal pathways," see also Brady (2008, 228).

25. Mahoney, Kimball, and Koivu (2009, 126) use an example from democratic peace research, according to which nondemocracy (as in a pair of countries that includes at least one nondemocracy) is a necessary condition for interstate war. Now, several attributes of political regimes are in themselves sufficient for nondemocracy (e.g., uncompetitive elections and no adherence to human rights), which means that each of these can be conceived of as SUIN conditions.

26. Explicit references to Mackie and INUS conditions in this context are given by, among others, Ragin (2000, 11), Goertz and Mahoney (2012, 24), Rohlfing (2012, 57), and Schneider and Wagemann (2012, 79). The INUS concept is also widely used by QCA practitioners (e.g., Basedau and Richter 2014; Ide 2015; Kim and Verweij 2016; Kirchherr, Charles, and Walton 2016; Mello 2014; Mross 2019; Oppermann and Brummer 2020; Pagliarin, Hersperger, and Rihoux 2020; Vis 2011; Wurster and Hagemann 2018).

27. Adding nuance to a discussion that is often cast in binary terms, Paul and Hall (2013, 15) note that even under determinism, "the causes of some event do not guarantee that nothing occurs that could prevent those causes from bringing about that event."

5 • Calibrating Sets

It is impossible to conduct meaningful fuzzy set-theoretic
analysis without attending to issues of calibration.

—CHARLES C. RAGIN

Calibration is a precondition for QCA. It is also a much-misunderstood part of the
method. Before the analysis can be run, all data must be *calibrated* into crisp or fuzzy
sets.[1] This procedure distinguishes QCA from other methods of empirical analysis,
because there are vital differences between traditional measurement and set-theoretic
calibration (Ragin 2000, 2008b; Schneider and Wagemann 2012). Opening with this distinction, this chapter introduces the main calibration techniques, talks about sources
of raw data, and introduces the technical routine for the direct method of calibration.
Throughout, the chapter also takes into account new perspectives on calibration methodology (Goertz 2020; Ragin and Fiss 2017). The chapter closes with several calibration examples from published studies, a summary of common misconceptions, and
good practices for calibration.

MEASUREMENT AND CALIBRATION

What is the difference between measurement and calibration? In the social sciences,
most numerical data are based on *uncalibrated* measures. Examples include economic
data, such as gross domestic product and the unemployment rate, and sociological
data on education history, health status, and household income. These measures can
be compared, aggregated, or placed in relation to an average or some other descriptive
statistical indicator. Yet without additional information, we would not know whether
a certain household income is "high" or "low" within a given country or region. Nor
would we be able to say how a given unemployment rate compares across countries or
in different parts of the globe.

By contrast, calibrated measures refer to *external standards*, which means that scores can be directly interpreted once these standards are known. For example, temperatures expressed in degrees Celsius can indicate qualitatively different states, because we know that water freezes at 0°C and boils at 100°C. Hence there is a *qualitative* difference between a lake at 10°C and the same lake at −10 °C, beyond the *quantitative* 20-degree difference in temperature.

Another advantage of calibrated measures is that they allow us to distinguish between meaningful and *less relevant variation* in the uncalibrated raw data. When transforming raw data into sets, we can specify which variation to emphasize. For example, let us suppose we expect the *economic strength* of a country to be a relevant factor in explaining its performance in implementing certain policies. We know that there are economic differences between, say, Switzerland and Denmark. But on a global scale, both these countries would be considered economically strong, which means that we may assign them the same fuzzy score (1, or full membership in the set of *strong economies*). However, for countries with weaker economies, even small differences in gross domestic product per capita mean a lot more in terms of economic development. With the calibration procedure, we can emphasize such differences by delineating the *relevant variation* based on our own substantive knowledge of the research area, as is explained below.

How do we arrive at calibrated measures? Calibration and the assignment of set-theoretic scores requires (1) *plausible and consistent rules* that apply equally to all the selected cases; (2) *content validity*, as in a close correspondence with the underlying social science concept that the target set shall reflect; and, importantly, (3) the definition of *external criteria* (Ragin 2008b, 82; Schneider and Wagemann 2012, 32). In essence, calibration is about "semantic transformations," as in connecting the meaning of a concept to numerical indicators (Goertz 2020, 74).

To delineate external criteria for set-theoretic calibration, three types of knowledge can be distinguished. The first type are *undisputed facts*. These can refer to authoritative statistics or other sources of official information (e.g., demographic data, economic indicators, and historical timelines of events). The second area contains conceptions that are *generally accepted* or widely used in a given field of research (definitions of terms, classification systems, and agreed-upon standards and benchmarks). The final area relates to *individual expertise*—which means that in order to arrive at meaningful calibration criteria, researchers should tap into their own knowledge of specific cases and concepts, and recent developments. In fact, this is a major advantage of QCA because it allows researchers to use their own substantive knowledge of a given field and to devise meaningful sets based on this knowledge.

Some may object that the role of individual knowledge inserts unwarranted subjectivity into the calibration procedure—resulting in what may be seen as arbitrary set membership scores, rather than objective, neutral measurements of the base concepts. This is a valid concern. However, it should be clear that decisions about social science concepts can never be entirely neutral, value-free assessments. Just take concepts like *poverty*, *equality*, or *terrorism*—clearly, there are different understandings of these terms. Depending on our conceptualization, the terms will be connected to different numerical indicators. This means that any decision made during concept formation will have an impact upon the analysis and eventual results. Yet this does *not* mean that these decisions are arbitrary. To the contrary, with every concept there will be a corridor of plausible, justifiable conceptualizations that need to resonate with the scholarly literature and prior research on a given topic (Goertz 2020, 77). This means that though calibration decisions are subjective, and typically are made by an individual researcher or research group, they are still *constrained* by previous studies and accepted knowledge in a given research area.

Against this backdrop, it is crucial that calibration decisions are made *transparent*, to indicate which part of the calibration rests on external standards, which understandings informed the concept formation, and which individual decisions were made and why. For example, we should highlight where we follow the literature in coding decisions (e.g., using a democracy threshold of 7 on the combined Polity scale), whether several plausible calibration strategies exist for a given concept (either because different indicators could be used, or due to disagreement in the literature), or whether the data for some of the included cases are not clear-cut (as when there is contradicting or ambiguous information on a given case). The latter two situations would call for *robustness tests*, understood as complementary analyses based on different calibration strategies to compare how such changes affect the analytical results. This resonates with recent efforts to increase research transparency in qualitative and multimethod research (Büthe and Jacobs 2015), including QCA (Schneider, Vis, and Koivu 2019; Wagemann and Schneider 2015).[2] We will return to these points in the good practices section at the end of this chapter.

CALIBRATION PROCEDURES

There are three approaches to calibration. The *manual approach*, quite simply, assigns scores by hand to individual cases. Like all calibration approaches, this requires a prior definition of the target set, as well as consistent coding rules and external criteria. But beyond that, the scores are manually attributed to each case. To be sure, the manual attribution can also be done via software, where values are assigned following specific rules determined by the researcher. The second approach, termed the *direct method* of calibration, uses a software-based routine to transform numerical raw data into crisp or fuzzy sets. Crucially, this involves a prior definition of three "empirical anchors" set by the researcher (Ragin and Fiss 2017, 61). Finally, the *indirect method* of calibration requires an assignment of preliminary scores to individual cases. In the second stage, a statistical estimation technique is then used to calculate predicted fuzzy values based on the raw data and the initially assigned scores (Ragin 2008b). This chapter focuses on the manual approach and the direct method as the most important approaches to calibration.[3]

When calibrating data, the first step is about conceptualizing and naming the target set. What is important here is that nouns should be turned into adjectives. So, instead of investigating *poverty* or *income*, we would define a set of *poor people*. Following the *Ragin Adjective Rule*, as Gary Goertz calls it (2020, 85), ensures that the target set entails a direction and that it can be interpreted correctly. Hence, we know what it means to have a case that has full membership in the set of *poor people*, whereas some numerical income level would have to be placed into context first.

The second step in calibration is about deciding whether we want to construct a crisp set or a fuzzy set. For crisp sets, we need criteria to define what constitutes membership as opposed to nonmembership in the target set. For fuzzy sets, we have to determine the *crossover point* of 0.5, which is also known as point of maximum ambiguity. This is the point where we cannot say whether a case is inside or outside a given set. This may be because of missing data, which means that we simply do not know enough about the case, or because the case shows idiosyncrasies, as in characteristics that make it difficult to classify in comparison with other cases.

Fuzzy sets can take on many forms, some of which are shown in table 5.1. Note that the examples given in this table should not preclude other conceivable scales. A simple four-value fuzzy set introduces gradations toward both ends of the scale (*more in than out* and *more out than in*). As we move further to the right in the table, the fuzzy scales become more differentiated, until we reach a continuous scale with fine-grained decimal scores between 0 and 1, calculated with the software-based calibration routine.

Note that there is no right or wrong with regard to the calibration scale. Crisp sets can be useful, especially for concepts with binary distinctions (a case is either inside or outside the set). Likewise, if the data allow for a more fine-grained calibration, then a continuous fuzzy set has its advantages. But there can also be substantive reasons to use other calibration scales, different from the ones suggested in table 5.1. Note also that crisp sets and fuzzy sets both evolve vis-à-vis the same fundamental distinction between a case's membership or nonmembership in a given set. Regardless of how nuanced a fuzzy set is, the essential question remains: what distinguishes cases that are more inside than outside a given set (scores above 0.5) from those that are more outside than inside (scores below 0.5)?

To illustrate the calibration process and differences based on the choice of the approach, let us take an example using unemployment data. Suppose we wanted to construct the set *high unemployment* for the 28 European Union member states, just before the departure of the United Kingdom in January 2020. Using official reports on the EU's progress toward its stated goals for the labor market as our benchmark (European Parliamentary Research Service 2019),[4] we may say that 10 percent unemployment and

Table 5.1 Calibration Scales

	Crisp Set	Fuzzy Sets			
Verbal Label	**Binary**	**Four Values**	**Five Values**	**Eleven Values**	**Continuous Scale**
Fully in	1	1	1	1 0.9	1
More in than out		0.7	0.7	0.8 0.7 0.6	$0.5 < X_i < 1$
Neither in nor out			0.5	0.5 0.4	0.5
More out than in		0.3	0.3	0.3 0.2 0.1	$0.5 > X_i > 0$
Fully out	0	0	0	0	0

higher can be considered *fully in* the set high unemployment, whereas 6 percent shall be the *crossover*, where a country falls right in between being inside and outside the set. Finally, 3 percent and lower is considered *fully out* of the set. For the direct method of calibration, these empirical anchors would let the software transform the raw data (given in percentages) into decimal fuzzy scores, ranging from 0 to 1. Note that we look into the technical steps of the transformation procedure in the next section.

Table 5.2 shows the raw data and the calibration results for a crisp set and two fuzzy sets. The raw data are the unemployment rate among EU countries (Eurostat 2020). The right-hand columns show a crisp set calibration, and two fuzzy set calibrations. These are based on the same criteria, using a crossover of 6 percent unemployment to distinguish between being inside or outside the set. For the crisp set, this results in the upper 10 countries receiving scores of 1 (reflecting unemployment rates between 6.3 and 16.4 percent) and the lower 18 countries receiving scores of 0 (with unemployment rates between 2.0 and 5.9 percent). The five-value fuzzy set uses the same crossover, but further distinguishes between *fully in* (1) for raw data scores equal to or above 10, *almost fully in* (0.7) for those below 10 and above 6, *almost fully out* (0.3) for those below 6 and above 3, and *fully out* (0) for those with scores of 3 and less. Note that there is no country that receives a set membership of 0.5, which would be assigned to a case with exactly 6 percent unemployment. Finally, on the right-hand side of table 5.2 is the continuous fuzzy set, which is based on the direct method of calibration that is processed with the software. We can see that this calibration approach yields the

Table 5.2   Raw Data and Calibrated Crisp and Fuzzy Sets

Case/Country	Raw Data	Calibrated Set, High Unemployment		
		Crisp Set	Fuzzy Set (Four Values)	Fuzzy Set (Continuous)
Greece	16.4	1	1	1
Spain	13.8	1	1	1
Italy	9.5	1	0.7	0.93
France	8.1	1	0.7	0.82
Sweden	7.0	1	0.7	0.68
Portugal	6.8	1	0.7	0.64
Lithuania	6.6	1	0.7	0.61
Finland	6.6	1	0.7	0.61
Latvia	6.5	1	0.7	0.59
Croatia	6.3	1	0.7	0.55
Cyprus	5.9	0	0.3	0.48
Luxembourg	5.6	0	0.3	0.40
Slovakia	5.4	0	0.3	0.36
Belgium	5.2	0	0.3	0.31
Denmark	4.8	0	0.3	0.24
Ireland	4.8	0	0.3	0.24
Estonia	4.7	0	0.3	0.22
Austria	4.3	0	0.3	0.16
Bulgaria	4.1	0	0.3	0.13
Romania	3.9	0	0.3	0.11
United Kingdom	3.8	0	0.3	0.10
Slovenia	3.7	0	0.3	0.09
Hungary	3.4	0	0.3	0.07
Malta	3.4	0	0.3	0.07
Germany	3.2	0	0.3	0.06
Netherlands	3.0	0	0	0.05
Poland	2.9	0	0	0.05
Czechia	2.0	0	0	0.02

Source: Eurostat (2020).

most fine-grained values and that it introduces further distinctions between some of the cases that still received the same values in the five-value fuzzy set.

Does it matter which calibration approach is chosen? Is there a best approach to calibration? Table 5.2 shows that irrespective of which procedure is adopted, the resulting scores across the three types of sets remain fairly similar. This can also be seen from figure 5.1, which visualizes the relationship between the raw data and the three different

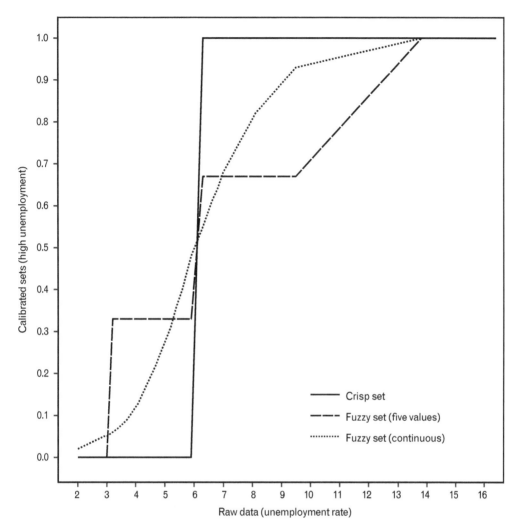

Figure 5.1   Raw Data and Different Calibration Scales

calibration scales. With crisp sets, there is a qualitative jump around the crossover. With the five-value fuzzy set, there are several such jumps, while the continuous fuzzy set approximates a smooth, s-shaped curve. This is so because the transformation is based on a logarithmic scale (see the discussion in the next section), which means that the default pattern is an s shape. Certainly, the continuous fuzzy set yields the most nuanced set membership scores, but this should not be taken to imply that the other approaches are subordinate to the direct method of calibration.

The most consequential decision in calibration is the assignment of the empirical anchors, and of these, the crossover has the largest *qualitative* impact because it can determine whether a case is inside or outside the target set. In practice, it is often helpful to begin the calibration process by thinking about the crossover as the distinguishing criterion. This mirrors the discussion in chapter 2 on the selection of positive and negative cases. As a preliminary step during calibration, one can create a crisp set for an initial analysis to find out whether the selected condition provides inferential leverage that helps to explain the phenomenon under study. Throughout this process, it may become clear that the crossover should be set differently, or that further distinctions and thus fuzzy sets are warranted.

TYPES OF DATA

Which types of data can be used for calibration? And what is needed in order to construct crisp and fuzzy sets? Clearly, a major advantage of QCA is the method's openness to both *qualitative* and *quantitative* data. Applied examples are given in box 5.1 (Swinkels 2020a) and box 5.2 (Giordono, Boudet, and Gard-Murray 2020). Although emphasis is often placed on the transformation of quantitative data (e.g., Ragin 2008b; Schneider and Wagemann 2012), calibration can equally draw on qualitative information gained from interviews, documents, field observations, or historical archives, just as it can be based on quantitative indicators, taken from existing or newly created data sets or surveys.[5] Importantly, different approaches can be merged in the same QCA study, as in having qualitative conditions alongside quantitative ones. There is no need to use the same calibration approach across all the conditions in a single study. Along the same lines, crisp set and fuzzy set conditions can be combined, as in having a fuzzy-set outcome and crisp-set conditions, or vice versa, if that suits the research aim.

Finally, depending on the context, it may be helpful to draw on several different data sources to inform the calibration procedure—for instance, by first using a generally accepted statistic to determine whether a case is inside or outside a set, and then using interviews and in-depth research to determine fine-grained scores above and below the 0.5 crossover. For such an approach, one could either devise a codebook and apply the rules manually to each case, or one could use a stepwise procedure in R to conduct the calibration. That being said, to use the direct method of calibration, one would usually work with interval- or ratio-level data, while all levels of measurement can be used for the qualitative calibration procedure that assigns values by hand.

Table 5.3 summarizes the levels of measurement commonly used in the social sciences, with the addition of fuzzy sets. The *nominal* level means that numbers or categories are used to classify observations or cases.[6] All cases in a category are treated as equal to each other, and there is no ranking between categories. The *ordinal* level of measurement means that observations can be placed in relation to each other. This is common in survey responses like "more happy" versus "less happy," or "stronger agreement" versus "moderate agreement," and so forth. Measurement at the *interval* level means that the exact distance between the observations is known and that it can be expressed in

Box 5.1   Using Fuzzy-Set QCA to Analyze the Influence of the Political and Economic Context on Leaders' Beliefs About the Economy

Marij Swinkels, Utrecht School of Governance, Utrecht University

Students and scholars of political leadership have long been puzzled by the question of what affects political leaders' beliefs, and in turn their political responses. In the literature, a general consensus exists that different groups of conditions affect belief change of political leaders. These range from environmental conditions to personal dispositions, e.g. a crisis, party ideology, or leaders' traits and motivations (Swinkels 2020b). While scholars in general acknowledge that varying sets of factors play a role in instigating belief-change, I found fewer studies that tested this idea of *causal complexity* empirically. Thus, I set out on an adventure to look for ways in which I could study the interaction of different factors and their influence on belief changes. I found QCA to be the most suitable method to study my question as it allowed me to do just what I was looking for: getting an understanding of the "multiple ways that lead to Rome (or in this case, Brussels)."

For my study (Swinkels 2020a), I selected 12 EU leaders during the euro zone crisis of whom I could obtain data about their core beliefs about the economy (Van Esch et al. 2018). These leaders were selected on the basis of "most-different" criteria, for example coming from countries with demand-led versus export-led growth models. For each leader, I studied whether their beliefs about the economy were more Keynesian or more ordoliberal, and how these beliefs changed throughout the Eurozone crisis. Subsequently, I wanted to know what configuration of political and economic conditions affected these observed different belief changes. QCA allowed me to systematically study the different pathways that led to the different outcomes in my study. For establishing the conditions, I used a combination of both *quantitative* and *qualitative data*. I believe this is another ideal feature of QCA, to be able to work with different types of data in your analysis.

My findings provide evidence for the idea that the socioeconomic situation of individual leaders in the EU affects their beliefs about the economy. As these socioeconomic situations of leaders continued to differ throughout the crisis, convergence of beliefs was constrained and potentially further complicated joint decision-making of leaders in the euro zone crisis. Furthermore, my findings allowed me to dive into alternative explanations for *deviant cases* commonly found in the existing scholarly literature (Culpepper 2014; Schoeller,

(continued)

Box 5.1 (*continued*)

Guidi, and Karagiannis 2017; Van Esch 2014). One of these alternative explanations was the influence of a broader European policy discourse on individual leaders' beliefs. I used this finding as the basis of my subsequent empirical study into why and when leaders' change their beliefs.

In my view, using QCA as a method provides me and other scholars in my subdiscipline of EU leadership in crises with a grounded approach to systematically trace the impact of different factors on certain leadership outcomes. On one hand, it introduces the idea of causal complexity to existing methodological approaches in my subdiscipline; on the other hand, it provides scholars with a systematic approach to study such causal patterns. Furthermore, QCA helps researchers to identify interesting cases for further study via process tracing or other intensive case study approaches (on multi-method research designs, see chapter 2).

Box 5.2   Using Fuzzy-Set QCA to Explain Local Adaptation Policy Responses to Extreme Weather

Leanne Giordono, Oregon State University; Hilary Boudet, Oregon State University; and Alexander Gard-Murray, Harvard University

Climate change is expected to yield more frequent, extreme and potentially devastating weather events at a global level (Allen, Dube, and Solecki 2018). Theoretically, we might expect such events to yield a window of opportunity during which policy actors take advantage of event-focused attention to adopt new policy oriented toward climate change adaptation or mitigation (Birkland 2006). Using 15 cases of localized extreme weather events during the period of 2012–15, we used fuzzy set Qualitative Comparative Analysis (fsQCA) to examine the conditions under which postevent policy adoption occurred and did not occur (Giordono, Boudet, and Gard-Murray 2020).

We chose to use fsQCA in this study for several reasons. First, underlying theory about policy change and climate change policy preferences is set-theoretic in nature—in other words, several necessary and/or sufficient conditions, acting

(*continued*)

Box 5.2 (*continued*)

in combination, form "recipes" for policy change. Second, the study included a mid-*N* number of cases—too many for traditional comparative methods, but ideal for QCA applications. Third, the study included access to rich case-specific qualitative data, as well as quantitative data. These data enabled us to leverage the "fuzzy" feature of fsQCA (i.e., assigning scores between 0 and 1) and engage in a dialogue between theory and evidence. Finally, we wanted to accommodate our expectations of equifinality, or the possibility that different combinations of conditions would lead to the main outcome of interest (policy change) and its negation (no policy change).

There are two related challenges of engaging in fsQCA that are not unique to this study. The method is data-intensive, due to the reliance on a mid-*N* number of cases and the need for in-depth knowledge of each case. Our data included 164 interviews and over 4,500 newspaper articles and editorials, as well as extant data from a variety of sources (e.g., the American Community Survey). Ideally, scores are assigned based on measurable indicators. For example, in our study, policy adoption was scored using an explicit combination of the number and types of policies adopted after an event. However, operationalizing and scoring the conditions still requires the researcher to balance her in-depth case knowledge with theoretically and empirically relevant expectations about how and when the underlying data would indicate that the case is "in" or "out" of the set.

This study benefited from being one of several studies in connection with a larger research project. Specifically, the research team had previously applied fsQCA methods to a different set of research questions (Boudet et al. 2019), yielding opportunities for learning. During the prior study, for example, the review process had taught us to provide extensive documentation to justify our analytic decisions and results, as emphasized throughout this book (summarized in table 10.1 in chapter 10 below). Moreover, we had learned to provide an up-front statement about our approach, namely that we had elected to apply a "case-oriented" approach, to ward off potential criticism from researchers who promote a competing "condition-oriented" approach (Thomann and Maggetti 2020; see also chapter 2 in this book). Ultimately, these last challenges—applying fsQCA in the context of a nascent and rapidly changing field—may prove to be the most demanding for researchers. They require a willingness to engage in critical dialogue, both with the method and other researchers, while acknowledging the motivations and reasoning of the original developers and those who follow in their footsteps.

Table 5.3 Five Levels of Measurement

Level	Equivalence	Greater Than	Fixed Interval	Natural Zero	Natural Maximum	Examples
Nominal	✓					Marital status, continent
Ordinal	✓	✓				Happiness, agreement
Interval	✓	✓	✓			Temperature (°C), intelligence (IQ)
Ratio	✓	✓	✓	✓		Years of education, gross domestic product per capita
Fuzzy	✓	✓	✓	✓	✓	Educated person, developed country

numerical terms, whereas the *ratio* level is typically considered the highest form of measurement because it entails a natural zero point (Frankfort-Nachmias and Nachmias 2008).[7] However, as Ragin (2000, 155) suggests, fuzzy sets could be considered an even higher form of measurement because these entail a natural zero and a natural maximum: "It could be argued that fuzzy-set membership is a higher form of measurement than the conventional ratio scale—it is a ratio scale with a fixed and meaningful minimum *and maximum*. Still, the purpose of a fuzzy set is parallel to that of the nominal scale—to indicate set membership" (emphasis in the original) (see also Goertz 2020, chap. 5).

With *qualitative data*, the main challenge is to find a consistent and systematic way of linking information to numbers, while staying as close as feasible to the underlying concept. As Debora De Block and Barbara Vis (2019) note, most of the methodological literature on calibration has focused on the transformation of quantitative data. This is sometimes taken as if QCA could only work with quantitative data sets, which is not the case. Yet the bottom line is that there are no firm rules about how to transform qualitative raw data into crisp or fuzzy sets. However, as with general aspects of calibration, it is useful to start by thinking about the crossover as the central criterion. So, regardless of how much qualitative, in-depth data you may have gathered, you should think about this part first. This is more easily illustrated with examples, which are provided after the technical discussion of the calibration routine in the next section.

THE DIRECT METHOD OF CALIBRATION

What is known as the direct method of calibration is a software-based routine to transform numerical raw data into fuzzy-set scores between 0 and 1 (Ragin 2008b). For the researcher, the key step is setting the three *empirical anchors* that guide this transformation (Ragin and Fiss 2017, 61). From there, the software applies a procedure that happens under the hood until we see the resulting calibrated scores. To shed light on this somewhat opaque process, I describe the calculations that are entailed in the calibration routine.[8] Clearly, readers without an inclination for mathematics may safely skip this description and still be able to apply the calibration procedure. Yet users often wonder how, exactly, the calibrated scores are calculated in QCA—a question that is answered in this section.[9]

How are the raw data transformed into fuzzy values? The calibration uses a logarithmic function, which is useful because the function is symmetric, and the transformed values will stay within the boundaries of 1 and 0. In fact, the values will never exactly reach the end points because the s-shaped curve flattens out near these values, toward positive and negative infinity. Hence, by convention values of 0.95 and 0.05 are interpreted as *full membership* and *full nonmembership* in a given set (Ragin 2008b, 87). One should thus not be surprised to see cases with values just below 1, even though their uncalibrated value is above the threshold for full set membership. This also means that small numerical differences in fuzzy sets should not be overinterpreted because they give a false impression of preciseness. This is one of the reasons why I recommend against reporting more than two decimal points for set-membership scores in publications (another reason being poor readability).

Table 5.4 shows the verbal labels for the three empirical anchors, the corresponding degree of membership, and two additional metrics that are needed for the transformation, as I illustrate just below: *associated odds* and *log odds*. Associated odds are calculated with this formula:

$$\text{associated odds} = \frac{\text{degree of membership}}{(1 - \text{degree of membership})}$$

In turn, log odds are calculated by taking the natural logarithm (ln) of the associated odds.[10] In essence, the three numerical columns of table 5.4 are merely different representations of the same values, starting with degree of membership.

Table 5.4   Metrics for the Direct Method of Calibration

Empirical Anchor	Degree of Set Membership	Associated Odds	Log Odds
Full set membership	0.95	19.000	2.944
Crossover	0.50	1.000	0.000
Full set nonmembership	0.05	0.053	−2.944

Table 5.5   Direct Method of Calibration, Human Development Example

Country	Raw Data (HDI, 2017)	Deviation	Scalars	Product	Fuzzy Set, High Human Development	Empirical Anchors
Switzerland	0.944	0.244	29.44	7.18	1	
Germany	0.936	0.236	29.44	6.95	1	
Lithuania	0.858	0.158	29.44	4.65	0.99	
Romania	0.811	0.111	29.44	3.27	0.96	0.80 (Fully in)
Turkey	0.791	0.091	29.44	2.68	0.94	
Brazil	0.759	0.059	29.44	1.74	0.85	
China	0.752	0.052	29.44	1.53	0.82	
Uzbekistan	0.710	0.010	29.44	0.29	0.57	0.70 (Crossover)
El Salvador	0.674	−0.026	19.63	−0.51	0.38	
India	0.640	−0.060	19.63	−1.18	0.24	
Kenya	0.590	−0.110	19.63	−2.16	0.10	
Pakistan	0.562	−0.138	19.63	−2.71	0.06	0.55 (Fully out)
Togo	0.503	−0.197	19.63	−3.87	0.02	
Ethiopia	0.463	−0.237	19.63	−4.65	0.01	
South Sudan	0.388	−0.312	19.63	−6.12	0	
Niger	0.354	−0.346	19.63	−6.79	0	

Note: HDI = Human Development Index.

With these three metrics in place, we can now turn to the actual calibration procedure. Table 5.5 shows raw data from the Human Development Index (HDI) of the United Nations for a sample of 16 countries out of a population of 189 countries for which HDI data are available. HDI scores closer to 1 indicate very high development, whereas scores closer to 0 refer to low development (these should not be confused with fuzzy scores). Conveniently, the methodology of the HDI entails a classification system according to which "high human development" is reflected in scores of 0.70 and higher, and "very high human development" relates to scores of 0.80 and above. At the low end of the scale, scores below 0.55 are considered "low human development" (United Nations 2018, 17). Hence, for our example, we can use these external standards as empirical anchors for the calibration of the fuzzy set *high human development*.

Accordingly, a raw data value of 0.80 and higher is taken to indicate that a country is fully in the set, 0.70 is considered the crossover, and 0.55 marks the threshold for being fully outside the set.

Once the empirical anchors are in place, we can calculate each cases' *deviation* (or numerical distance) from the crossover of 0.70. This results in positive scores for the cases above the crossover and negative scores for those below. In the next step, we take the *log odds* for full set membership (+2.944; see table 5.4) and full set nonmembership (−2.944) and divide them by the deviation of the threshold for fully in (0.10) and fully out (−0.15), which gives us *scalars* of 29.44 and 19.63, respectively. For each case, these scalars are then multiplied by the cases' deviation, which yields a *product*, as shown in the respective column of table 5.5. Finally, the product is transformed into scores between 0 and 1, by taking the *exponent* of the product and dividing it by itself plus 1 as in the next example. The result is rounded to two digits, which yields a fuzzy set membership of 1 in the case of Switzerland. In the same way, we calculate the fuzzy values for all the countries, as shown in the second-to-last column of table 5.5:

$$\text{Switzerland} = \frac{\exp(7.18)}{(1 + \exp(7.18))} = \frac{1312.91}{1313.91} = 0.9992 \approx 1$$

The effects of the calibration procedure and the choice of the empirical anchors can be visualized with an X–Y plot that displays the raw data against the calibrated data. Figure 5.2 shows the s-shaped curve that is typical of a logarithmic function. The x axis displays the complete raw data from the HDI (United Nations 2018), which ranges from 0.354 (Niger) to 0.953 (Norway), covering 189 countries, as opposed to the selected 16 countries show in table 5.5. The y axis displays the calibrated fuzzy values. The figure also includes three dashed vertical lines for the empirical anchors and a solid horizontal line for the 0.5 cutoff that separates cases that are inside the fuzzy set (above the horizontal line) from those that are outside the fuzzy set (below the horizontal line). Finally, the X–Y plot shows the location of selected cases across the range of raw data shown in table 5.5 (from low to high: Chad, Kenya, Iraq, Samoa, Brazil, and Norway). As can be seen in the figure, the calibrated values rise steeply around the cutoff and between the anchors for full exclusion and full inclusion. Beyond those, the line flattens out on both ends, closing in on 0 and 1, respectively. This means that any empirical variation beyond the thresholds is deemphasized. Countries receive

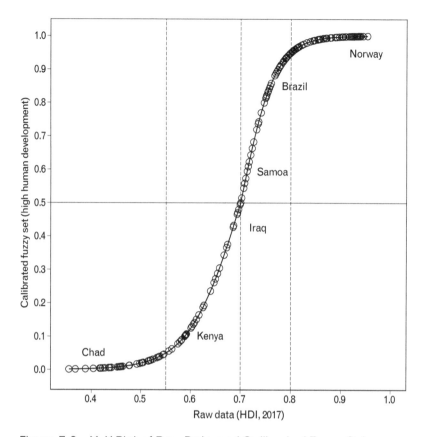

Figure 5.2   X–Y Plot of Raw Data and Calibrated Fuzzy Set

similar fuzzy values beyond the empirical anchor chosen for full exclusion (0.55) and full inclusion (0.8), whereas small increases in the raw data in the center (around the crossover, between these thresholds) lead to substantially higher fuzzy values, as visualized in the steep ascent of the curve. Note that, for presentational purposes, the x axis is truncated because there are no countries with less than 0.354 HDI (Niger's score).

What fuzzy set calibration does, and what can be gleaned from the X–Y plot, is that it essentially *stretches* the raw data that are located in the center, above and below the crossover, and it *flattens* the raw data that are located around the edges, below full exclusion and above full inclusion in the set. This procedure emphasizes small differences in the area that is deemed most relevant (above and below the crossover), and it deemphasizes variation that is held to be less relevant for the phenomenon under study. Plotting the raw data against the calibrated fuzzy set makes this immediately visible, which is one reason why such plots should be included in online appendixes or supplementary material for empirical applications of QCA (see guidelines in the final section of this chapter).

APPLIED EXAMPLES OF CALIBRATION

This section provides several calibration examples from published studies (Cacciatore, Natalini, and Wagemann 2015; Fagerholm 2014; Kuehn et al. 2017; Mello 2020; Ragin and Fiss 2017; Schmitt 2018). These were selected to cover a range of different calibration scenarios—including procedures for qualitative calibration, the transformation of quantitative raw data, the combination of several conditions into a macrocondition, the weighting of indicators, and asymmetric concepts. The examples presented are illustrative—without going into the context and details of the respective studies, nor discussing their QCA results. Here it must suffice to introduce the concept of the respective condition or outcome, the underlying data, calibration thresholds, and the results of the calibration process.

Example 1: Parental Income

In their book-length study *Intersectional Inequality*, Charles Ragin and Peer Fiss (2017) explore life chances and social inequality based on various configurations of race, gender, educational achievement, and family background. Two of their fuzzy-set conditions are based on parental income in relation to the household-adjusted poverty level: *low-income parents* and *high-income parents*. What makes this interesting for our purposes is that these are examples of *asymmetric concepts*. As Ragin and Fiss (2017, 69) note, there is a difference between individuals with high-income parents and those with parents who are not low-income. The former group of people is certainly smaller than the latter and hence it makes sense to analyze these as separate sets. This is visualized in figure 5.3, where we can see the area between the two vertical crossover lines. Individuals in this area are outside *both* sets (with fuzzy scores below 0.5). Ragin and Fiss base their calibration criteria on prior studies, official government thresholds, and national surveys, noting that there are "value judgments" involved because "there is no consensus within the scientific community on exactly where the poverty line should be drawn" (Ragin and Fiss 2017, 67). Against this backdrop, Ragin and Fiss opt for what the authors describe as a "conservative cutoff value," which is substantiated by recommendations from the National Research Council (2017, 67). The authors use the direct method of calibration on raw data that reflects multiples of the income-to-poverty ratio to construct the fuzzy sets *low-income parents* (fully out, 5.5; crossover, 3; fully in, 2) and *high-income parents* (fully out, 3; crossover, 5.5; fully in, 8).

Example 2: Path Dependence

In their study of Europeanization and the implementation of national reform programs among EU member states, Federica Cacciatore, Alessandro Natalini, and Claudius Wagemann (2015, 1191) include a *path dependence* condition ("ACCESS") that builds

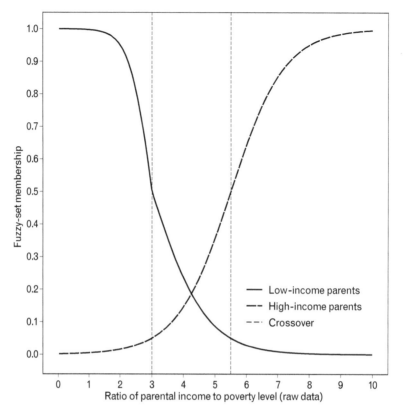

Figure 5.3   Low-Income and High-Income Parents
Source: Ragin and Fiss 2017.

on theoretical expectations derived from historical institutionalism—namely, that a country's familiarity with EU institutions and practices "will determine the domestic implementation success" of new European legislation. The authors use a straightforward metric to operationalize the path dependence logic by measuring the number of years that passed since a member state joined the European institutions. The fuzzy set is calibrated using the direct method of calibration, with the empirical anchors being 5 years (fully out), 20 years (crossover), and 40 years (fully in), as summarized in table 5.6. The table shows only a selection of cases to illustrate the calibration procedure, but it should be noted that the study includes three observations per country (in the years 2011–13). As can be seen from the table, the empirical anchors effectively distinguish the EU's founding and early members from those that joined it in later accession rounds. The authors discuss their calibration strategies in a supplementary document, where they argue that their choice for the calibration thresholds for the path dependence condition ACCESS "seems to be an appropriate time span for a country to fully achieve and

Table 5.6   Condition "Path Dependence"

Country (Selection)	Year of EU/EC Accession	Years in EU/EC	Fuzzy Set ACCESS	Empirical Anchors
Belgium	1952	51	0.99	
Germany	1952	51	0.99	
Italy	1952	51	0.99	
Denmark	1973	40	0.95	
United Kingdom	1973	40	0.95	Fully in ⩾ 40 years
Greece	1981	32	0.86	
Portugal	1986	27	0.74	
Spain	1986	26	0.71	
Sweden	1995	18	0.40	Crossover = 20 years
Finland	1995	18	0.40	
Hungary	2004	9	0.10	
Slovenia	2004	8	0.08	Fully out ⩽ 5 years

Source: Cacciatore, Natalini, and Wagemann (2015, online appendix).

assimilate the EU's political culture and mechanisms" (Cacciatore, Natalini, and Wagemann 2015, online appendix, 5). Arguably, with numerical indicators such as these, there will always be some leeway, and others might opt for a higher or lower threshold. What the authors highlight, however, is that during the three observed years, none of the cases passed the crossover from being considered less accustomed to more accustomed with EU institutions (Cacciatore, Natalini, and Wagemann 2015).

Example 3: Civilian Control of the Military

In their study of civil–military relations in 28 new democracies, David Kuehn and colleagues (2017) operationalize the fuzzy-set outcome *civilian control of the military* by taking weighted averages across five fuzzy-set dimensions: elite recruitment (ER), public policy (PP), internal security (IS), national defense (ND), and military organization (MO). Due to its centrality for the functioning of democratic institutions, ER receives a fivefold weight, whereas PP and IS are weighted twofold and the other conditions receive single weights (Kuehn et al. 2017, 432). The authors justify this weighting system with a body of theoretical work on this topic. This yields the following formula for the calculation of the outcome:

$$\text{Civilian control} = \frac{\text{ER} \times 5 + \text{PP} \times 2 + \text{IS} \times 2 + \text{ND} + \text{MO}}{11}$$

Table 5.7   Outcome "Civilian Control"

Country (Selection)	Civilian Control (Outcome)	Elite Recruitment	Public Policy	Internal Security	National Defense	Military Organization
Brazil 1, 1985–87	0.13	0.2	0.2	0	0	0
Brazil 2, 1988–98	0.65	0.85	0.85	0.4	0	0.4
Nepal 1, 1999–2001	0.74	1	0.85	0.6	0	0.2
Nepal 2, 2006–10	0.86	1	1	0.55	0.4	1
Taiwan 1, 1992–2001	0.89	1	1	1	0.4	0.4
Taiwan 2, 2002–10	1	1	1	1	1	1

Source: Kuehn et al. (2017, online appendix).

The study by Kuehn et al. (2017) illustrates how a complex condition can be modeled with fuzzy sets and how individual indicators can be assigned different weights. Here, the authors use the *average* across the included indicators, but one could have also constructed a fuzzy set from combinations of conditions that are joined by Boolean operators, as introduced in chapter 2 of this book. For instance, Goertz (2020) provides illustrative examples of how multiple-level theories and concepts can be modeled in this way. Table 5.7 shows the calibrated data for the outcome and its constituent conditions for 5 of the 28 cases of the study. The use of higher-order concepts—such as *civilian control*, which is employed by Kuehn and others (2017)—has the advantage that a broad array of indicators can be taken into account to inform the calibration of a single condition. One downside of this is that the interpretation of the eventual scores is complicated, and it may be necessary to reexamine a case's scores in the constituent conditions to make sense of empirical patterns (e.g., Nepal 2 and Taiwan 1 receive similar scores in the outcome, but they differ substantively on *internal security* and *military organization*, as two of the outcome's five dimensions). Another concern is the weighting system, because one could plausibly justify different weights, but changes in this regard would affect the outcome scores. Hence, when considering an *index condition*, it is vital to justify the constituent conditions and their weighting (especially when these are not weighted equally), and to consider alternative analyses as robustness tests.

Example 4: The Utility of Junior Partners in Coalition Warfare

The book-length study *Allies that Count* by Olivier Schmitt (2018) investigates the role of junior partners in coalition warfare, such as the multinational military operations in Iraq and Afghanistan. The book primarily comprises intensive case studies based on archives, interviews, participatory observation, and secondary sources. These are complemented by a crisp-set QCA for a systematic exploration of the qualities that make a junior partner useful in coalition warfare. Schmitt (2018, 202–3) defines the outcome *utility* as a junior partner's "capacity to positively assist in the achievement of the desired result." The calibration involves in-depth qualitative assessments for each of the observed coalition members. As Schmitt explains, "The question asked in assessing the utility was, would the campaign planning and conduct have been substantially different in the absence of this ally?" This question is addressed for each of the observed cases and conflicts. For example, as for the United Kingdom and France as coalition partners in Afghanistan, Schmitt argues:

> In Afghanistan, the nonparticipation of France or the United Kingdom would have forced the United States to devote key resources to strategically important areas of operations such as the Helmand and Kapisa Provinces. Although the performance of the British and French troops can certainly be criticized, whether another ally would have done better is unclear. In any case, the absence of these two states would have negatively impacted the legitimacy of the operation and the strategic planning by draining US resources. The French and British participation were coded as 1. (Schmitt 2018, 203)

The study by Schmitt is an example of a *qualitative* calibration procedure that boils down to value judgments, the results of which cannot easily be transformed into numbers.[11] Against this backdrop, Schmitt chooses the crisp-set variant of QCA, which emphasizes qualitative differences rather than differences in degree. His book also provides a thorough discussion of its calibration decisions in its appendix.

Example 5: Ecological Change

In his study of ecological change within social democratic parties, Andreas Fagerholm (2014) examines the ecological orientation of parties' election programs. His study makes use of data from the Comparative Manifesto Project (Klingemann et al. 2006; Volkens et al. 2013), which contains several variables that are related to ecological

Table 5.8 Outcome "Ecological Change"

Social Democratic Party (Selection)	Ecological Change (Outcome)	Ecologism		
		1970–79	1980–89	1990–99
PvdA (Netherlands)	1	6.40	5.72	8.12
SPS (Switzerland)	1	5.24	15.74	7.31
SPÖ (Luxembourg)	1	2.97	8.10	7.10
SPD (Germany)	1	−0.84	3.30	15.27
PSOE (Spain)	0	−0.75	−0.82	3.40
LP (United Kingdom)	0	0.50	1.91	3.10
PS (France)	0	0.60	−3.03	0.95

Source: Fagerholm (2014).

preferences. Specifically, Fagerholm focuses on mentions of "anti-growth economy: positive" (per416) and "environmental protection: positive" (per501) and subtracts mentions of "productivity: positive" (per410), using the following formula to calculate an indicator for social democratic parties' ecologism:

$$\text{Ecologism} = [(\text{per}416 + \text{per}501) - \text{per}410] \geq 5.0$$

Given this formula, ecologism is seen as present when "ecological issues outnumber non-ecological issues by a difference of at least 5 percent," as Fagerholm (2014, 5) explains. Table 5.8 shows selected raw data for 7 of Fagerholm's 19 social democratic parties (abbreviated for purposes of illustration). The study analyzed party programs over three periods, between 1970 and 1999. The ecologism indicator was used as a basis to calibrate the crisp-set outcome *ecological change*. This was coded positively when ecologism scored above 5 percent during at least one of the observed periods. From table 5.8, we can see that this is the case for social democratic parties in the Netherlands, Switzerland, Luxembourg, and Germany but not in Spain, the United Kingdom, and France. The study by Fagerholm is another example where several indicators inform the calibration of a single condition. Here, the same indicator (ecologism) is taken at three different points in time to determine what is conceptualized as *ecological change*. This way, the study also takes into account *temporality*—an aspect that is typically neglected by the static comparisons of QCA. Why did the study use a crisp-set outcome? Fagerholm (2014, 11) argues that emphasis was placed on "case-based knowledge, since *differences in kind* are deemed to be more important than fine-grained *differences in degree*" (emphasis added). This is a plausible argument, similar to the one in the previous example by Schmitt (2018). Yet, given that the study already has fine-grained Comparative Manifesto Project data at hand, it would also have been feasible to calibrate a fuzzy-set outcome.

Example 6: Fatalities

In my own study of coalition defection during the Iraq War (Mello 2020), I included a condition that takes into account civilian and military deaths that resulted from terrorist attacks—as a potential influence on democratic leaders' decision-making. The study drew on two databases: the Iraq Casualties Project, for military casualties; and the Rand Database of Worldwide Terrorism Incidents, for civilian casualties. I calibrated these data starting with a *qualitative* criterion—distinguishing "primarily between leaders who experienced casualties and those who did not" (Mello 2020, 15). This means that government leaders without any casualties received fuzzy values of 0, while those with casualties received fuzzy values between 0.51 and 1.0.

To determine the exact value for the condition, the direct method of calibration was used on a quantitative measure of the ratio between casualties and the number of deployed troops, using the thresholds 0.005 (fully out), 0.006 (crossover), and 0.50 (fully in). The crossover effectively means that countries with *at least one fatality* receive scores above 0.51 and above (and are thus considered inside the set). Table 5.9 summarizes the raw data and calibrated fuzzy-set values for 12 of the 51 leaders included in the study. For example, we can see that El Salvador received a fuzzy set value of 1, whereas Japan only received a value of 0.98. This is because the ratio of fatalities per deployment is higher for El Salvador under President Flores (2.5 percent)

Table 5.9   Condition "Fatalities"

Country (Selection)	Government Leader (Selection)	Raw Data			Fuzzy-Set Fatalities
		Fatalities per Deployment (percent)	Fatalities (Nominal)	Deployed Number of Troops	
Albania	F. Nano	0.00	0	80	0.00
Australia	J. W. Howard	0.19	2	1,048	0.75
Denmark	A. F. Rasmussen	0.83	4	480	0.99
El Salvador	F. Flores	2.50	1	40	1.00
Estonia	A. Ansip	0.00	0	40	0.00
Hungary	F. Gyurcsány	0.00	0	300	0.00
Japan	J. Koizumi	0.67	4	600	0.98
Netherlands	J. P. Balkenende	0.23	3	1,288	0.79
Poland	L. Miller	0.06	1	1,667	0.58
Portugal	J. M. D. Barroso	0.00	0	120	0.00
Spain	J. L. R. Zapatero	0.08	1	1,300	0.61
United Kingdom	G. Brown	0.34	16	4,770	0.88

Source: Mello (2020).

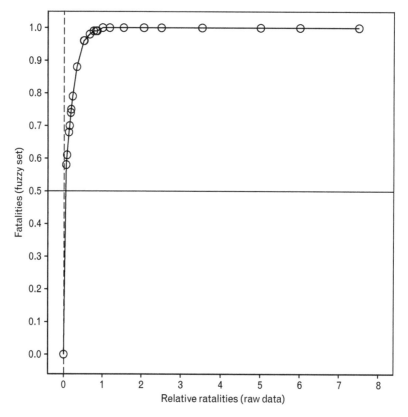

Figure 5.4   Raw Data and Calibrated Fuzzy-Set Fatalities

than for Japan under Prime Minister Koizumi (0.67 percent). Figure 5.4 visualizes the calibration.

Hence, the fuzzy set *fatalities* is another example of an *asymmetric condition* (see example 1). Moreover, the condition is conceptualized in a way that allows for scores between 0.51 and 1, but not for scores larger than 0 and less than 0.51 (because either there are civilian or military deaths or there are none). Alternatively, a crisp-set condition could have been used. The advantage of a crisp-set calibration would have been the simpler, more straightforward metric, but, unlike the fuzzy set, this could not have taken into account gradations based on fatalities per deployment.

COMMON MISCONCEPTIONS ABOUT CALIBRATION

At the outset of this chapter, I mentioned that calibration is a much-misunderstood part of QCA. What do I mean by that? First, sometimes you encounter a view that holds calibration to be an essentially "arbitrary" process of "making up" crisp and fuzzy values. Clearly, that is not the case. As this chapter has shown, there are *well-defined standards* for calibration. Additionally, many published studies go to great lengths to clarify what data they used and how this was transformed into set-membership scores. But it is understandable that the process may seem opaque when one is not used to working with calibrated measures. And, surely, there are also QCA articles where it is difficult to decipher the calibration process, much less to replicate the results.[12] In sum, the best way to address concerns about calibration is with conceptual clarity, data transparency, and plausible calibration criteria (see also the good practices for calibration in the next section).

Second, calibration is occasionally approached as a mechanical exercise of transforming numerical raw data into crisp and fuzzy scores. As mentioned in this chapter, it makes no sense to simply take descriptive statistics like the average or median and use these as cutoffs for the calibration. Nor does it make sense to take maximum and minimum scores in the empirical data and use them as upper and lower bounds. Such approaches miss the fundamental advantage of QCA, namely, that *meaningful variation* can be separated from irrelevant variation (Ragin 2000, 161). This can only happen on a substantive basis and therefore requires conceptual work.

Third, there are also misconceptions about crisp and fuzzy sets. Regardless of the choice, users should justify *why* they opted for crisp or fuzzy sets. Some argue that crisp sets are the more conservative, or safer, choice when there are not enough data or when it is difficult, and thus potentially arbitrary, to introduce gradations in set membership. This may be true for some research endeavors, and there are certainly concepts that have a greater affinity for crisp sets. But often it appears that users apply crisp sets simply because it is more convenient and less research-intensive to work with binary values. Moreover, a widely held view is that it is easier to identify consistent set-theoretic relationships with crisp sets than with fuzzy sets (Ragin 2009a, 114; Schneider and Wagemann 2012, 69). Hence, a weak set-theoretic relationship can look stronger because crisp sets were used. This seems to resonate with the experience of many applied QCA researchers, who find that fuzzy sets provide for more demanding tests of consistency and coverage (we look into the calculation of these metrics in chapter 6). However, in a recent contribution, Ingo Rohlfing (2020) reaches the conclusion that the relationship between crisp sets, fuzzy sets, and consistency scores is "ambiguous" and, as such, can go in both directions, depending on the structure of the empirical data. Hence it may be unwarranted to claim that crisp sets *generally* lead toward higher consistency scores.

Finally, it is sometimes implied that the choice of the calibration approach can greatly affect the results. This leaves new users wondering about the "correct" choice when calibrating their data. However, as shown in the example using unemployment data (table 5.2), the differences in the results are rarely substantial. What matters are the positions of the empirical anchors, especially the crossover, but it is of secondary concern whether the direct method of calibration was used or whether the values were assigned manually, based on previously defined calibration rules. We will return to these issues in later chapters.

GOOD PRACTICES FOR CALIBRATION

The discussion of common misunderstandings lends itself to this list of good practices for calibration (this goes in line with efforts to formulate coherent methodological standards for QCA):[13]

- Studies should clearly document the conditions that were used throughout the analysis. Ideally, the publication includes at least a summary table with this kind of information. (This is particularly relevant for studies that use various models of conditions; see chapter 2.)
- Data sources must be made transparent. The raw and calibrated data should be made available, either on the journal website or in an openly accessible data repository. For qualitative data, this can be more demanding, and even raise ethical issues (as in protecting sources and sharing sensitive information). In that case, researchers should use discretion to decide what information can be shared and what needs to be aggregated or anonymized before publication (on transparency, see the contributions to the symposium edited by Büthe and Jacobs 2015).
- For analyses conducted within the R software environment, the R script should be made available on an openly accessible data repository.
- The method of calibration and calibration thresholds should be reported. For conditions calibrated with the direct method, histograms and plots for raw and calibrated data should be provided in supplementary documents.
- Calibration thresholds must be verbally justified, and their impact should be discussed (why cases were considered below/above the threshold, what their inclusion/exclusion means for the results). For critical cases, there should be an alternative analysis based on different calibration thresholds.
- Set labels should be as concise and unambiguous as possible (acronyms do not work particularly well if there is no legend provided in the table).
- Set names should adhere to the adjective rule to indicate the directionality of a given set (e.g., *generous* welfare state, *supportive* public, and *high* unemployment).

NOTES

Epigraph: Ragin (2008b, 8).

   1. The chapter focuses on crisp and fuzzy sets. On multivalue conditions, see chapter 8.

2. In 2015, the American Political Science Association initiated a process that led to wide-ranging "qualitative transparency deliberations" across four thematic clusters (the discussion forums can still be accessed at www.qualtd.net). This also led to a report with specific transparency recommendations for QCA (Schneider, Vis, and Koivu 2019).

3. There are few empirical applications of the indirect method of calibration, which is probably due to its more complicated, twofold procedure (when compared with the direct method). For a technical discussion, see Ragin (2008b, 94–97) and Duşa (2019b, 92–94).

4. It should be highlighted that whether the three percentage scores are plausible empirical anchors would need to be justified within the research context of a given study.

5. On challenges specific to the transformation of qualitative data, see De Block and Vis (2019). Qualitative calibration examples are also provided in Kahwati and Kane (2020, 76–86).

6. Goertz (2020, 138) argues that it is "fundamentally misleading" to perceive of the nominal level of measurement as a scale, because a nominal condition is really "two (or more) concepts."

7. This distinguishes temperature measured in degrees Kelvin from temperature measured in degrees Celsius. Although Celsius has a zero point, it is arbitrary, whereas Kelvin has a meaningful zero.

8. This section is based on Ragin's (2008b, 85–105) detailed account of the calibration process. See also Duşa (2019b, 74–92), who describes how the procedure happens inside the QCA package for R and who also introduces an alternative to the logarithmic function on which the standard calibration procedure is based.

9. This is complicated by the fact that the numbers for the metrics given in Ragin (2008b, 88) are rounded up, which is why a manual recalculation with his data does not produce identical results.

10. These metrics are geared toward the thresholds of 0.95, 0.50, and 0.05. The three-digit values for associated odds and log odds are approximations that are rounded for convenience. Because the software works with the exact numbers, a manual recalculation may yield slightly different results (Duşa 2019b, 87).

11. On qualitative calibration, see also De Block and Vis (2019).

12. For my QCA courses, one of the tasks is for students to replicate published studies. This exercise showed that few studies could be replicated with matching results, as many articles missed information on raw data, calibration thresholds, and analytical decisions. Clearly, this issue applies more broadly and is not limited to set-theoretic methods.

13. On standards of good practice, see Schneider and Wagemann (2010). A survey of empirical applications and their alignment with formulated standards is given by Mello (2013). For guidelines, see also Oana, Schneider, and Thomann (2021).

6 • Measures of Fit

Set relations are important . . . in the same way that
assessments of significance and strength are important
in the analysis of correlational connections.

—CHARLES C. RAGIN

In the course of its development over the past 30 years, QCA has undergone substantial methodological sophistication. As a Boolean approach, the method initially only worked with binary values and did not allow for contradictory truth table rows where some cases show the outcome and others do not—such configurations needed to be resolved through measures of *research design*, before one could proceed with the analysis (Ragin, Mayer, and Drass 1984; Rihoux and De Meur 2009; Rihoux and Ragin 2009). However, perfect set relations can rarely be found in the social sciences. More often, one identifies a relationship that comes close to necessity or sufficiency but where some empirical cases in the data do not fit such patterns. How to move on under these circumstances? What proportion of cases will be *enough* to merit a set-theoretic relationship?

Hence, after the introduction of fuzzy sets (Ragin 2000), which allowed for differentiated degrees of set membership, Charles Ragin (2006a) put forth the measures of fit *consistency* and *coverage* to assess imperfect set-theoretic relationships in empirical data. These were a major step forward in the methodological development of QCA. Although these metrics should never replace case knowledge and substantive interpretation, they were a valuable addition to the method because they gave researchers benchmarks to assess and compare their results. They also furthered transparent standards for applied research (Oana, Schneider, and Thomann 2021; Rihoux and Ragin 2009; Schneider and Wagemann 2010, 2012).

Consistency and coverage can be compared with the well-known statistical indicators of significance and strength, as highlighted in the above quotation. Similar to statistical significance, *consistency* measures the degree to which an empirical relationship between a condition or combination of conditions and the outcome comes close to set-theoretic necessity and/or sufficiency. Similar to statistical strength, *coverage* measures the empirical importance or relevance of a condition or combination of conditions (Ragin 2008, 45). That said, set relations should *not* be equated with the metrics of statistical association. They measure different things but serve similar purposes.

Although consistency and coverage remain the standard indicators to formally assess set-theoretic relationships, over the years it has been pointed out that these measures could not detect issues that may occasionally arise in empirical data. Hence, researchers developed several additional metrics. Among these, "proportional reduction in inconsistency" (PRI) addresses simultaneous subset relations (Ragin 2006b; Schneider and Wagemann 2012), and "relevance of necessity" (RoN) seeks to distinguish trivial from relevant necessary conditions (Schneider and Wagemann 2012). Both these metrics have been incorporated into the major software packages, and it has become customary to report them in publications.[1] As with other parts of the method, measures of fit are an area of continuous development and methodological refinement. In this vein, several other metrics have been proposed, including alternative measures of consistency and coverage (Haesebrouck 2015; Stoklasa, Luukka, and Talášek 2017; Veri 2018, 2019), to assess the distance of an empirical pattern from a set-theoretic relationship (Eliason and Stryker 2009), measures to evaluate the importance of single conditions in QCA solutions (Damonte 2018), distinct approaches to assess the degree of necessity (Dul, Van der Laan, and Kuik 2020; Vis and Dul 2018), and metrics for combinations of conditions that are jointly necessary (Bol and Luppi 2013).

Building on the introduction of set relations in chapter 4, this chapter introduces the standard measures of fit that are essential for QCA, explains how they are calculated, and provides illustrative examples to demonstrate the issues at stake. This means that the discussion is focused on consistency, coverage, PRI, and RoN—whereas a broader treatment of metrics is beyond the scope of this chapter. Of course, for a standard application of QCA, users do not need to *manually* calculate the measures of fit—that is done by the software—but they will benefit from going through the calculations to understand how different scores are derived and how these can be interpreted.

Before proceeding, one caveat is in order. The measures of fit discussed in this chapter can help to identify set-theoretic relationships in empirical data, but any interpretation, particularly a *causal interpretation* of the identified patterns, must always be grounded in theory and substantive knowledge (see the discussion in chapter 4). Like the old adage *correlation is not causation*, we should acknowledge that *set relation is not causation*. Whether identified patterns are meaningful always depends on the research design of a study (chapter 2), the strength of the empirical evidence, and its theoretical and substantive interpretation by the researcher.

SET-THEORETIC CONSISTENCY

The measure *consistency* is used to assess "the degree to which the cases sharing a given combination of conditions . . . agree in displaying the outcome in question" (Ragin 2008b, 44). In other words, consistency helps to determine the "fit of the empirical evidence with an assumed set-theoretic relationship" (Mello 2017, 127). As such, the measure is applied to assess the consistency of necessary conditions and of sufficient conditions, and it can be used on combinations as well as individual conditions.

In formal terms, consistency is calculated to reflect the extent to which there is a set relation between instances of a condition and an outcome. When all values for the outcome Y are equal to or less than the respective values for X, then Y is a *subset* of X (and, vice versa, X is a superset of Y), and hence X is a *necessary condition* for Y. Likewise, if all values for Y are greater than or equal to the respective values for X, then Y is a *superset* of X (which also means that X is a subset of Y), and X is thus a *sufficient condition* for Y. This means that when all values for the outcome Y and the condition X are exactly equal (in an X–Y plot with fuzzy data, all points would be on the diagonal line), then X is *both* a necessary and sufficient condition for Y.

Before moving to the calculation of consistency, it is useful to depict the set-theoretic relationships of necessity and sufficiency in visual terms. Recalling the illustrations from chapter 3, the Euler diagrams given in figure 6.1 show these relationships for crisp sets, assuming data with binary values. X_1 is a perfectly consistent necessary condition, whereas as X_2 is a perfectly consistent sufficient condition for Y. The X–Y plots in figure 6.2 show the equivalent set-theoretic relationships for fuzzy sets, with graded set-membership values. In these plots, the cases either all populate the area *below* or on the main diagonal (necessary condition X_1), or they are located on or *above* the diagonal line (sufficient condition X_2).

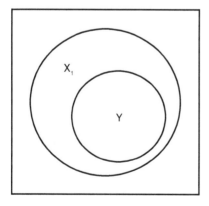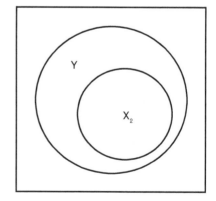

Figure 6.1   Necessary Condition and Sufficient Condition (Crisp Sets)

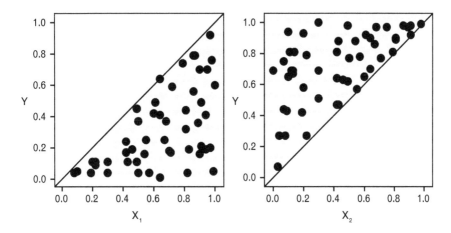

Figure 6.2 Necessary Condition and Sufficient Condition (Fuzzy Sets)

How can we express these relationships numerically? The consistency of necessary and sufficient conditions is calculated with the following two formulas, which differ only in the denominator (Ragin 2006a, 297; 2008):

$$\text{Consistency}_{\text{Necessity}}(Y_i \leq X_i) = \frac{\sum \min(X_i, Y_i)}{\sum Y_i}$$

$$\text{Consistency}_{\text{Sufficiency}}(X_i \leq Y_i) = \frac{\sum \min(X_i, Y_i)}{\sum X_i}$$

Aimed to detect formal subset relationships, each formula divides the sum of the minimum set membership scores for the condition and the outcome by the sum of the scores for the outcome (for *necessary* conditions), or by the sum of the scores for the condition (for *sufficient* conditions). For perfect subset relations, this calculation yields consistency scores of 1. For imperfect set relations, where one or more cases violate a statement of necessity or sufficiency, the resulting scores will be less than 1. The similarity in the formulas reflects the inverse relationship between necessity and sufficiency.

What is an appropriate level of consistency? At which point can we declare a condition or a combination necessary and/or sufficient for an outcome? Generally speaking, the closer consistency scores approximate 1, the more confident we can be about a set relation. For sufficient conditions, the analysis involves the minimization of the truth table (covered in chapter 7). Here, the recommended *minimum* benchmark for the inclusion of truth table rows is 0.75 consistency (Ragin 2008, 46; Schneider and Wagemann 2012, 279). But it must be noted that this is but *one step* on the way to the

QCA solution terms. Typically, the truth table analysis will include several rows with consistency levels that are higher than the threshold of 0.75. Thus the overall solution term will most often *exceed* the minimum consistency threshold. For necessary conditions, the analysis does not entail the truth table procedure and the theoretical focus typically rests on single conditions. Hence, it is recommended to use a consistency threshold of 0.90 for necessary conditions (Schneider and Wagemann 2012, 278).

Of course, these thresholds are *rules of thumb*, and one should always use case knowledge and individual judgment when interpreting empirical data. Especially, the set-theoretic requirement of 0.90 consistency for necessary conditions is fairly demanding. This means that it is not often reached in empirical settings, even when there are patterns in the data. For example, in a study of military coalition defection (Mello 2020), the condition "upcoming elections," which was deemed to be theoretically important, yielded a consistency of 0.83 and was thus, formally speaking, not necessary. However, a standard chi-square test of association showed that there was a statistically significant difference between groups that faced elections and those who did not, because 16 out of 18 cases showed the pattern (Mello 2020, 60).

Besides, one also must take into account the *number of cases* involved. The smaller the number of cases, the higher one should set the consistency threshold. For example, in a QCA study with only 12 cases, we would expect intimate knowledge of the selected cases, and thus there should be very high or even perfect consistency. On the contrary, for a QCA study with 50 or even 80 cases, a lower level of consistency is anticipated and would certainly be acceptable (but consistency must still meet the minimum thresholds for set relations).

AN EXAMPLE OF CALCULATING CONSISTENCY

Let us look at an example on how consistency is calculated. Suppose the members of a group of office workers in a small company have all been tested positively for the coronavirus. After their infection with the COVID-19 illness, some of them developed serious symptoms, whereas others only showed mild symptoms, or none at all. How to explain this variation? Table 6.1 lists hypothetical data on the eight workers and their membership in the fuzzy sets *serious symptoms* (outcome), and two supposed explanatory conditions: *weak health* and *old age*. Weak health takes into account the severity of prior medical conditions, such as lung disease or diabetes, among other risk factors. Old age acknowledges that older adults are at a significantly higher risk of experiencing complications from the illness. Scores above 0.5 indicate that the person is *inside* the set, whereas a score of 1 refers to *full membership* in the respective set.

Before coming to the calculation of consistency, we can visualize the conditions and the outcome to see whether there are indications of set-theoretic relationships. Figure 6.3 shows separate X–Y plots for the conditions *weak health* and *old age* against

Table 6.1   Example: Coronavirus and Risk Factors

Person	Weak Health	Old Age	Serious Symptoms (Outcome)
Linda	1.0	0.7	0.9
George	0.9	0.9	0.9
Megan	0.8	0.6	0.7
Carlos	0.7	0.4	0.6
David	0.3	0.0	0.2
Sara	0.5	0.1	0.1
Tamira	0.6	0.3	0.4
Jamar	0.8	0.2	0.6

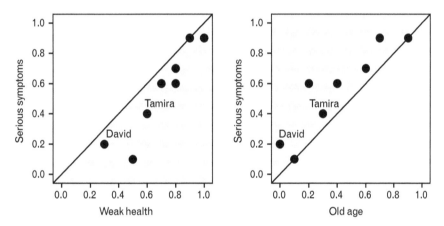

Figure 6.3   X–Y Plots: Risk Factors and Serious Symptoms

the outcome *serious symptoms*. Two cases are labeled for illustrative purposes. In the left-hand plot, we can see that the condition weak health fits the pattern for a perfectly consistent *necessary condition*, because all the cases are on or below the diagonal line. This indicates that all set membership values for weak health are equal to or larger than the respective set membership values for the outcome. In other words, the condition fully encloses the outcome (formally speaking, the condition is a *superset* of the outcome). When we look at the cases, we can see that the five people who are in the set *serious symptoms* also hold membership in *weak health* above 0.50. There is no person with serious symptoms without weak health. Yet weak health is not sufficient for the outcome, as evidenced by the office worker Tamira, who has weak health but is outside the set serious symptoms.

Likewise, the right-hand plot shows that the condition old age fits the pattern for a perfectly consistent *sufficient condition*, because all cases are located on or above the diagonal line. This reflects a situation where all set membership values for the condition are smaller than or equal to the respective set membership values for the outcome. This means that the condition old age is a *subset* of the outcome, because the latter fully encloses the former. For the cases, this means that whenever a person holds membership in *old age*, then they also show *serious symptoms*. For our group of workers, this applies to Linda, George, and Megan.

How to calculate consistency? To do that, we can apply the formulas introduced above to the data from our example. Table 6.2 shows the data plus the sums of the fuzzy-set membership values of our office workers for the two conditions and the outcome, as well as the minimum values across each condition and the outcome, as required for the calculation of consistency. For set-theoretic *necessity*, the outcome should be a perfect subset of the condition. For weak health (X_1), this is calculated by taking the sum of the minimum values across X_1 and Y and dividing this score by the sum of the values for the outcome. This means that we divide 4.4 by 4.4, which equals 1. This confirms that weak health is a perfect necessary condition for serious symptoms, as we already knew from the X–Y plot. For old age, we divide 3.2 by 4.4, which equals 0.73. This is well below the threshold of 0.9, and hence old age cannot be considered a necessary condition for serious symptoms. This is reflected in the fact that the office workers Carlos and Jamar are both inside the set serious symptoms and outside the set old age (which we can see from table 6.1).

Given the data in table 6.2, the calculation of consistency is:

$$\text{Consistency}_{\text{Necessity}}(X_1) = \frac{4.4}{4.4} = 1 \qquad \text{Consistency}_{\text{Necessity}}(X_2) = \frac{3.2}{4.4} = 0.73$$

For set-theoretic *sufficiency*, the relationship should be inverted, which means that the respective condition should be a subset of the outcome. We calculate the consistency of sufficient conditions by taking the sum of the minimum values across the condition and the outcome and dividing this score by the sum of the values for the condition. For *weak health* (X_1), we thus divide 4.4 by 5.6, which equals 0.79. This means that the condition weak health can be considered a *weak* sufficient condition for the outcome serious symptoms, because the relationship is far from perfect, but is above the minimum threshold of 0.75.[2] We can see this reflected in our data, where a close correspondence exists between the values for weak health and serious symptoms. Yet values in the former frequently exceed those in the latter. In qualitative terms, Tamira is one person who is inside the set weak health but outside the set serious symptoms, which also speaks against weak health being a perfectly sufficient condition. For the condition *old age* (X_2), we divide the sum of the minimum values across the condition and the outcome 3.2 by the sum of the values for the condition 3.2, which equals 1. Hence, for this hypothetical example, old age is a perfectly sufficient condition for the

Table 6.2   Calculating Consistency: Coronavirus Example

Person	Weak Health (X_1)	Old Age (X_2)	Serious Symptoms (Y)	Minimum (X_1, Y)	Minimum (X_2, Y)
Linda	1.0	0.7	0.9	0.9	0.7
George	0.9	0.9	0.9	0.9	0.9
Megan	0.8	0.6	0.7	0.7	0.6
Carlos	0.7	0.4	0.6	0.6	0.4
David	0.3	0.0	0.2	0.2	0.0
Sara	0.5	0.1	0.1	0.1	0.1
Tamira	0.6	0.3	0.4	0.4	0.3
Jamar	0.8	0.2	0.6	0.6	0.2
Sum	5.6	3.2	4.4	4.4	3.2

outcome serious symptoms. There are three people in our group of workers who are inside this set (Linda, George, and Megan), and all three of them also show high fuzzy-set membership in the outcome serious symptoms. Based on the data in table 6.2, we calculate this:

$$\text{Consistency}_{\text{Sufficiency}}(X_1) = \frac{4.4}{5.6} = 0.79 \qquad \text{Consistency}_{\text{Sufficiency}}(X_2) = \frac{3.2}{3.2} = 1$$

SET-THEORETIC COVERAGE

The measure of *coverage* is used to assess "the degree to which a cause or causal combination 'accounts for' instances of an outcome" (Ragin 2008b, 44). Put differently, coverage is used to determine "the *relevancy* of a condition in empirical terms" (Mello 2017, 128). For sufficient conditions, coverage indicates how much of the empirical evidence is explained by a given condition or combination. For instance, we may identify a condition that, whenever present, leads to the outcome. Yet only a single case of our population shows this condition. Formally speaking, this may be a sufficient condition, but its contribution to the explanation of the outcome is rather small.

For necessary conditions, coverage helps to distinguish *relevant* from *trivial* necessary conditions. For example, a condition may formally fulfill the criteria for set-theoretic necessity (as when X is a perfect *superset* of the outcome Y), but this might still be a trivial finding because the condition is almost always present, and thus it is difficult to establish a causal link between the condition and the outcome. For example,

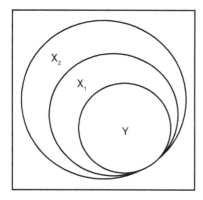 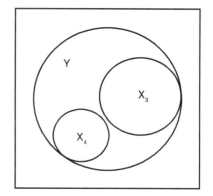

Figure 6.4   Coverage in Necessary and Sufficient Conditions
(Crisp Sets)

oxygen is nearly ubiquitous. Formally speaking, it may thus be a necessary condition for a range of phenomena, including the outbreak of civil war. However, stating "oxygen is a necessary condition for civil war" would have no analytical value because of the omnipresence of oxygen.

Figure 6.4 illustrates these relationships. The left-hand Euler diagram shows an outcome Y and the conditions X_1 and X_2 that are perfect supersets of Y. Thus, formally speaking, both of these can be considered necessary conditions for the outcome. Yet we see that X_2 occurs more often than X_1 (the box represents our universe of phenomena in this simple setting). Hence, in the absence of any other information, X_2 can be considered less relevant than X_1.

Now consider the right-hand Euler diagram. Here, we have an outcome Y and two perfect subsets: X_3 and X_4. This means that whenever a case holds membership in either of these conditions, it also holds membership in the outcome. Thus, both X_3 and X_4 are sufficient conditions for Y. But we also see that X_4 is smaller than X_3, which means that there are fewer cases with membership in it. If our aim was to provide an account of Y, then X_3 would be the more relevant condition, simply because it covers more instances of Y. However, in an applied setting, both might be part of a solution term that entails several pathways to the outcome. For each pathway, we can calculate its *raw coverage* and *unique coverage*. The former is the total coverage of this pathway, irrespective of any empirical overlap with other pathways. The latter is limited to the unique contribution of the individual pathway (including only those cases that are not also covered by other pathways). We will return to this point when we examine solution terms in chapter 7.

How are these set relations calculated? Mirroring the computation of consistency, the *coverage* of necessary and sufficient conditions is calculated with these two formulas, which differ in their denominator (Ragin 2006a, 63; 2008b):

$$\text{Coverage}_{\text{Necessity}}(Y_i \leq X_i) = \frac{\sum \min(X_i, Y_i)}{\sum X_i}$$

$$\text{Coverage}_{\text{Sufficiency}}(X_i \leq Y_i) = \frac{\sum \min(X_i, Y_i)}{\sum Y_i}$$

It is apparent from the formulas for consistency and coverage that these are inversely related. Yet what must be noted is that consistency is the *primary* measure of fit, and as such it should always be calculated and examined first. Coverage is only meaningful when a consistent set-theoretic relationship has been identified in the analysis. In this sense, one should always proceed stepwise, starting with consistency. As Ragin (2008b, 55) says, it is "pointless" to examine and interpret coverage for a condition that is not a consistent subset or superset of the outcome. But once consistency has been established, then the calculation of coverage can help to assess the empirical relevance of the identified set-theoretic relationship.

AN EXAMPLE OF CALCULATING COVERAGE

Again, let us illustrate the calculation of coverage using the data from the coronavirus example, as listed in table 6.1. In the previous stage, we identified *weak health* (X_1) as a perfectly necessary condition for the outcome *serious symptoms*. Let us now calculate its coverage. For this, we take the sum of the minimum values (for each office worker) across the condition and the outcome and divide it by the sum of the values for the condition. This means that we divide 4.4 by 5.6, which yields 0.79. This coverage value suggests a fairly close fit between the condition and the outcome. We will return to this example when calculating the relevance of necessity toward the end of the chapter.

We also identified *old age* (X_2) as a sufficient condition for the outcome. To calculate its coverage, we divide the sum of the minimum values across the condition and the outcome (3.2) by the sum of the values for the outcome 4.4, which equals 0.73. This is a good coverage score. Yet it also indicates that part of the outcome serious symptoms cannot solely be accounted for with the condition old age. For instance, the office workers Jamar and Carlos are both inside the outcome serious symptoms, but outside the set old age, suggesting that their weak health accounts for the outcome. Based on the data in table 6.1, we calculate coverage as:

$$\text{Coverage}_{\text{Necessity}}(X_1) = \frac{4.4}{5.6} = 0.79 \qquad \text{Coverage}_{\text{Sufficiency}}(X_2) = \frac{3.2}{4.4} = 0.73$$

The last step in the calculation means that the sufficient condition old age covers 0.73 of the *fuzzy-set membership values* of the outcome serious symptoms. This is an

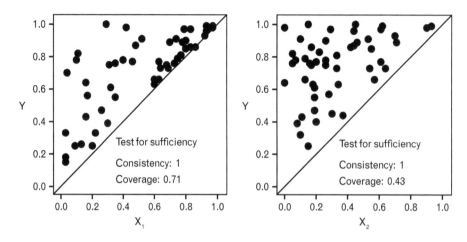

Figure 6.5   Sufficient Conditions with Varying Coverage (Fuzzy Sets)

important distinction: on first observation, one may think that coverage reflects the *share* or *percentage* of covered cases. But with fuzzy sets, the calculation is based on cases that hold various degrees of set membership. Moreover, cases with less than 0.50 set membership are also included in the calculation. We can check this with a look at the data given in table 6.2. As we can see, there are five persons with membership above 0.50 in the outcome. Three of these are accounted for by the condition old age X_2. If it were just about the share of cases, the coverage of X_2 should be 0.60. However, as we calculated above, its actual coverage is 0.73.

Although consistency is a straightforward metric, coverage can be more difficult to grasp. Essentially, coverage is about the fit between a condition and the outcome. The larger the gap between the values for the outcome and those for the respective condition, the lower the coverage score. This is illustrated in the two sufficient conditions shown in figure 6.5. The left-hand condition X_1 has many cases that are clustered close to the main diagonal, indicating equal membership in the condition and the outcome. The condition X_1 has a *coverage* score of 0.71 (and perfect consistency). For condition X_2 the relationship is different. Many cases are further removed from the main diagonal, which means that the values for the outcome far exceed those for the condition. Like the other condition, X_2 is also a perfectly consistent sufficient condition, but its *coverage* is only 0.43.

PROPORTIONAL REDUCTION IN INCONSISTENCY

Proportional reduction in inconsistency (PRI) is a measure to identify *simultaneous subset relations* in the analysis of sufficient conditions. What does this mean? Simultaneous subset relations may happen with fuzzy-set data when a condition or combination

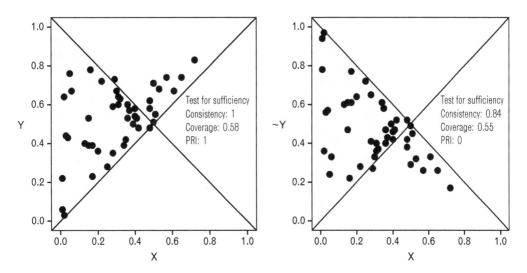

Figure 6.6   Simultaneous Subset Relations

of conditions is both a subset of the outcome and a subset of the nonoutcome. This would be a *logical contradiction*. However, based solely on the measures consistency and coverage, it would be difficult to determine whether X should be treated as sufficient for the outcome or the nonoutcome. To identify such situations and provide guidance for the correct interpretation of the set-theoretic relationship, the PRI measure was introduced into the fs/QCA software by Ragin (2006b) and was first described in the textbook by Carsten Schneider and Claudius Wagemann (2012, 237–44).[3] The PRI measure has become a standard feature in most QCA software, including the QCA package for R developed by Adrian Duşa (2019, 134–36).

To illustrate simultaneous subset relations, let us look at an example with hypothetical data on 45 cases. Figure 6.6 shows X–Y plots for the condition X, the outcome Y, and the nonoutcome ~Y. In the left plot, we can see that X is a sufficient condition for Y with a consistency of 1 and coverage of 0.58. Yet, as shown in the right plot, X also appears to be a sufficient condition for the *nonoutcome*, with a consistency of 0.84 and coverage of 0.55.

How can this be? When we look at the empirical distribution of cases for the left plot, two observations stand out. First, apart from a few exceptions, most cases hold low scores in X with membership scores of less than 0.5, located on the left side of the crossover. Second, most cases are placed inside the left triangle that is shaded gray. The additional diagonal line divides the plot into four triangles. All cases inside the left triangle fulfill the criteria for being subsets of the outcome *and* the nonoutcome, formally defined as X ≤ Y and X ≤ ~Y (Ragin 2011). This explains why consistency is high in both settings and thus formally passes the test for sufficiency. However, examining the data in these plots should raise doubts about treating X as a sufficient condition for ~Y

Table 6.3   Simultaneous Subset Relations

Case	A	Y	~Y	min(A, Y)	min(A, ~Y)	min(A, Y, ~Y)
France	0.2	0.3	0.7	0.2	0.2	0.2
Greece	0.5	0.6	0.4	0.5	0.4	0.4
Italy	0.4	0.5	0.5	0.4	0.4	0.4
Portugal	0.6	0.7	0.3	0.6	0.3	0.3
Spain	0.3	0.4	0.6	0.3	0.3	0.3
Sum	2	2.5	2.5	2	1.6	1.6

because there are no cases with values above 0.5 in X that also show values above 0.5 in the nonoutcome. This contrasts with the left plot, where we at least have a handful of cases that are inside both the condition and the outcome (> 0.5).

Before coming to the calculation of PRI as a solution to the problem described above, let us look at a simple example that involves just a few cases. Table 6.3 shows five hypothetical countries and their fuzzy-set membership values in the condition A, the outcome Y, and the nonoutcome ~Y. On the right side, the table provides three metrics needed to calculate consistency, coverage, and PRI.

Let us now calculate the consistency for A as a *sufficient condition* for the *outcome* Y and the *nonoutcome* ~Y. We use the standard consistency formula introduced earlier in this chapter:

$$\text{Consistency}_{\text{Sufficiency}} (A \le Y) = \frac{2}{2} = 1 \quad \text{Consistency}_{\text{Sufficiency}} (A \le \sim Y) = \frac{1.6}{2} = 0.8$$

Taking the sum values from the bottom line of table 6.3, we divide the sum of the minimum values across A and Y (2) by the sum of the values for A (2), which equals 1. This means that A is a perfect sufficient condition for Y. What about the *nonoutcome?* Here, we divide the sum of the minimum values across the condition and the nonoutcome (1.6) by the sum of the values for A (2), which yields 0.8. Because the consistency value for A and ~Y is above the 0.75 threshold, we might also treat A as a sufficient condition for the nonoutcome, especially if this consistency score referred to a truth table row. Yet doing so would mean that the condition equally leads to the outcome and its negation, which would be a logical contradiction. How to resolve this paradox? The measures of fit consistency and coverage do not help us in this scenario, but PRI detects the problem. The formula for the proportional reduction in inconsistency is (Ragin 2011; Schneider and Wagemann 2012, 242):

$$\text{PRI} = \frac{\sum \min(X_i, Y_i) - \sum \min(X_i, Y_i, \sim Y_i)}{\sum X_i - \sum \min(X_i, Y_i, \sim Y_i)}$$

Table 6.4   Simultaneous Subset Relations and PRI

Metric	A → Y	A → ~Y
Consistency	1	0.80
Coverage	0.80	0.64
PRI	1	0

We apply this formula to assess the relationship between A and Y as well as A and ~Y:

$$\text{PRI}_{(A, Y)} = \frac{(2 - 1.6)}{(2 - 1.6)} = \frac{0.4}{0.4} = 1 \qquad \text{PRI}_{(A, \sim Y)} = \frac{(1.6 - 1.6)}{(2 - 1.6)} = \frac{0}{0.4} = 0$$

The PRI value for A as a sufficient condition for Y is 1, whereas the PRI for A and ~Y is 0. Although consistency and coverage are relatively similar for both outcome and nonoutcome (see the summary in table 6.4), the PRI scores give a clear indication that we should treat A only as a valid sufficient condition for Y and not as a sufficient condition for ~Y.

As a general rule, with statements of sufficiency one should always observe whether there is a substantial difference between PRI and consistency. When that is the case, one should examine the nonoutcome for simultaneous subset relations. The problem of simultaneous subset relations *may* occur when there are too many cases with low values in a condition, especially if most of these are located in the left triangle depicted in figure 6.6. Hence, as a precaution, it is always useful to create *histograms* of individual conditions and to plot these against the outcome before the actual analysis, to examine whether any of these may later cause analytical problems. Apart from theoretical considerations, this is another reason why one should strive to have a *reasonably even distribution* of membership values for each condition.

RELEVANCE OF NECESSITY

As introduced above, the standard coverage measure helps to distinguish trivial from relevant necessary conditions. The example used earlier was *oxygen* being a trivial necessary condition for the outbreak of *civil war*. In this example, the large difference between the "size" of the condition (or the frequency with which it appears) and the outcome will yield low coverage, indicating a trivial necessary condition. Put differently, in such a situation the data entail many instances where the condition is present, but very few or almost no cases where the outcome is also present. Formally, this may still indicate perfect set-theoretic consistency, but coverage would be low. This can

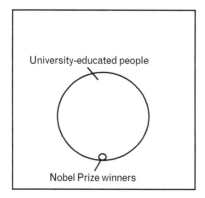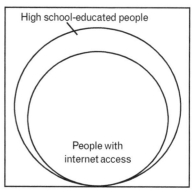

Figure 6.7 Two Types of Trivial Necessary Conditions

happen especially when the condition is a widespread phenomenon and the outcome of interest is a rare event.

To take another example, consider the relationship between obtaining a university education and winning a Nobel Prize. Albeit a few exceptions, a university education may be formally necessary for winning a Nobel Prize in the sciences, but this is a trivial finding because the set of people who won such a prize is tiny when placed in relation to those who completed a university education. This is illustrated in the left-hand Euler diagram in figure 6.7. In fact, the depiction of Nobel Prize winners should be even smaller than shown here. The illustration underlines that there is little to be gained from knowing that the condition university education is formally necessary for becoming a Nobel Prize winner because there is such a large gap between the sizes of the respective sets. Hence this relationship points at a *trivial* necessary condition.

Apart from this common scenario, there can be circumstances where potentially trivial necessary conditions in the empirical data would *not* be detected with the existing formula for the calculation of coverage. Therefore, several alternative measures of necessary conditions' relevance and trivialness have been suggested (Braumoeller and Goertz 2000; Goertz 2006; Schneider and Wagemann 2012).

The source for such a form of trivialness is what can be termed a *constant* condition, as when a condition shows little variation across the observed cases. To stay with the education example, suppose we are interested in explaining the internet penetration rate, looking at the outcome *people with internet access*. In the United States, this would be a large set of about 86 percent of the population. Now one of our conditions may be the set of *high school–educated people*, which would be an even larger set that constitutes about 90 percent of the US population. If we placed these sets in relation (and assume for illustration's sake that there is a perfect overlap between them), then it would turn out that being in the set of high school–educated people is a necessary condition for having internet access. This is shown in the right-hand Euler diagram in figure 6.7. The set-theoretic analysis would yield perfect consistency and high coverage scores. What is wrong with this? The problem in this scenario is that the condition comes close to being a constant. Hence, we could explain almost *any* outcome on the basis of high school education, even when there is no relationship. If our outcome is similarly omnipresent, then the standard coverage metric would not alert us to this issue in our data.

To identify this second type of trivial necessary conditions, Schneider and Wagemann (2012) put forth the "relevance of necessity" (RoN) measure, based on an earlier metric suggested by Gary Goertz (2006). This has become a standard indicator in testing for the relevance of necessary conditions (Oana, Schneider, and Thomann 2021). By conception, the RoN measure can yield values between 0 and 1, where lower scores indicate *trivialness* and higher scores denote *relevance*. The more a condition X resembles a constant, the closer to 0 the RoN metric will be. The formula for the calculation of RoN is (Schneider and Wagemann 2012, 236):

$$\text{Relevance of necessity} = \frac{\Sigma(1 - X_i)}{\Sigma\left(1 - \min(X_i, Y_i)\right)}$$

How does this look in practice? To illustrate the use of the RoN measure, let us take a simple example involving the condition X, the outcome Y, and hypothetical data on just four cases. Table 6.5 shows that, formally speaking, X is an almost perfect *superset* of Y because the values for X are almost always larger than or equal to the values for Y. On this basis, the condition X might be considered a necessary condition for Y.

The right-hand side of table 6.5 further shows the results for the calculation of the *consistency* and *coverage* for necessary conditions, and the *relevance* of necessity. As expected, we can see that at 0.95, the set-theoretic consistency is very high, satisfying the formal threshold for necessary conditions (equal to or above 0.90). The coverage is lower, but at 0.59 it would not immediately prompt concern. However, we can see that the RoN indicator is closer to 0 than to 1, suggesting a potentially *trivial* necessary condition.

Why is this? This being a hypothetical example, we have no substantive knowledge of the underlying data. But what we can see is that X shows little variation, with three of four cases at values equal to or close to 1. With data patterns like this,

Table 6.5   The Relevance of Necessity

Case	X	Y	Test for Necessity: X ← Y	
1	1.0	0.9	Consistency	0.95
2	0.9	0.4	Coverage	0.59
3	1.0	0.3	Relevance of necessity	0.38
4	0.3	0.4		

the consistency measure would always satisfy the criterion for a necessary condition. However, the RoN measure suggests that we should be *cautious* before treating it as a relevant necessary condition for the outcome. Ultimately, dealing with data patterns like this is a matter of interpretation. There can be situations where a condition is almost a constant, but still the condition may have substantive importance and relevance as a necessary condition. However, such an interpretation would need to be justified explicitly. As a rule of thumb, any *potential* necessary condition that meets the consistency benchmark of 0.9 should be checked for its coverage and relevance. If the latter two metrics fall below 0.5, this suggests that we may be dealing with a *trivial necessary condition*. In order to make an informed judgment on this, we should always examine the empirical distribution of our cases and their set-theoretic membership scores. A good way to do this are histograms and X–Y plots of the raw and calibrated data (on this, see also chapter 10).

NOTES

Epigraph: Ragin (2008b, 45).

1. On the methodology of necessary conditions see Braumoeller and Goertz (2000), Goertz (2003b), and Goertz and Starr (2003b). More recent contributions include Thiem (2016); Vis and Dul (2018); and Dul, Van der Laan, and Kuik (2020).

2. As noted, sufficiency is typically analyzed through the truth table procedure (see chapter 7).

3. On the PRI measure, see also Duşa (2019, 134–36).

7 • Set-Theoretic Analysis

Necessary conditions pose traps to the researcher
because of their deceptive simplicity.

—GARY GOERTZ AND HARVEY STARR

A truth table . . . is a direct examination of the kinds
of cases that exist in a given set of data.

—CHARLES C. RAGIN

Earlier chapters introduced *set theory* as the foundation on which QCA rests, showed
how raw data can be *calibrated* into crisp and fuzzy sets, and discussed *measures of fit*
for the assessment of set-theoretic relationships. With these essentials in place, this
chapter turns to the set-theoretic analysis of empirical data.

Set-theoretic analysis comprises testing individual conditions and combinations of
conditions for their necessity and/or sufficiency. These tests are done separately, beginning with the analysis of necessary conditions, before moving to the truth table procedure, which is directed at testing for sufficient configurations and subsequent Boolean
minimization. This is the analytical core of QCA.

ANALYZING NECESSARY CONDITIONS

It is considered *good practice* to analyze necessary conditions in a separate step before
engaging in the truth table procedure (Ragin 2000, 204; Schneider and Wagemann
2010, 404). Knowing about the existence of a necessary condition helps to make
informed choices during the minimization of the truth table and the treatment of logical remainder rows, which we will cover toward the end of this chapter.[1] Moreover,
necessary conditions are not directly observable from the analysis of sufficient conditions, especially if the set-theoretic relationship of necessity is imperfect. This may

happen, for instance, when there is at least one case that shows the outcome despite the absence of the condition. In such a situation, one might overlook a necessary condition if the focus rests solely on the truth table procedure and its minimization.

As discussed in previous chapters, having a necessary condition means that whenever the outcome occurs, the condition is also present. In formal terms, the outcome is thus a *subset* of the necessary condition and, vice versa, the necessary condition is a *superset* of the outcome. The primary measure of fit for necessary conditions is *consistency*. By convention, conditions have to pass *at least* 0.9 set-theoretic consistency to be considered necessary (Mendel and Ragin 2011, 21; Schneider and Wagemann 2012, 143).

Besides the formal benchmark of set-theoretic consistency, one also has to consider *coverage*, because conditions may be formally necessary but empirically less meaningful or even irrelevant. This is complemented by the parameter *relevance of necessity*, as an additional metric for necessary conditions (Schneider and Wagemann 2012; and see the discussion in chapter 6). Together, the three parameters *consistency*, *coverage*, and *relevance* should be considered when testing for necessity. For conditions that do not pass 0.9 consistency, the other measures are meaningless. But once the consistency threshold has been passed, then one should further consider coverage and relevance to assess the condition under study. As a rule of thumb, when the metrics *coverage* or *relevance* are below 0.5, then this suggests that we may be dealing with a *trivial* necessary condition. To make an informed judgment in such a setting, we should always examine the empirical distribution of our cases and their set-theoretic membership scores (as discussed in chapter 6).

What about *combinations* of conditions? In most situations, you may either have no expectation about a potential necessary condition or, when you do, then you would typically expect a single condition to be necessary on its own. However, in some situations you may also have an expectation about a particular combination of factors, each of which has to be present for the outcome to occur. In logical terms, when we expect several conditions to be *jointly necessary*, then each single element of that conjunction must also be necessary. Hence, a test for individual conditions should suffice to show whether the expected conditions are truly necessary for the outcome.

However, occasionally a theory may propose the *substantive equivalence* of two or more conditions—where the presence of *either of them* may be necessary for the outcome. For example, suppose we are interested in the relationship between party politics and the perceived legitimacy of the European Union. Based on our theory, we may say that in order to increase the EU's perceived legitimacy, political parties either need to organize and campaign on the European level (as opposed to electoral campaigns based on national boundaries) or parties need to agree upon common candidates for leadership positions in the EU before the elections. Both of these would be expected to increase the perceived legitimacy of the EU in the eyes of the public, but *at least one of them* must be present for the outcome.

The software allows the specification and testing of such *disjunctional expectations* for necessary conditions. However, a note of caution is warranted: while it is possible to search for any kind of necessary combination, I advise against "fishing" for necessary disjunctions when there is no prior expectation about a set-theoretic relationship. We may discover some complex combinations of conditions (linked by a Boolean OR) to be necessary, but without prior theory it will be challenging to interpret such findings and to fill them with meaning. This resonates with advice not to apply the method "mechanically," in a data-driven way, without due emphasis on existing knowledge and substantive interpretation (Ragin 1987, 120; Schneider and Wagemann 2010, 410).

To illustrate the procedure of testing individual conditions for necessity, let us look at an example. Table 7.1 shows fuzzy-set values for five cases across three conditions (A, B, C) and the outcome Y. The right-hand side of the table displays the results for the calculation of set-theoretic consistency, coverage, and relevance of necessity (RoN), based on the formulas introduced in chapter 6. We can see that all three conditions pass the formal threshold of 0.9 consistency. In fact, all of them have *perfectly consistent* set relations of necessity, because the set-membership values for each condition and case are equal to or exceed those for the outcome. This means that A, B, and C are all *supersets* of the outcome Y.

However, although all three conditions pass the formal benchmark for the consistency of necessary conditions, their coverage and relevance scores indicate that some of them are more important than others. For condition A, both coverage and RoN are close to 1 (0.8 and 0.83), which means that, based on these metrics and without considering the substantive background, A can be considered a relevant necessary condition. Condition B has a fairly low coverage (0.54) and even lower RoN (0.43). This suggests that condition B is clearly a *less relevant* necessary condition than condition A. Whether condition B should further be considered a trivial necessary condition is a matter of substantive interpretation for which we would have to take into account a study's theory and research context. Finally, with condition C, the pattern is more pronounced. C has a slightly lower coverage than B (0.43), but the RoN value drops

Table 7.1 Necessary Conditions: Consistency, Coverage, and Relevance

	Conditions			Outcome		Test for Necessity		
Case	A	B	C	Y		Consistency	Coverage	Relevance
1	0.9	1	1	0.9	A	1	0.80	0.83
2	0.8	1	1	0.7	B	1	0.54	0.43
3	0.3	0.7	1	0.2	C	1	0.43	0.10
4	0.4	0.8	0.9	0.2				
5	0.1	0.2	0.8	0				

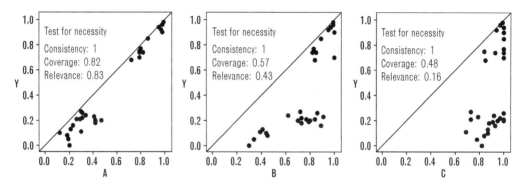

Figure 7.1   Necessary Conditions: Consistency, Coverage, and Relevance

close to zero (0.1). Looking at the values for condition C across the five cases, we can see that C is *always present* (all cases hold membership values above 0.5). Hence, there is not much gained from saying that "C is a necessary condition for Y" because C is a constant in this setting. Given these data, C should thus be considered a *trivial* necessary condition.

Figure 7.1 illustrates these relationships of necessity for a larger number of cases (30 cases across conditions A, B, C). We can see that all 3 conditions fit the measure of set-theoretic consistency, because all of them are located on or below the main diagonal. However, as can be seen from the 3 X–Y plots, there are considerable differences in coverage and relevance of necessity. Although condition A in the first plot should be considered a relevant necessary condition, the pattern in the second plot indicates that condition B is a less relevant necessary condition. Finally, condition C clearly is a trivial necessary condition, as indicated by its low coverage, and particularly by its relevance of necessity, which is close to zero.

We can also glean from the plots how certain values in the metrics correspond to specific patterns in the data. For relevant necessary conditions, the cases are located closer to the diagonal line, whereas irrelevance increases the further cases are lined up on the right-hand axis. This becomes evident with condition C, which approximates a constant where the cases populate a small range of values for the condition, between 0.7 and 1, whereas they show the full range of values for the outcome. This is evidence against a meaningful relationship between the condition and the outcome. Hence, condition C should be considered a *trivial necessary condition*.

To sum up, the analysis of necessity should *precede* the truth table analysis. Each condition and its negation should be tested for their necessity vis-à-vis the outcome and the nonoutcome. For studies that focus on explaining the outcome, it suffices to document tests for necessity for the outcome. Yet due to causal asymmetry, it is recommended to also conduct and report separate tests for the nonoutcome, with all conditions and their negation. As the primary measure of fit, *consistency* determines whether the other metrics are examined (because these are not meaningful otherwise). Conditions with *at least* 0.9 consistency can be considered necessary conditions *if* they also have high enough coverage and relevance of necessity scores. Otherwise, they may be considered trivial and should not be treated as necessary conditions. How *high* do coverage and relevance of necessity have to be? In the absence of firm benchmarks for coverage and relevance, a rule of thumb is that coverage and relevance scores *below* 0.5 indicate that the respective necessary condition may be trivial.[2] Against that backdrop, the illustrative data patterns shown in table 7.1 and figure 7.1 are meant to provide yardsticks for the comparison of empirical relationships. But as with all metrics, the numerical indicators should never replace *substantive interpretation* and *case knowledge* when trying to make sense of one's analytical findings.

TRUTH TABLE CONSTRUCTION

The core of QCA is the truth table analysis. Because the method is grounded in *combinatorial logic*, the truth table represents the number of combinations that are logically possible with the selected number of conditions. Each row of the truth table stands for a specific combination of conditions (*configuration*), and the number of rows equals the overall number of possible configurations. The formula for this is 2^k, where k is the number of conditions included in a study. Hence, when the analysis comprises 3 conditions, then there are 8 rows of configurations, 4 conditions result in 16 rows, and 5 conditions yield 32 rows, and so forth. We can see that the truth table *grows exponentially* with every additional condition. This distinguishes truth tables from a conventional spreadsheet, where each row represents a single observation or case, and where the size of the data matrix is circumscribed by the number of observations and variables.

The truth table shows possible configurations, but it also provides information about the empirical distribution of cases, and their connection to the outcome. Therefore, each row of the truth table is also a *statement of sufficiency*. Some rows may consistently lead toward the outcome, where each case with the respective combination shows the phenomenon of interest, whereas other rows might have no cases that show the outcome. There can also be *contradictory rows* in the truth table, where some cases have a positive outcome and others have a negative outcome (Rihoux and De Meur 2009; Rubinson 2013; Yamasaki and Rihoux 2009).

We can illustrate the construction of a truth table with a simple example. Table 7.2 shows a truth table for crisp set data on 20 cases; the conditions A, B, and C; and the outcome Y. Based on previous research, we expect the 3 conditions to be sufficient for the outcome, either individually or in combination. The table shows all logically possible combinations of the 3 conditions, where each row reflects 1 specific combination. In total, there are 8 rows, as 2^3 equals 8. For instance, row 6 refers to the absence of condition A, the presence of condition B, and the absence of condition C. There

Table 7.2   A Simple Truth Table

	Conditions			Outcome	Cases
Row	A	B	C	Y	N
1	1	1	1	1	4
2	1	1	0	1	5
3	1	0	1	1	2
4	0	1	1	0	1
5	1	0	0	0	3
6	0	1	0	0	2
7	0	0	1	?	0
8	0	0	0	0	3

are 2 empirical cases that share this combination of conditions, and both cases do not show the outcome Y. We can also see that 1 combination (row 7) is not filled with an empirical case. This means that there is no case that holds membership above 0.5 in this configuration. Hence, we cannot say whether this row is connected to the outcome or the nonoutcome (indicated by the question mark in the table). This is the issue of *limited diversity*, to which we will return when discussing solution terms. Finally, we can see that the combinations in the first 3 rows of the truth table are associated with the outcome. These will be the rows to focus on for an explanation of the phenomenon of interest.

The truth table provides valuable information about the empirical distribution of cases —the "kinds of cases" to which Ragin refers in this chapter's introductory quotation. The truth table also helps us to think systematically about theoretical expectations. For instance, what about the configuration in row 7? If there were an empirical case with membership above 0.5 in this configuration, would this case show the outcome? And why is it that row 4 does not have a positive outcome, although 2 of the 3 conditions we expected to lead to the outcome are present?

The truth table helps to analytically explore the data and to formulate such questions, which is particularly useful when there are even more conditions and possible configurations to consider. During the early phases of designing a QCA study, a preliminary truth table can be used to guide the selection of conditions because it shows whether the included conditions are *difference makers* that adequately distinguish the observed cases. If many cases cluster in just a few rows of the truth table and the remaining rows are empty, then one should explore whether some conditions should be reconceptualized, recalibrated, or replaced by conditions previously omitted. Such changes in research design can help to differentiate between clustered cases and can result in a more evenly spread distribution across the truth table rows.[3] Likewise, if each case has a "row of its own," then this indicates that the research design may be overly differentiated—a situation that can be improved, for instance, by eliminating certain conditions or by merging some of them into macro-level conditions (see chapter 3).

TRUTH TABLE ANALYSIS

The truth table is in itself a valuable tool for descriptive data analysis. However, because each row in the truth table is a statement about sufficiency, we can use Boolean algebra to minimize the truth table to derive solution terms for an outcome, which is what QCA is all about. This section summarizes and illustrates the Boolean minimization procedure that was developed by Ragin (1987, 93–102; 2000; 2008b) and consolidated by Schneider and Wagemann (2012, 104–15; 2013), among others (see also Duşa 2019; and Oana, Schneider, and Thomann 2021). The final sections of this chapter also look into some refinements of what is known as the *standard analysis*.

The truth table analysis is done via software, but the procedures rest on Boolean algebra and as such they can be reproduced by hand. The technical steps are described in the R Manual, referred to in the appendix. Let us take an example from a published study, simplified for our purposes, to illustrate the analysis of the truth table. In his article on the politics of religion, Luis Felipe Mantilla (2012) explores the conditions under which the Catholic Church promoted democratization in South America.[4] The study uses eight countries as cases and the explanatory conditions *resources, opportunity*, and *cultural framing* to explain the outcome *democratization support*, as shown in table 7.3.

Based on these crisp-set data, we can construct a truth table. Table 7.4 shows how the empirical cases distribute across the logically possible configurations. We can see

Table 7.3   Data Frame: Politics of Religion

Country	Resources (R)	Opportunity (O)	Framing (F)	Outcome (Y)
Brazil	1	1	1	1
Chile	1	1	1	1
Peru	1	1	0	1
Ecuador	0	1	0	0
Bolivia	0	0	1	0
Uruguay	0	1	1	0
Argentina	1	1	1	1
Paraguay	0	0	1	0

Source: Mantilla (2012).

Table 7.4 Truth Table: Politics of Religion

Row	Resources (R)	Opportunity (O)	Framing (F)	Outcome (Y)	N	Country
1	1	1	1	1	3	Argentina, Brazil, Chile
2	1	1	0	1	1	Peru
3	0	0	1	0	2	Bolivia, Paraguay
4	0	1	1	0	1	Uruguay
5	0	1	0	0	1	Ecuador
6	1	0	1	?	0	—
7	1	0	0	?	0	—
8	0	0	0	?	0	—

that the eight cases fill five rows, two of which lead consistently toward the outcome (the top two rows). There are also three *empty rows* at the bottom of the table, indicated by a question mark. These are combinations of conditions without empirical cases in the data, and thus we cannot say whether the respective configurations consistently lead to the outcome (these rows are also termed *logical remainders*). However, one advantage of QCA is that it allows for counterfactual reasoning through a systematic treatment of these logical remainder rows. This is the issue of *limited diversity*, to which we will return when discussing solution types.

How to proceed with the truth table *analysis*? In a manual application, the first step would be writing down the configurations that are linked to the outcome. In our example, these are the first two rows of table 7.4, both of which show the outcome. The cases included in these rows are Argentina, Brazil, and Chile for row 1, and Peru for row 2.

We write down the combinations as individual conditions linked by a Boolean AND (·). For convenience, we may also omit this operator and simply write the letters that represent the conditions next to each other, as in "ROF" to indicate the combination in the first line. The combinations themselves are linked by a Boolean OR (+), to indicate the existence of multiple paths, where each is sufficient for the outcome. Hence, the formal notation for the conditions *resources* (R), *opportunity* (O), *framing* (F), and the outcome *democratization support* (Y) is:

$$R{\cdot}O{\cdot}F + R{\cdot}O{\cdot}{\sim}F \rightarrow Y \tag{1}$$

This reads as "resources *and* opportunity *and* framing *or* resources *and* opportunity *and not*-framing are sufficient for democratization support." To simplify this expression, we can apply the rule of *Boolean minimization*: "If two Boolean expressions differ in only one causal condition yet produce the same outcome, then the causal condition that distinguishes the two expressions can be considered irrelevant and can be removed to create a simpler, combined expression" (Ragin 1987, 93).[5]

Based on this rule, we can delete F and ~F from expression 1, because both combinations lead toward the outcome (with and without the condition *framing*). In the next step, we can eliminate one of the duplicate expressions of R·O, which leaves us with:

$$R \cdot O \rightarrow Y \qquad (2)$$

This reads as "resources *and* opportunity are sufficient for democratization support." In other words, when both R and O are present, then this leads to Y. We can see that this solution matches the information contained in the truth table (table 7.4). There are only two possible combinations that entail the expression R·O (rows 1 and 2), and both of these show the outcome.

This is a simple example, but it helps to illustrate the way Boolean minimization works. Each truth table row that is associated with the outcome yields a *primitive expression*. This is the Boolean notation of the combination contained in the respective row. If there are two or more primitive expressions (i.e., truth table rows associated with the outcome), then the minimization rule can be applied to derive a simpler expression, which consists of so-called *prime implicants*. In another step, this can be further simplified by seeing if some of the prime implicants are *redundant* because primitive expressions may be covered by several of the prime implicants.

To illustrate this point, let us imagine a truth table that yields four combinations of the conditions A, B, C; each of which is sufficient for the outcome Y:

$$B \cdot C + A \cdot B \cdot \sim C + \sim A \cdot B \cdot C + \sim A \cdot \sim B \cdot C \rightarrow Y \qquad (3)$$

Again, we can apply the rule of Boolean minimization to derive a shorter statement. To do so, each primitive expression can be compared with one or several of the other expressions until no further minimization is possible. In the next minimization, the brackets indicate which two expressions from line 4 are used to create the simpler statement in line 5. Note that the procedure shown here does not exhaust all possible comparisons, but these will not yield other solutions. For the minimization, each expression must be compared with at least one other expression or carried over to the next row. We can see that the first expression A·B·C is compared with both the second expression A·B·~C and with the third expression ~A·B·C:

$$A \cdot B \cdot C + A \cdot B \cdot \sim C + \sim A \cdot B \cdot C + \sim A \cdot \sim B \cdot C \rightarrow Y \qquad (4)$$

$$A \cdot B \ + \ B \cdot C \ + \ \sim A \cdot C \ \rightarrow Y \qquad (5)$$

This first step in the minimization procedure eliminates expressions that are deemed *superfluous* for the solution because their presence *and* absence both lead to the outcome, given the presence of the other conditions. This applies, for instance, to the conditions C and ~C in the first two expressions in line 4. They are part of the combinations A·B·C and A·B·~C. Hence, when A and B are both present, then it does not matter whether they combine with C or ~C, because both combinations lead to the outcome. Hence this can be minimized to A·B, as stated in line 5. The other two minimizations follow the same logic.

For the second step of the Boolean minimization procedure, a *prime implicant chart* is constructed (Ragin 1987, 97). Again, this process is implemented in the software, but it helps to go through the sequence in order to understand how QCA solution terms are derived. Users should also be familiar with the prime implicant chart because they may need to work with it (e.g., in the fs/QCA software, but also in R). The prime implicant chart displays as columns all the truth table rows that are sufficient for the outcome (the *primitive expressions*). The results from the first minimization step (the *prime implicants*) are listed as rows. Table 7.5 shows the chart for the hypothetical truth table data used above.

The columns of the prime implicant chart list the configurations (truth table rows) that were linked to the outcome. The crosses in the cells indicate which expression is covered by which prime implicant. This means that the respective prime implicant is a *superset* of the covered primitive expression(s). In our example, we can see that each prime implicant covers two primitive expressions, but the second prime implicant is *redundant* because its primitive expressions are also covered by the other two prime implicants. In short, there is no information gained from keeping the expression B·C in the solution term and thus it can be *deleted* to yield a more parsimonious solution:

$$A·B + ~A·C \rightarrow Y \tag{6}$$

Why can we erase the expression B·C from the solution? The Venn diagram in figure 7.2 shows why the shorter statement in line 6 is equivalent to the statement in

Table 7.5 Prime Implicant Chart

Primitive Expressions					
A·B·C	A·B·~C	~A·B·C	~A·~B·C		
×	×			A·B	
×		×		B·C	**Prime Implicants**
		×	×	~A·C	

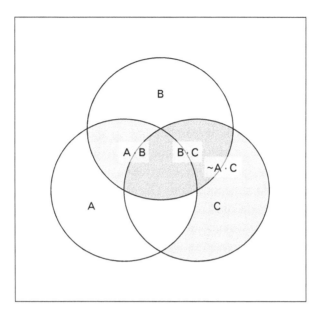

Figure 7.2   Venn Diagram: Prime Implicants and
Redundancy

line 5 above. Quite simply, there is nothing gained from saying B·C, because its gray-shaded area in the Venn diagram is *entirely covered* by the other two prime implicants A·B and ~A·C. Hence, in this setting, saying that "A *and* B *or not-*A *and* C are sufficient for Y" *implies* that B·C is also sufficient for Y. B·C is thus a redundant prime implicant.

   The prime implicant chart also helps to understand why different solution terms might be derived from the same data. This phenomenon is known as *model ambiguity*, a concept that describes how, depending on the structure of the truth table and the assumptions made, several logically equivalent solution terms may be derived from the same data (Baumgartner and Thiem 2017). Importantly, even when there are multiple solutions, in principle, these are all equally "correct," in the sense that they are the result of an accurate Boolean minimization procedure, based on the empirical information that is entailed in the truth table. However, some solutions may include *redundant elements* and other solutions may entail *untenable simplifying assumptions* about logical remainder rows. These aspects are examined in the next section (also see chapter 9).

SOLUTION TERMS

The two-stage minimization procedure described in the previous section is incorporated into QCA's software routine, which draws upon the *truth table algorithm* to minimize expressions and to derive solution terms. Initially, this was based upon the

Quine-McCluskey (QMC) algorithm and the enhanced Quine-McCluskey (eQMC) algorithm, which have been replaced by the Consistency Cubes algorithm (Duşa 2018) as the default minimization method in recent versions of the QCA package (Duşa 2019b). From a user's perspective, the differences between these algorithms mainly concern their performance and reliance upon computer resources, as they reach identical minimization results.[6]

Before the minimization, the researcher has to specify a *consistency threshold* to indicate which rows of the truth table should be treated as positive instances of the outcome and included in the analysis. For these, the outcome column is coded as 1. Rows below the threshold are coded as 0. The standard threshold for this step is 0.75 consistency. Apart for exceptional reasons, researchers should not include rows with a consistency lower than this conventional threshold (Ragin 2008, 144; Rubinson et al. 2019, 4; Schneider and Wagemann 2012, 292).[7] What is important to understand about the consistency threshold is that it merely defines the *lower bound* that determines which rows shall be included in the minimization. Hence, the eventual solution consistency will typically be *higher* than the consistency threshold because there will also be rows of a higher consistency.

Users can further define a *frequency threshold* to indicate how many cases with membership greater than 0.5 must be entailed in a truth table row for it to be included in the minimization procedure. Usually, this is set to 1, which means that a single case suffices, but in large-*N* research settings with high numbers of cases it can be expedient to increase the frequency threshold so that only those rows are included that hold a certain number of cases with membership above 0.5 in the respective configuration. For example, in their large-*N* QCA study on the persistence of electoral autocracies (with 156 cases of elections across 48 autocratic regimes), Carsten Schneider and Seraphine Maerz (2017, 222) select a frequency cutoff of *at least 2* empirical cases per row because this helps to guard against the chance of misclassified cases. Notably, the frequency threshold did not substantively alter their QCA results.

Once the consistency and frequency thresholds have been specified, the QCA software is applied to derive three different solution terms: the *conservative solution*, the *parsimonious solution*, and the *intermediate solution*. The differences between these solution types originate from their treatment of logical remainders.

The Conservative Solution

The *conservative solution* has its name because it only works with the empirical rows that are associated with a positive outcome, above the specified consistency and frequency thresholds. As the term *conservative* conveys, this solution does *not* make assumptions about empty rows in the truth table, and thus it sidesteps counterfactual reasoning. In fact, the conservative solution treats all logical remainder rows as false (Ragin 2008b, 173; Schneider and Wagemann 2012, 162). One consequence of this approach is that it tends to yield lengthier solution terms than the other types. This is so because the conservative solution can use only rows with empirical cases above the specified thresholds for the pairwise Boolean minimization, whereas the other solutions both incorporate logical remainder rows to different extents. This is why the conservative solution is also called the *complex solution* (Ragin 2008b, 173). Complexity in this sense refers to the number of conditions and operators that are entailed in a solution term. The more conditions and operators, the greater the complexity of the solution. As Adrian Duşa (2019, 177) notes, "no other solution can be more complex than the conservative one," yet other solutions can be *similarly* complex.[8]

The Parsimonious Solution

The *parsimonious solution* considers all truth table rows with logical remainders and uses those that allow it to derive a less complex solution through pairwise Boolean minimization. Those logical remainders that are used for minimization are called "simplifying assumptions" (Ragin 2000, 305; 2008b, 136). These logical remainders are *simplifying* because they enable further minimization through Boolean comparisons. Some logical remainders may have no utility for the minimization, but these would simply not be used by the parsimonious solution. Those logical remainders that are used are further called *assumptions* because using them rests on the counterfactual conjecture that if cases with the respective configuration existed, then these would show the outcome. Because the parsimonious solution is allowed to examine all logical remainders, it can work with the broadest pool of configurations, and thus its minimization procedure tends to yield the least complex solution terms. Yet what the parsimonious solution does *not* consider is the *plausibility* of the simplifying assumptions that were used to derive it. This means that the parsimonious solution may rest on unrealistic assumptions about hypothetical data. Hence, the parsimonious solution should always be scrutinized for its simplifying assumptions (Ragin 2008b, 162), which means examining the logical remainder rows that were included in its calculation. We will return to this point in the next section.

The Intermediate Solution

Finally, as its name implies, the *intermediate solution* is positioned between the conservative and parsimonious solutions because it includes logical remainders, but only those that are deemed sensible. With the intermediate solution, the researcher can decide which logical remainder rows to include in the minimization and which ones should be excluded from the procedure. As Ragin (2009a, 118) puts it, the intermediate solution "incorporates only the logical remainders that are consistent with theoretical and substantive knowledge," as defined by the researcher. Here, as a heuristic device, a distinction is made between *easy* and *difficult counterfactuals* (Ragin (2008b,

160–67; Ragin and Sonnett 2005). Both of these are simplifying assumptions that are used for the parsimonious solution. Easy counterfactuals are defined as those assumptions that are theoretically meaningful and reasonable in light of case knowledge. A shortcut to the assessment of easy counterfactuals are "directional expectations" about the presence or absence of a condition and its respective relationship to the outcome (Ragin 2003b, 9).[9]

For example, based on theory, we may expect the *presence* of an electoral system that is based on proportional representation to lead to a multiparty system. In principle, logical remainders where such an electoral system is present should thus be considered easy counterfactuals. By contrast, *difficult counterfactuals* are assumptions that conflict with theory and substantive knowledge. For instance, this may be the case when a logical remainder entails the *absence* of conditions whose presence is expected to lead to the outcome. The basic idea behind the intermediate solution is to include easy counterfactuals while excluding difficult counterfactuals from the analysis (Ragin 2008b, 174).

How is this done in practice? One way to derive an intermediate solution is by *excluding* specific truth table rows (Schneider and Wagemann 2012, 171). This can be fine when there are few simplifying assumptions but can be complicated with large truth tables that contain many empty rows. Another way to do this is through the formulation of *directional expectations* for each condition (Schneider and Wagemann 2012, 168). Based on this information, the algorithm in the software then selects simplifying assumptions in line with the formulated expectations (Duşa 2019).

However, even though the software takes directional expectations into account, this does not mean that all counterfactuals that meet the criteria will be considered in the calculation of the intermediate solution term. The scope for the intermediate solution is *circumscribed* by the other two solution terms. The starting point is the conservative solution, which rests entirely on the empirical cases. The parsimonious solution seeks to arrive at simpler expressions, but it may be based on unrealistic assumptions about certain logical remainder rows. For the intermediate solution, those logical remainders that are deemed *plausible counterfactuals* may be used for the minimization, which should in principle result in a solution term that is situated between the conservative and the parsimonious solution in terms of complexity (see also the next section on counterfactual analysis).[10]

AN ILLUSTRATION OF SOLUTION TERMS

The relationship between the three different types of solution terms is best illustrated with an example. Table 7.6 shows a truth table for fuzzy-set data across 3 conditions and 25 cases. Note that the software indexes the truth table rows and that these designators are kept throughout the analysis. Because the truth table is sorted by consistency and frequency, the numerators are not in sequence any longer, but each row retains its

Table 7.6   Example of a Truth Table

Row	A	B	C	Outcome	N	Consistency	PRI
6	1	0	1	1	6	0.95	0.95
4	0	1	1	1	5	0.95	0.94
7	1	1	0	1	5	0.95	0.94
2	0	0	1	0	5	0.37	0.16
5	1	0	0	0	5	0.26	0.14
1	0	0	0	?	0	—	—
3	0	1	0	?	0	—	—
8	1	1	1	?	0	—	—

unique identifier throughout the analysis. This may become important, for instance, when seeking to exclude a certain logical remainder row from the minimization.

From table 7.6, we can see that 3 rows are associated with the presence of the outcome. We can summarize this information in Boolean notation:

$$A \cdot {\sim}B \cdot C + {\sim}A \cdot B \cdot C + A \cdot B \cdot {\sim}C \rightarrow Y \tag{7}$$

The truth table further shows that there are 3 logical remainder rows, as in rows without empirical cases. What can we say about these? Given the pattern in the first 3 rows and the way the conditions were calibrated, we may expect that the joint presence of all 3 conditions would also lead to the outcome if such cases existed. This applies to the logical remainder in row 8 (A·B·C), which is thus an *easy counterfactual*. But what about row 1 (~A·~B·~C) and row 3 (~A·B·~C)? Both of these could be considered *difficult counterfactuals* because the conditions point in the "wrong" direction. We also know from the rows associated with the outcome that it seems to require at least 2 of the 3 conditions to bring about the outcome, so the absence of all of them (row 1) or 2 of them (row 3) may not suffice for the outcome.

We can now derive the three solution terms from the truth table. In this example, the *conservative solution* is identical to the top three rows of the truth table because these cannot be further minimized without using logical remainders:

$$A \cdot {\sim}B \cdot C + {\sim}A \cdot B \cdot C + A \cdot B \cdot {\sim}C \rightarrow Y \tag{8}$$

Next, we derive the *parsimonious solution*, for which the software considers all logical remainders and uses those that enable it to derive a simpler, more parsimonious solution term. This process yields this solution:

$$A \cdot C + B \rightarrow Y \tag{9}$$

This parsimonious solution rests on simplifying assumptions about logical remainder row 3 (~A·B·~C) and row 8 (A·B·C), both of which are treated as if they were sufficient for the outcome. How is this result achieved? The minimization that is entailed in the parsimonious solution can be reproduced manually by adding the two expressions for the logical remainders. I should highlight that what follows is a *stylized example* that simplifies the algorithmic routine to illustrate what is *effectively* going on with the parsimonious solution. First, the order in which the expressions appear is sorted for a more convenient illustration:

$$A\text{·}{\sim}B\text{·}C + A\text{·}B\text{·}C + A\text{·}B\text{·}{\sim}C + {\sim}A\text{·}B\text{·}C + {\sim}A\text{·}B\text{·}{\sim}C \;\rightarrow Y \qquad (10)$$

$$A\text{·}C \;+\; B\text{·}C \;+\; B\text{·}{\sim}C \;+\; {\sim}A\text{·}B \;\rightarrow Y \qquad (11)$$

$$A\text{·}C \;+\; B \;+\; {\sim}A\text{·}B \;\rightarrow Y \qquad (12)$$

$$A\text{·}C \;+\; B \;\rightarrow Y \qquad (13)$$

Through pairwise Boolean comparison, indicated by lines and brackets, we reduce the original term of five expressions in statement 10 to four expressions in statement 11. From here, we can further eliminate ~C and C, which yields the three expressions in statement 12. The final minimization rests on Boolean logic because the expression ~A·B in statement 12 is covered by the single condition B. This can be confirmed with a prime implicant chart or a Venn diagram (see the earlier sections of this chapter). Hence the parsimonious solution is the statement in line 13, which cannot be further minimized.

However, we know that this parsimonious solution rests on the inclusion of a difficult counterfactual (row 3). Hence, we create an *intermediate solution*, which allows us to specify which logical remainder rows should be used. Here, we may want to treat row 8 as an *easy counterfactual* because all conditions are present, but we specify that the software should *exclude* row 3 from being used in the solution because this constitutes a difficult counterfactual with the presence of only a single condition. If we pass this criterion on to the software, it returns the following intermediate solution, which rests on the inclusion of a single logical remainder (row 8):

$$A\text{·}C + B\text{·}C + A\text{·}B \rightarrow Y \qquad (14)$$

Table 7.7   Conservative, Intermediate, and Parsimonious Solutions

Path		Relation	Consistency	PRI	Raw Coverage	Unique Coverage
Conservative solution			0.97	0.97	0.87	–
1	A·~B·C	+	0.95	0.95	0.37	0.29
2	~A·B·C	+	0.95	0.94	0.32	0.24
3	A·B·~C	→ Y	0.95	0.94	0.32	0.24
Intermediate solution			0.97	0.97	0.88	–
1	A·C	+	0.96	0.95	0.40	0.29
2	B·C	+	0.96	0.95	0.35	0.24
3	A·B	→ Y	0.95	0.95	0.35	0.24
Parsimonious solution			0.96	0.96	0.90	–
1	A·C	+	0.96	0.95	0.40	0.29
2	B	→ Y	0.96	0.95	0.61	0.51

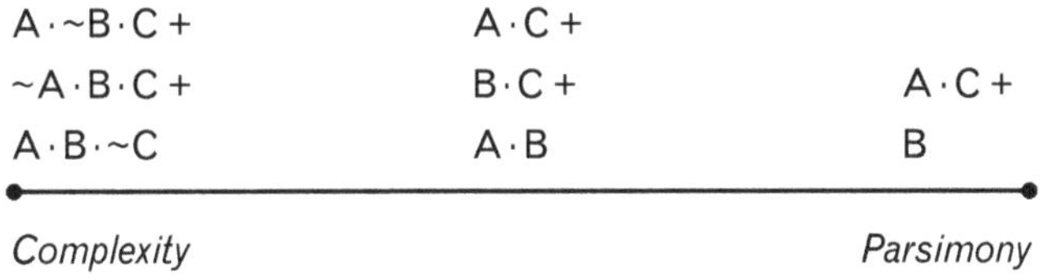

A·~B·C +   A·C +

~A·B·C +   B·C +   A·C +

A·B·~C   A·B   B

Complexity   *Parsimony*

Figure 7.3   The Complexity/Parsimony Dimension

Table 7.7 shows the three different solution types and their measures of fit. This confirms that the parsimonious solution is the *superset* of the other solutions and that the conservative solution is a *subset* of the intermediate and parsimonious solutions. This general relationship between the solution types will always apply, the only exception being identical solutions. In this example, we see that the three paths that constitute the conservative solution are fully covered by the two paths of the parsimonious solution (A·~B·C is covered by A·C, whereas ~A·B·C and A·B·~C are both covered by B). The same principle applies for the intermediate solution, which is a *superset* of the conservative solution and a *subset* of the parsimonious solution.

As for measures of fit, in this example the intermediate and conservative solutions yield nearly identical scores, whereas the parsimonious solution has slightly higher coverage and less consistency than the other solutions. Depending on the empirical data, the differences may be more pronounced. Typically, the parsimonious solution has the highest coverage, whereas the conservative solution tends to have the highest consistency.

The relationship between the solution types is summarized in figure 7.3, which places the three solutions on a single dimension that runs from *complexity to parsimony*, whereas the Venn diagrams in figure 7.4 depict the subset–superset relations

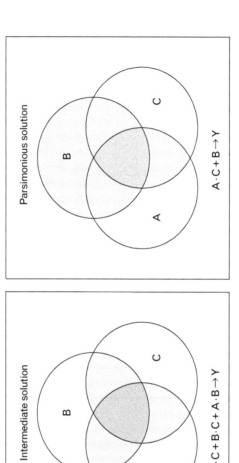

Figure 7.4   Conservative, Intermediate, and Parsimonious Solutions

that govern the solutions.[11] The illustration shows that the parsimonious solution is the *most general* as it covers the largest area in the diagram. Yet, we should note that this parsimonious solution is based on a difficult counterfactual. Hence it should always be scrutinized and compared to the other solutions, as discussed above. The conservative and intermediate solutions are subsets of the parsimonious solution, and hence it can be said that they are *more specific*, which also shows in the smaller areas covered in the Venn diagrams.

Which solution type should be given preference? As this section has shown, the solution types are not ordered in a hierarchical fashion but rather are characterized by their *interdependence*.

In general, *all three solutions* should be derived and examined. Ideally, the three solutions should also be reported in publications, either in the main text or in online supplements. That said, published studies typically emphasize a single solution type in their substantive interpretation. Most often, this is the *intermediate solution* because it allows researchers to determine the treatment of logical remainders based on their theoretical expectations and substantive knowledge of the research area. This is also why the intermediate solution has been emphasized in the QCA literature (Ragin 2008b, 175; Schneider and Wagemann 2012, 279). However, the *conservative* and *parsimonious solutions* are equally valid, under the precondition that the latter is checked for untenable assumptions. After all, the choice of which solution type to focus on for the substantive interpretation will also be based upon the research aims of a given study, the complexity of the analysis, and the extent to which reasoning about logical remainders is possible in a given field of research. The next section examines the topic of logical remainders and counterfactual analysis, whereas chapter 9 looks into further aspects of solution terms.

Although the layout of table 7.7 is suitable for a comparison of the different solution terms, the Boolean notation is fairly abstract and may pose a challenge for readers who are not used to set-theoretic methods. Hence, for publications it is often a good idea to use a more reader-friendly layout where conditions are spelled out and case membership is listed, both of which enhance the communication of the analytical results (a topic to which we will return in chapter 10).

Table 7.8 shows an abbreviated example from a recent study by Tobias Ide and colleagues (Ide et al. 2020). Their study on the conditions leading to water-related conflict in the Middle East and North Africa resulted in two pathways. Following the notation introduced by Charles Ragin and Peer Fiss (Fiss 2011; Ragin and Fiss 2008), black circles (•) indicate the presence of a condition, whereas crossed-out circles (⊗) refer to the absence of a condition (this simple example only entails the presence of conditions). We can see that of the four conditions included in the study, listed at the top left side of the table, the first path combined *cleavages* between social groups and an *autocratic regime*, whereas the second path contained *cleavages* in combination with *water cuts*. The condition *nightlight emissions* did not appear in any of the two solution paths. The

Table 7.8 Example: Solution Term and Solution Paths

Solution Term	Path	
	1	2
Cleavages	●	●
Autocratic regime	●	
Nightlight emissions		
Water cuts		●
Consistency	1.00	0.91
Raw coverage	0.53	0.59
Unique coverage	0.18	0.24
Covered cases / uniquely covered cases (underlined)	AinBerda	Aidah
	Annaba	AinBerda
	Batna	Annaba
	Damascus	Aramta
	Damru	Batna
	El Burullus	Damru
	ElChatt	Diyarbakir
	Guercif	El Burullus
	Ouargla City	El Chatt Nablus
		Nablus
Solution consistency	0.93	
Solution coverage	0.77	

Source: Ide et al. (2020, 8).

center of the table entails information on measures of fit, including consistency, the raw coverage of each of the two paths (irrespective of empirical overlap), and their unique coverage. The bottom of the table lists cases by path membership. We can see that six cases hold membership in both solution paths (the nonunderlined cases), while seven cases are underlined to indicate that they are uniquely covered by one of the two paths. The overall solution consistency and coverage are listed at the low end of the table.

This layout can be easily customized to include further information, for instance on *unexplained cases* not covered by the solution or on *deviant cases* that hold membership in the solution but not in the outcome (see chapter 10). Presenting QCA results in this layout has the advantage that all the condition names can be spelled out in full, while adding a visual element that makes it easier to grasp the combinations of conditions. Moreover, unless there is a very large number of cases, all the covered cases can be listed by path membership and uniquely covered cases can be highlighted. This enhances both the connection between the abstract analysis and the case-oriented nature of QCA.

COUNTERFACTUAL ANALYSIS

One of the strengths of QCA is that it uncovers limited diversity among social phenomena, which creates an opportunity for *counterfactual analysis* (Ragin 2008b, 151). The truth table is the tool to identify configurations filled with empirical cases, rows that lead consistently toward the outcome, the ones that are inconsistent, and configurations for which there are no empirical cases—the logical remainder rows. Logical remainders are *potential* counterfactual cases. They are combinations of conditions without empirical instances for which the plausibility of the outcome can be evaluated by the researcher.

As noted in the discussion of theories of causation (chapter 4), counterfactual analysis has an established pedigree in the social sciences, where it infused both qualitative (e.g., Fearon 1991; Harvey 2012; Levy 2008; Tetlock and Belkin 1996) and quantitative approaches (e.g., Emmenegger 2011; King and Zeng 2007; Morgan and Winship 2007). In QCA, logical remainders are included in the parsimonious solution, but for this solution type the algorithm is in the driver's seat, because it selects solely on the basis of whether the remainders enable further minimization, aiming for the least complex solution. Hence, there is no counterfactual *reasoning* involved in the parsimonious solution.

The intermediate solution remedies this shortcoming because it allows researchers to engage in counterfactual reasoning for the incorporation of logical remainders. How is this to be done? The first criterion is the distinction between easy and difficult counterfactuals (Ragin 2008b; Ragin and Sonnett 2005). *Easy counterfactuals* are simplifying logical remainders for which the presence of the outcome can be expected, based on theoretical and substantive knowledge. *Difficult counterfactuals* are simplifying assumptions that conflict with such knowledge. The conceptual distinction between easy and difficult counterfactuals thus emphasizes the importance of theoretical expectations and familiarity with the cases as preconditions for counterfactual reasoning (see also Mendel and Ragin 2011).

However, an applied researcher might ask *how* the distinction between easy and difficult counterfactuals ought to be made. On which grounds can we justify the use or nonuse of logical remainders? Charles Ragin described the core idea behind simplifying assumptions concisely in *Fuzzy-Set Social Science* (Ragin 2000, 305), where he also stressed the need for transparent documentation:

> Ultimately, the selection of simplifying assumptions for incorporation into a causal generalization must be grounded as much as possible in theoretical and substantive knowledge. The purpose of each evaluation—that is, thought experiment—is to *assess the plausibility of a nonexistent combination of conditions as a simplifying assumption*. The researcher asks: If this combination of conditions existed empirically, would it generate the outcome? If the answer is "yes," then

the simplifying assumption is permitted. Of course, if any simplifying assumptions are incorporated into a causal generalization, they should be carefully documented and thus made available for evaluation by the audience for the research
[emphasis added].

It is against this backdrop that subsequent studies elaborated the work on counterfactual reasoning and simplifying assumptions (Rihoux and De Meur 2009; Schneider and Wagemann 2012, 2013; Yamasaki and Rihoux 2009). Clearly, these and other
works have advanced the discussion of logical remainders and enriched the analytical toolkit of QCA. Yet, this has also led to a virtual "logical remainder soup" with a
plethora of related terms that can easily confuse new users, as well as those who are
acquainted with set-theoretic methods. With that in mind, my aim in this section is
to cut through the thicket and to provide a *concise* account of counterfactuals, their
analytical potential, and the hazards of unwarranted assumptions.[12]

To begin with, three types of logical remainders elude the distinction between easy
and difficult counterfactuals. The first of these are *contradictory counterfactuals*, which
are defined as logical remainders that are treated as if they were sufficient for both the
outcome and the nonoutcome (Rihoux and De Meur 2009, 64; Yamasaki and Rihoux
2009, 136).[13] Because the analysis of the outcome and the nonoutcome are conducted
separately, it may happen unwittingly that the same logical remainder is used to derive
solutions for both of these. This would be a *logical contradiction* that should be solved,
either by limiting the use of the logical remainder to the analysis where it is plausible
(either for the outcome *or* the nonoutcome), by excluding the logical remainder altogether, or by addressing the underlying issue through changes in the research design.
The first two approaches would be technical solutions introduced during the analysis,
whereas the third approach takes a step back to find ways how to improve the research
design to prevent such contradictions (see chapter 2).

The second type of logical remainders to avoid are *impossible counterfactuals*, which
are remainders that are simply *not possible* by what we know about the physical or
social world (Schneider and Wagemann 2012, 206). This can mean that the respective
configuration is either generally impossible or that it simply has never happened in
history (irrespective of whether it might happen in the future). A crude but frequently
used example is the combination of the sets *pregnant people* and *nonwomen*—"pregnant men"—which will be empty due to its impossibility. As another example for the
second type, imagine a study that seeks to explore the conflict involvement of United
Nations member states. The conditions include *permanent membership* in the UN Security Council and *possessing nuclear weapons*. Though both of these can be considered
relevant conditions, this design would create logical remainders that combine permanent UN Security Council membership with the *absence* of nuclear weapons—an
impossibility at the time of writing, though it is conceivable that at some point in the

future the UN Security Council might comprise permanent member states that do not possess nuclear weapons.

Impossible counterfactuals can occur whenever the selection of conditions allows for combinations that are not possible, but which would still be created as logical remainder rows in the truth table. Hence, such impossible counterfactuals may inform the parsimonious solution. Clearly, the best remedy to this situation is an improved research design. With QCA, only a limited number of conditions can be included and each of these should, in principle, be conceived in a way that allows for combinations with all other conditions. This mirrors the guidelines for case selection, where the *possibility* of a case showing the outcome is a crucial criterion (Mahoney and Goertz 2004). Wherever an adapted research design is not feasible, then the impossible counterfactuals should be excluded from the parsimonious and intermediate solutions.

Finally, the third type of logical remainders that should be avoided are *incoherent counterfactuals*, which are assumptions that conflict with a statement of necessity made earlier in the analysis (Schneider and Wagemann 2012, 201).[14] For example, we may have identified a relevant (nontrivial) necessary condition during the first step of the set-theoretic analysis (see chapter 6). Now it could be seen as a logical contradiction if we treated remainders that do *not* include the necessary condition as sufficient for the outcome. Hence, any necessary condition that was identified during the first step of the analysis should constrain the set of logical remainders that are available for the parsimonious and intermediate solutions. In principle, only those remainders that contain the presence of the necessary condition should be allowed.

However, this principle should not be followed blindly. In a given empirical setting, there may be logical remainders for which it can reasonably be argued on the grounds of theoretical and substantive knowledge that the outcome can be expected, although these might not entail the necessary condition. At the least, this possibility should *not be ruled out* per se, without thoroughly investigating the remainders and assessing their plausibility.

What does this mean for the analysis? The essential point for the truth table analysis is that counterfactuals should be located in the shaded area at the center of figure 7.5. I term these *plausible counterfactuals*, which are those logical remainders that meet all these criteria: (1) theoretical and substantive knowledge suggests the presence of the outcome, (2) the respective configuration is not contradictory, (3) empirically possible, and (4) does not conflict with a statement of necessity.[15] Whenever researchers engage in counterfactual reasoning with QCA, they should ensure to only include plausible counterfactuals in the analysis. A discussion of how this is done with the software is provided in the *online material* for this book (see the appendix for instructions).

Apart from the guidelines discussed above, two specific approaches have been developed to refine the treatment of logical remainders. The *enhanced standard analysis*

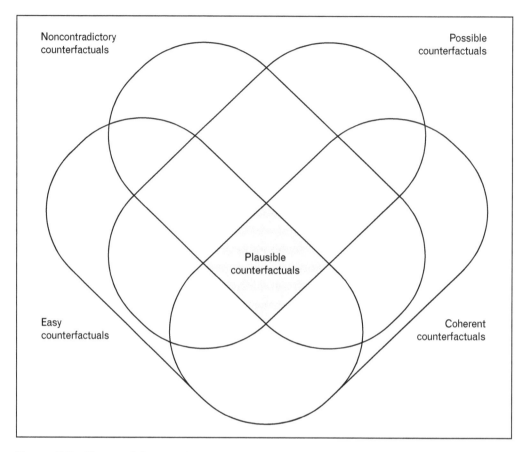

Figure 7.5   Types of Counterfactuals

(ESA) by Carsten Schneider and Claudius Wagemann (2012) is a procedure designed to avoid "untenable assumptions" based on contradiction, incoherence, or impossibility during the minimization of the truth table. This yields so-called *enhanced* parsimonious and intermediate solutions, which tend to be more complex than those derived with the standard routine. The ESA procedure is detailed by Schneider and Wagemann (2012, 198–211) and Duşa (2019, 183–96). This approach is complemented by a second approach, the *theory-guided enhanced standard analysis* (TESA, Schneider and Wagemann 2012, 211), which specifically allows for the inclusion of nonsimplifying remainders. The key point with TESA is that it emphasizes *theoretical resonance* over parsimony, and hence the produced solution terms will tend to be more complex than with the other approaches.

With their emphasis on tenability and analytical aims beyond parsimony, Schneider and Wagemann (2012, 2013) have advanced the methodological debate on the treatment of logical remainders in QCA. Notably, the SetMethods package for R has introduced a variety of advanced functions for set-theoretic analysis (Oana and

Schneider 2018; Oana, Schneider, and Thomann 2021). Yet, the suggested analytical procedures for the treatment of logical remainders in ESA have also drawn critiques. Barry Cooper and Judith Glaesser (2016, 311) contend that ESA "goes beyond the available evidence" in ruling out logical remainder rows that do not show a previously identified necessary condition. Alrik Thiem (2016) holds that ESA effectively yields conservative solutions, due to the constraints imposed by previously identified necessary conditions. In their replies, Schneider and Wagemann emphasize the importance of meaningful criteria for the relevance of necessary conditions, underlining that ESA does *not* force researchers "to declare as necessary any condition that is a superset of the outcome" (Schneider 2018; Schneider and Wagemann 2016, 317). This underscores a point made throughout this book, namely, that it is upon researchers to justify their analytical choices in the light of their case knowledge and theoretical expectations, which should not be replaced by mechanical routines.

Broadly conceived, counterfactual analysis is currently one of the most dynamic areas of QCA research—as it touches upon the linkage between theory and empirical analysis, the assumptions that go into solution terms, and the technical implementation of these procedures. Doubtless, this area will see further development as new procedures will be suggested for the treatment of logical remainders. We revisit this topic in chapter 9, when examining the current debate surrounding the validity of different solution terms in QCA.

NOTES

Epigraphs: Goertz and Starr (2003a, 3); Ragin (2014, xxvii).

1. At some stage, it has been recommended to *exclude* conditions that are found to be necessary from the following truth table procedure, while retaining them for the substantive interpretation (Ragin 2009a, 110). However, removing necessary conditions from the analysis may decrease inferential leverage (Mello 2013, 13). Notably, Ragin shifted his position on this issue (Mendel and Ragin 2011, 24).

2. The 0.9 consistency benchmark for necessary conditions is now widely accepted. Yet it should be pointed out that in some of his earlier work, Ragin (2000, 229; 2003a, 194) applied the linguistic qualifiers known from fuzzy sets also to the analysis of necessary conditions (as in "more in than out" and other verbal qualifiers to characterize partial set membership; see chapter 5). Hence, conditions with a consistency of at least 0.8 were considered "almost always" necessary for the outcome (Ragin 2003a, 194). For relevance of necessity, Schneider and Wagemann (2012, 237) point out that "low values indicate trivialness and high values relevance," and Oana et al. (2021, 205) suggest a threshold of 0.6, above which conditions may be deemed relevant.

3. On omitted variables in QCA, see Radaelli and Wagemann (2019).

4. The example has been simplified for the purposes of illustration. Among other differences, Mantilla (2012) uses fuzzy-set QCA and includes two observations for Peru (based on different time periods).

5. Schneider and Wagemann (2012, 105) rightly underline that the removed condition should be considered "irrelevant" only under the presence of the remaining conditions.

6. For a detailed technical discussion of the algorithmic differences, see Duşa (2019b, 197–208).

7. Exceptions may be permissible when consistency levels are generally low for a given truth table or when there is a respective row that carries a lot of empirical weight, and which comes near the 0.75 consistency threshold (e.g., a row with 0.74 consistency with an important case that should be retained for the truth table analysis). However, rather than using a low threshold, I recommend revisiting the research design (chapter 2) and the calibration of conditions (chapter 5) in order to construct a more consistent truth table.

8. Duşa's (2019b, 177) argument departs from Schneider and Wagemann (2012, 166), who suggest that "the formula without any assumptions is not necessarily the most complex one." Irrespective of these differences, it is apt to use the term *conservative* solution, as Schneider and Wagemann (2012, 162) propose, because this solution makes no counterfactual assumptions.

9. The intermediate solution is at times reduced solely to these "directional expectations." However, Ragin apparently used the term only in a working paper (Ragin 2003b), whereas his many discussions of simplifying assumptions make no reference to it but convey a broader understanding that emphasizes *plausibility* as a key criterion (Ragin 2000, 2008a, 2009b). As Ragin notes (2008b, 162), the distinction between easy and difficult counterfactuals "is not a rigid dichotomy, but rather a continuum of plausibility" that rests "primarily on the state of existing theoretical and substantive knowledge in the social scientific community at large." For broader conceptions of the intermediate solution in empirical applications, see, among many others, Maggetti and Levi-Faur (2013), Mello (2020), and Vis, Woldendorp, and Keman (2013).

10. The solution terms can occasionally be *identical*. Apart from the situation of a complete truth table without logical remainder rows (which happens rarely), this can occur when the logical remainders do not allow for further minimization or when the assumptions made for the intermediate solution effectively match those for the other solutions.

11. The Venn diagrams serve to illustrate the relationship between the solution types, without taking into account degrees of fuzzy-set membership in the underlying data.

12. To foster this aim, I have streamlined the terminology and reduced it to what I regard as essential differences between the concepts used by various authors. Readers are encouraged to consult the referenced sources for complementary accounts.

13. These are also referred to as "contradictory simplifying assumptions" (Yamasaki and Rihoux 2009, 136) and are subsumed under the category "incoherent counterfactuals" (Schneider and Wagemann 2012, 198). To avoid ambiguity, I use the latter term only for remainders that conflict with necessary conditions.

14. Ragin notes this problem in his conversation with Jerry Mendel, recommending the exclusion of logical remainders that do not show an identified necessary condition (Mendel and Ragin 2011, 25).

15. I use the term *plausible counterfactuals* because it resonates closely with the core idea of "plausibility" in counterfactual reasoning (Ragin 2000, 300–308; 2008a; 2009b). A related but broader term is "good counterfactuals," which further entails nonsimplifying logical remainders (Schneider and Wagemann 2012, 212).

8 • QCA Variants

It is the set-theoretic foundation from which all other
features of this family of methods derive.

—CARSTEN SCHNEIDER AND CLAUDIUS WAGEMANN

This book has focused on the crisp-set and fuzzy-set variants of QCA. These are the most popular and widely used variants of the method, as was shown in the cross-discipline survey of empirical QCA applications (chapter 2). Yet QCA comprises a whole family of approaches under the big tent of *set-theoretic methods*, as indicated in the opening quotation by Carsten Schneider and Claudius Wagemann (see also Rihoux and Ragin 2009).[1] This chapter introduces four major variants and approaches of QCA, to complement the foregoing discussion and to give new users an idea of the respective strengths and limitations. These are multivalue QCA, temporal QCA, fuzzy-set ideal type analysis, and two-step QCA. For some of these, a vast literature has developed. Rather than trying to summarize all the contributions that have been made over the years, my aim for this chapter is to provide concise introductions, so that readers can make an informed choice about what to pursue for their specific research aims. The chapter concludes with a brief look into additional variants and alternatives to QCA, such as Necessary Condition Analysis (NCA), MDSO-MSDO designs, and Coincidence Analysis (CNA).

MULTIVALUE QCA

When designing QCA studies, a recurrent challenge with crisp and fuzzy sets is that the former require the data to be dichotomized and the latter call for the definition of a crossover between being *inside* as opposed to *outside* the target set. Hence, despite their gradations, fuzzy sets effectively entail only two qualitative states. These limitations spurred the development of multivalue QCA (mvQCA), pioneered by Lasse

Cronqvist, who also developed the accompanying Tosmana software (Cronqvist 2004; Cronqvist and Berg-Schlosser 2009).[2]

As the name implies, the idea behind multivalue QCA is that conditions are allowed to take on several different values. This means that *categorical data* with three or more different values can be used in the analysis. These kinds of data are also referred to as *polychotomous*, as in being divided into many classes or parts. The advantage of mvQCA is that polychotomous data can be used more or less *as they are*, without having to introduce a dichotomous threshold for crisp sets or empirical anchors for fuzzy-set calibration.

For example, imagine we wanted to study the relationship between individuals' employment status and their life satisfaction. Rather than distinguishing solely between *employed* and *unemployed*, we may also want to include a separate category for *employed at minimum wage*, because we expect this group of people to show different characteristics from those who are working for a regular salary above the minimum wage. With multivalue QCA, we can include a condition with different values in our study: *unemployed, employed at minimum wage*, and *employed above minimum wage*. Of course, one could also introduce two crisp-set conditions to capture these differences. Apart from creating additional conditions, the downside of such an approach would be that it can easily create impossible combinations like *unemployed at minimum wage* (see the discussion of untenable assumptions in chapter 7).

Although multivalue QCA follows the same protocol for the analysis of necessary conditions and the minimization of the truth table, there are three important differences when compared with crisp- and fuzzy-set QCA (Cronqvist and Berg-Schlosser 2009). First, the *notation* is different, because for each condition, the value or *level* must be specified. By convention, this is done in curly brackets: In our example, *employment*{2} refers to employment above minimum wage, whereas *employment*{1} indicates employment at minimum wage, and *employment*{0} reflects unemployment.[3]

The second difference relates to the size of the *truth table*. Because multivalue conditions exist at different levels, each of them can logically combine with other conditions at their respective levels. This means that the truth table *grows exponentially* with each multivalue condition. To calculate the total number of possible combinations, we thus need to multiply the *number of levels* for each condition. For example, in a study with 4 conditions, 3 of which have 3 levels each and where the 3rd condition is a crisp set with 2 possible levels, the calculation of the size of the truth table yields 54 rows:

$$3_A \times 3_B \times 3_C \times 2_D = 54 \text{ rows}$$

By contrast, if the same study had used only crisp- or fuzzy-set conditions, the truth table would have consisted of only 16 rows:

$$2^{(A, B, C, D)} = 2^4 = 16 \text{ rows}$$

The final difference relates to *Boolean minimization* and the polychotomous nature of the conditions, which means that multivalue QCA requires an adapted version of the Boolean minimization rule (Ragin 1987, 93), introduced in chapter 7: "A condition can be considered irrelevant if a number of logical expressions differ in only this condition and produce the same outcome, *and if all possible values of this condition are included in these logical expressions*" (emphasis added) (Cronqvist and Berg-Schlosser 2009, 74).

How does this affect the minimization procedure? To illustrate the process, let us take an example with a crisp-set condition C, a multilevel condition M (with three levels), and the outcome O. Imagine that the truth table contains three rows that consistently lead to the outcome. All of these contain the presence of the crisp-set condition C, combined with M at each of the possible levels:

$$C\{1\} \cdot M\{0\} + C\{1\} \cdot M\{1\} + C\{1\} \cdot M\{2\} \rightarrow O \tag{1}$$

Under these circumstances, we can consider M *irrelevant*, because whenever C is present, it leads to the outcome O, irrespective of M's level (and all three levels are covered). Hence, we can minimize the primitive expressions from line 1 to reach this simpler statement in line 2:

$$C\{1\} \rightarrow O \tag{2}$$

This simple example demonstrates that multivalue conditions *increase the requirements* for Boolean minimization. To erase a multivalue condition from a complex expression, we need empirical cases for each level, and all of them need to share the remaining configuration and the outcome.

An Applied Example of Multivalue QCA

How does mvQCA look in practice? To illustrate some of the differences and similarities, let us look at a published study. In his article on judicial independence, Pablo Castillo Ortiz (2017) examines the conditions under which councils of the judiciary are perceived by judges as impediments to their judicial independence (see box 8.1). The article draws on a cross-national survey conducted by the European Network of Councils of the Judiciary, which informs several of the conditions used. The study includes 17 cases, representing different European jurisdictions. The four explanatory conditions include three crisp sets and one multivalue condition, whereas the outcome is also multivalue (the calibration of the multivalue condition and outcome are summarized in table 8.1).

The outcome *disrespectful council* is a multivalue condition based on the share of respondents who indicate that their judicial independence has not been respected

Box 8.1 Using Multivalue QCA to Study Councils of the Judiciary and Judges' Perceptions with Respect to Their Independence

Pablo Castillo-Ortiz, School of Law at the University of Sheffield

The multivalue QCA study (Castillo Ortiz 2017) is part of my research line about higher judicial actors in Europe, in which I have explored mainly constitutional courts and judicial councils. My academic work on these institutions is at the crossroads of law and politics, and it has focused on aspects such as the causes of the design of these institutions, their process of decision-making, and their effect on public perceptions of the judiciary as a whole.

In my academic work, I have often used Qualitative Comparative Analysis as my main method of research. In fact, QCA methods have seldom been used to tackle law-related research inquiries. Although there are some precedents in the area of legal and judicial studies, the use of configurational methods in the field of legal research is still rather limited. By way of hypothesis, my intuition is that this might simply be the result of the predominance of doctrinal and theoretical pieces in the legal field, to the detriment of empirical research methods in general. This is regrettable, because QCA has an enormous potential for researchers seeking to understand legal dynamics and phenomena.

In this piece in particular, I decided to use QCA because I wanted to understand the interactions between explanatory conditions in the production of outcomes. From the outset, I hypothesized that the phenomena that I wanted to explore—judges' perceptions of disrespect for their independence by judicial councils—had a configurational causation. This was based on my preliminary knowledge of certain cases that I had studied beforehand, notably the Spanish case. In Spain, two interesting circumstances converged: the judicial council is powerful, and the system of appointment of its members had been criticized as too political. QCA allowed me to understand interactions between explanatory conditions like these in a systematic and rigorous way. In this paper, the multivalue version of QCA was used, because there were conditions that were multichotomous in nature; for instance, the system of appointment of members of judicial councils, which I classified into political, apolitical, or hybrid.

The evidence offered by the paper is preliminary, and future research will be necessary to confirm the results, especially with analyses at the level of individual judges and with more high-quality data. However, I believe that the findings of the paper are interesting and that they tell something relevant

(*continued*)

Box 8.1 (*continued*)

about judicial councils. In particular, the paper shows that certain institutional designs of judicial councils—for instance, powerful judicial councils controlled by political actors or interest groups—can have a negative impact on the self-perception of the independence of judges, so such designs might have to be rethought or simply avoided. Thus, QCA has also a strong potential for evidence-based assessment and the design of legal-political institutions.

Table 8.1 Multivalue Condition and Outcome

Multivalue Condition/ Outcome (Selection)	Multivalue Operationalization	Sources
Outcome: High perception of disrespect for judicial independence	$\{2\} = X_i > 9.5\%$ $\{1\} = 4.5\% > X_i > 9.5\%$ $\{0\} = X_i < 4.5\%$	European Network of Councils of the Judiciary questionnaire, share of respondents who indicated that their independence as judges had been not respected by the council of the judiciary
Condition: Nature of the appointment procedure for members of the councils of the judiciary	$\{2\}$ = Primarily political $\{1\}$ = Hybrid $\{0\}$ = Primarily judicial or apolitical	EU Justice Scoreboard and European Network of Councils of the Judiciary website (fact sheets on member states), secondary literature

Source: Castillo Ortiz (2017).

by judicial councils. For cases where this exceeds 9.5 percent, a level of 2 is assigned, whereas a level of 1 is given for a share between 4.5 and 9.5 percent, and a share of less than 4.5 percent results in a level of 0. The multilevel condition *appointment* reflects whether the nomination procedure for the judicial council is controlled by the judiciary itself without any political influence (level 0), whether the procedure is controlled by political actors (level 2), or whether the appointment procedure shows traces of both and can thus be considered a hybrid (level 1).

As mentioned above, the analytical protocol for mvQCA follows the standard procedure described in chapter 7. Yet, because the study by Castillo Ortiz (2017) contains a multilevel outcome, each level needs to be analyzed on its own. Hence, the article contains separate analyses for a *high perception of disrespect* (outcome $\{2\}$), a *low perception of disrespect* (outcome $\{0\}$), and a *moderate perception of disrespect* (outcome $\{1\}$).

Table 8.2   Truth Table with Multivalue Conditions

A	P	C	T	OUT	N	Consistency	PRI	Cases {Outcome Value}
0	1	1	1	1	1	1.00	1.00	BGR {2}
0	1	1	2	1	1	1.00	1.00	PRT {2}
1	1	0	0	1	1	1.00	1.00	ITA {2}
1	1	0	2	1	1	1.00	1.00	ESP{2}
1	0	0	0	0	3	0.33	0.33	LVA {1}, GBR-NIR {2}, GBR-SCO {0}
0	0	0	0	0	3	0.00	0.00	IRL {0}, POL {0}, GBR-ENG {0}
0	0	0	1	0	2	0.00	0.00	BEL {0}, DNK {0}
0	1	0	1	0	2	0.00	0.00	ROU {1}, SVN {1}
0	0	0	2	0	1	0.00	0.00	NLD {0}
0	0	1	1	0	1	0.00	0.00	SVK {1}
0	1	1	0	0	1	0.00	0.00	LTU {1}
0	0	1	0	?	0	—	—	—
0	0	1	2	?	0	—	—	—
0	1	0	0	?	0	—	—	—
0	1	0	2	?	0	—	—	—
1	0	0	1	?	0	—	—	—
1	0	0	2	?	0	—	—	—
1	0	1	0	?	0	—	—	—
1	0	1	1	?	0	—	—	—
1	0	1	2	?	0	—	—	—
1	1	0	1	?	0	—	—	—
1	1	1	0	?	0	—	—	—
1	1	1	1	?	0	—	—	—
1	1	1	2	?	0	—	—	—

Source: Castillo Ortiz (2017).
Note: A: Association; P: Powers; C: Corruption; T: Appointment.

Table 8.2 shows the truth table for the outcome high perception of disrespect (OUT). For illustrative purposes, the table also contains logical remainder rows, and cases' outcome values are given in curly brackets in the right-hand column. We can see how multilevel conditions further differentiate the truth table: Bulgaria and Portugal, in the first two rows, have nearly identical configurations, and both show the same level in the outcome. But because the countries differ in the multivalue condition *appointment*, they end up on different truth table rows.

With one multivalue condition and three crisp-set conditions, the number of truth table rows equals $3 \times 2 \times 2 \times 2 = 24$ rows. Eleven of these are filled with empirical cases, while 13 are logical remainders. By comparison, if the study had used solely crisp and/or fuzzy sets, then there would have been only 16 rows (2^4), and nine of these would have been filled with empirical cases. Here, the difference is rather small, because there is only one multivalue condition. But the calculation illustrates the exponential increase of limited diversity that is at stake when multivalue conditions are introduced.

Finally, let us have a look at some of the study's results, which are summarized in table 8.3. The table displays the *intermediate solution*, based on directional expectations, where the presence of a crisp-set condition and level 2 of the multilevel condition are associated with the outcome, as reported by Castillo Ortiz (2017, 327). This yields four paths, the first two of which are populated by Spain and Italy, which share the expression A · P, but differ in their appointment procedure (multilevel condition T). Similarly, Bulgaria and Portugal both show the conjunction P · C but differ in their values for T. Apart from notational differences, the mvQCA results can be reported in the same fashion as other QCA studies. Yet, because the levels must be included, the notation becomes more complex and less intuitive to read.

In sum, multivalue QCA presents a viable alternative for studies where conditions cannot be adequately transformed into crisp sets or where researchers want to keep a distinction between more than two qualitative levels in a condition that cannot be expressed with fuzzy sets. Moreover, given the integration of mvQCA in the QCA package for R (Duşa 2019b) and the existence of the stand-alone software Tosmana (Cronqvist 2019), it is straightforward for users to implement the multivalue variant, also because the analytical procedure closely resembles a standard QCA routine. Previously, it was not possible to have a multivalue outcome (Cronqvist and Berg-Schlosser 2009, 84), but this limitation has been resolved with recent software developments (Duşa 2019b), and is shown in the example above (Castillo Ortiz 2017).

That being said, the *increased complexity* of mvQCA presents a challenge that is not easily overcome. The truth table becomes substantially larger with every multivalue condition. For this reason, most mvQCA applications limit the number of actual multivalue conditions and use mostly crisp-set conditions. This is in line with recommendations on multivalue QCA (Cronqvist and Berg-Schlosser 2009), namely, to use a *maximum of two to three multivalue conditions*, irrespective of the overall number of conditions included in a study. We can see this in many published applications of mvQCA, for example, in the studies by Feliciano de Sá Guimarães and Maria Hermínia Tavares de Almeida (2017), Tim Haesebrouck (2018), and Giulia Mariani (2020), apart from the study by Pablo Castillo Ortiz (2017) discussed above and introduced by the author in box 8.1. All these articles include just one or two conditions that take on multiple values and use crisp sets for the remaining conditions (see also the review by Alrik Thiem 2013).

The challenges and critical points about multivalue QCA are reflected in a debate about the relative merits of this approach. Critics point out that the logic of polychotomous conditions is difficult to reconcile with set theory because membership in crisp or fuzzy sets "is essentially different" from membership in multivalue conditions (Vink and van Vliet 2009; 2013, 213). As Schneider and Wagemann (2012, 259) argue, "If

Table 8.3 Multivalue QCA: Intermediate Solution Term

Path		Relation	Consistency	PRI	Raw Coverage	Unique Coverage	Cases
Intermediate solution			1.00	1.00	0.80	–	–
1	A{1}·P{1}·T{2}	+	1.00	1.00	0.20	0.20	Spain
2	A{1}·P{1}·T{0}	+	1.00	1.00	0.20	0.20	Italy
3	P{1}·C{1}·T{1}	+	1.00	1.00	0.20	0.20	Bulgaria
4	P{1}·C{1}·T{2}	→OUT	1.00	1.00	0.20	0.20	Portugal

Source: Castillo Ortiz (2017).
Note: A: Association; P: Powers; C: Corruption; T: Appointment. Directional expectations: A {1}, P {1}, C {1}, T {2}.

there is no non-membership, it suggests that multi-value variables are indeed not sets." Moreover, mvQCA amplifies limited diversity and this brings along the problem of *untenable assumptions* once logical remainders are used to minimize the truth table, especially if the standard parsimonious solution is used (Schneider and Wagemann 2012, 261). This problem is magnified by the recommendation that in mvQCA "logical remainders have to be included in larger data sets to obtain meaningful results" (Cronqvist and Berg-Schlosser 2009, 76). Supporters of mvQCA have responded by showing the value added in using mvQCA rather than crisp- or fuzzy-set variants, pointing to examples of published research (Haesebrouck 2016) and arguing that some of the criticism against mvQCA is misguided (Thiem 2013).

To conclude, the decision whether to use multivalue QCA should be primarily based on the target concept. If this cannot suitably be expressed as a crisp or fuzzy set, then one should consider mvQCA. In any event, multiple-value conditions should be used sparingly and, as always, solution terms must be scrutinized for their simplifying assumptions (see chapter 7). Although limited diversity is an issue for all QCA variants, mvQCA is particularly prone to large numbers of logical remainders, due to the further growth of the truth table once multivalue conditions are introduced.

TEMPORAL QCA

One particular limitation of QCA is that it is a *static* approach, as noted in chapter 2 on research design. This means that all the conditions in a QCA study are treated in the same way and the analysis does not consider the timing or sequence in which the included conditions appeared. For many research aims, this is fine. However, for some topics, *timing* is crucial, and it may even be the most important part of the analysis (Büthe 2002; Sewell 1996).

For example, most scholars of democratization would agree that a successful democratic transition requires a minimum level of peace and stability, functioning state structures, free and fair elections, and an independent judiciary. Yet there is disagreement about which of these factors should come first. Should democratic elections be held as early as possible, or should these be preceded by the creation of political institutions? With a standard QCA analysis, these factors would only be compared as static conditions, which would allow us neither to assess when something occurred (*timing*) nor which condition preceded another condition (*sequence*).

That said, there are suitable approaches to how timing and sequence can be incorporated in the *research design* of a QCA study. Clearly, the most forthright way is by including observations (cases) at different points in time. For example, instead of looking at a single case per country, we could include separate cases for each government cabinet, or we could use predefined periods of time as cases (as in yearly observations, months, or days). In fact, many QCA applications have used such approaches to *indirectly incorporate time* in their *casing* (e.g., Fagerholm 2014; Mello 2020; Vis 2011; Wurster and Hagemann 2018).

Another option is to address timing and sequence in the *conceptualization and calibration* of conditions. In this vein, instead of calibrating a set "economic strength" on the basis of gross domestic product at a given point in time (based on yearly statistics), we could conceptualize "economic growth" from one point in time to another. The resulting percentages in growth could serve as a basis for the calibration procedure. Finally, time could also be taken into account by assigning *time-sensitive membership scores* to cases. As such, we might attribute different scores to cases based on whether an event happened sooner or later. This is done by Mello (2012, 433), where the outcome "military participation" in the Iraq War takes into account the *time of deployment*, assigning lower scores to later events, because the legal status of the military operation changed over time and thus arguably affected political calculations. Another way to address time is by *reconstructing the historical sequence* after the QCA analysis, as is done by Stefan Lindemann and Andreas Wimmer (2018, 315) in their analysis of conflict escalation. Notably, the authors find that across the 21 cases covered by their solution, "there is only one temporal sequence to ethnic war." These are examples of the many feasible ways in which timing and sequence can be incorporated at the research design stage.

Apart from these approaches to acknowledge timing and sequence through research design, inroads have been made to formally incorporate time in the analytical procedure of QCA (Caren and Panofsky 2005; García-Castro and Ariño 2016; Hino 2009; Pagliarin and Gerrits 2020; Ragin and Strand 2008). The first attempt was made by Neal Caren and Aaron Panofsky (2005), who developed temporal QCA (tQCA) as an approach to manually combine QCA with the analysis of sequences. This was taken up by Charles Ragin and Sarah Strand (2008), who showed how tQCA could be implemented in the existing software, but who also pointed out pitfalls in the analytical procedure of tQCA. Notably, Airo Hino (2009) developed a related approach, which he termed time-series QCA (TS/QCA).

Essentially, tQCA introduces another logical operator to indicate whether a condition came before another condition (as in *A before B* or *B before A*). Cases are coded accordingly: they can receive a score of 1 (if A happened before B), a score of 0 (if both conditions are present but A did not come before B), or a dash sign "−" to indicate *don't care* cases. These are cases where either of the two conditions is not present and where it is thus not possible to say that one preceded the other.

To illustrate the procedure, let us take a simple example: with three conditions—A, B, and C—there are six logically possible sequences how these conditions can appear in empirical data, as summarized in table 8.4. Notably, this is based on the assumption that sequences can only comprise the *presence* of conditions, understood as their

Table 8.4   Possible Sequences with Three Conditions

Sequence	1st	2nd	3rd
1	A	B	C
2	A	C	B
3	B	A	C
4	C	A	B
5	B	C	A
6	C	B	A

occurrence (*A happened before B, which happened before C*, and so forth). Otherwise, there would be many more combinations of conditions.

These possible sequences need to be added to the truth table. To take our example, this would mean that there is not just a single row with the configuration, where all three conditions are present (A·B·C), but *six rows* with different sequences of these three conditions. Based on this logic, we can see that the truth table grows explosively with tQCA. This is the reason why tQCA should only be used with very low numbers of conditions. Again, this is a trade-off: we can either focus on two or three conditions and also explore their sequence (if that is imperative for our research aim), or we can include more conditions for a more comprehensive account, but then we cannot include timing in a formalized way as through tQCA.

Questions of temporality remain an intriguing area of research. Along those lines, Roberto García-Castro and Miguel Ariño (2016) developed diagnostic tools for the set-theoretic analysis of panel data with cross-sectional observations. Recently, Sofia Pagliarin and Lasse Gerrits (2020) proposed Trajectory-Based QCA (TJ-QCA), to account for within-case time variation, building on the approach put forth by Hino (2009). For further discussions of timing and sequence, see De Meur, Rihoux, and Yamasaki (2009, 161–63); Schneider and Wagemann (2012, 269–73); Duşa (2019b, 209–13); and Kahwati and Kane (2020, 189–95). For a discussion of temporality with a focus on policy processes in comparative public policy, see Fischer and Maggetti (2017).

TWO-STEP QCA

One of the persistent challenges of comparative research is *limited diversity*. In the set-theoretic context, this means that the number of logically possible configurations exceeds the number of empirical cases (see chapter 2). This problem increases with each condition that is added to the analysis, which is one reason why researchers should not use more than a moderate number of conditions for most types of QCA applications. The other reason is that solutions tend to become increasingly complex and difficult to interpret with more conditions.

This was the starting point for Schneider and Wagemann (2006) to suggest a *two-step approach* to QCA. Distinguishing between *remote* and *proximate* conditions, this approach splits up the analysis into separate truth table procedures. The first stage entails running an analysis solely with remote conditions. These can be conceived of as "context" or "structure" conditions that are expected to influence the outcome, but only in an *indirect way* through actors, institutions, organizations, and the like. The latter are examples of proximate conditions, which can be regarded as factors that are *causally closer* to the outcome, and which can have an immediate impact on the phenomenon of interest. For instance, these could be politicians who vote on a motion, bureaucrats who formulate a directive, institutions in charge of implementing policies, or judges deciding on legal cases.

During the first step of two-step QCA, an analysis is conducted with all the remote conditions, to identify "outcome-enabling conditions" (Schneider and Wagemann 2006, 761). Because this part of the analysis is intentionally "underspecified," a lower consistency threshold is deemed acceptable (Schneider and Wagemann 2012, 254). For the second step, the solution paths from the first step are placed in QCA analyses, together with all the proximate conditions. In practice, this means that new conditions are created, one for each of the solution paths from the first step, and these are inserted into separate truth table procedures during the second step.[4]

Effectively, two-step QCA thus reduces the number of conditions that are used in a single analysis by splitting up the procedure and eliminating some of the remote conditions after the first step, which reduces limited diversity. It also allows a comparison between different outcome-enabling contexts. Another reason why two-step QCA has been well received lies in the adaptability of the concept of remote and proximate conditions. These resonate with many social science theories and can thus be easily applied to research designs across academic fields.

Two-step applications have examined such diverse topics as women in political leadership positions (Inguanzo 2020), regulatory agencies in policymaking (Maggetti 2009), democratic regression and breakdown (Tomini and Wagemann 2018), policies addressing deforestation (Brockhaus et al. 2017; Korhonen-Kurki et al. 2014),[5] equal pay laws and their institutionalization (Laux 2016), contributions to UN peacekeeping operations (Haesebrouck 2015a), large dam projects and resettlements (Kirchherr, Ahrenshop, and Charles 2019), and e-mobility policies (Held and Gerrits 2019). In the next subsection, we look at the study by Tomini and Wagemann (2018) to illustrate the two-step research process. For another example, see box 8.2, where Maria Brockhaus and colleagues share insights on the research project behind their QCA studies (Brockhaus et al. 2017; Korhonen-Kurki et al. 2014), and why they chose two-step QCA for these.

**Box 8.2   Using Two-Step QCA to Explain (the Lack of)
Transformational Policy Change for REDD+**

*Maria Brockhaus, University of Helsinki; Jenniver Sehring,
IHE Delft; Kaisa Korhonen-Kurki, University of Helsinki;
and Monica Di Gregorio, University of Leeds*

Deforestation in the tropics is one of the most persistent environmental, social, and economic problems of our times, embedded in complex domestic and international politics, economics, and power relations. In the early 2000s a global mechanism to reduce emissions through avoided deforestation and forest degradation and other activities (called REDD+) was introduced under the UN Framework Convention on Climate Change. Shortly thereafter, we had the opportunity (the funding, and access to a widespread network of fellow researchers in the tropics working for decades on the issue of deforestation), to investigate the question of what enables (or hinders) policy change to effectively halt deforestation.

As part of a global research effort on REDD+ led by the Centre for International Forest Research, we designed a comparative analysis of 15 countries, through case studies and analysis of institutions, discourses, policy networks, and policy documents (Brockhaus et al. 2017; Korhonen-Kurki et al. 2014). We chose QCA, because of its potential to deliver rigorous analysis to inform policy and practice on the expected complex and diverse pathways to achieve carbon-effective, cost-efficient, and equitable REDD+ policy design, implementation, and outcomes.

Country experts played a key role in the identification, selection, and assessment of factors to be included as remote and proximate conditions for our two-step QCA. They made the first round of assessment of conditions for their case; and after that, all the assessments were discussed and compared in a joint workshop. Through this process, country experts could set their case knowledge in relation to other cases while project coordinators and researchers at the global level could strengthen their overview across the cases. We found this particularly important to ensure a joint understanding of the indicators and thresholds for each condition and consistency in the assessment (there were more than 60 country experts involved). Data collection and assessment were conducted in 2012, in 2014, and in 2016, with a further round in progress.

One of the benefits for us as researchers was that QCA helped us structure our data and engage with case specifics without losing track of theory. The two-step QCA reflects our theoretical assumptions about a wider enabling

(*continued*)

Box 8.2 *(continued)*

institutional environment (*remote conditions*), and the factors mostly related to the actors in the policy arena (*proximate conditions*), which are closer to the outcome and less stable over time.

One of the biggest challenges for our QCA analysis was the lack of stability and the dynamics in the emerging REDD+ policy domain, which made it hard to measure the outcome consistently with the same indicators. Ideally, the outcome would have been measured in reduced emissions in tCO_2 from deforestation per country, but our analysis was too early for measurable results of REDD+ at a national scale. We solved this by using a *process-oriented outcome*, which required a careful definition of the assessment criteria to avoid overlap with the conditions supposed to explain presence or absence of our outcome. In order to reflect the developments in the policy arena, we increased the threshold for a positive assessment in the second and third rounds. We also included other conditions in the analysis based on new insights and discussions. Although this solved the issues with the individual analysis in each year, it makes comparison over the three rounds of data collections challenging.

Another challenge we faced was to explain the application of QCA in our publications and presentations, so that it is was accessible enough for readers (and reviewers) interested in REDD+ and not familiar with the method, while being detailed enough for those who are—starting with the specific *terminology*. As a result, we often ended up with contradicting reviews—asking for either more or less case material, or more or less methodical reflections. We would have wished to learn more from and with reviewers on the method, in particular the two-step application, and our thematic area, but the combination of both is hard to find. Our advice would be to think carefully about reviewers to suggest who can provide you with a sound review of the application of the method.

AN APPLIED EXAMPLE OF TWO-STEP QCA

To illustrate how two-step QCA works in practice, let us have a look at an example. Luca Tomini and Claudius Wagemann (2018, 695) apply the two-step approach to explain under which conditions *democratic breakdown* occurs, which is understood as the transformation of democracies into hybrid or authoritarian regimes. Their analysis entails 59 cases of democratic regression, as in countries that experienced "a negative trend in democratic performance." Tomini and Wagemann include a total of nine conditions, which are split into six remote conditions and three proximate conditions. The *remote conditions* are (1) economic development, (2) economic inequality, (3) the fragmentation of the party system, (4) the duration of democracy, (5) ethnolinguistic fractionalization, and (6) the external context, which relates to the political systems of neighboring countries. The *proximate conditions* are (7) concentration of executive power, (8) the volatility of the party system, and (9) social instability. As we can see, these conditions cover a wide range of economic, political, and social aspects that can be expected to impact upon democratic breakdown. However, if all these were used in the same analysis, this would yield a truth table with 512 rows (2^9), an overwhelming majority of which would be logical remainders.

Here, the two-step approach helps to keep the number of conditions manageable, by dividing the analysis into two parts. During the first step, the six remote conditions are analyzed on their own, the results of which are summarized in table 8.5. We can see that four of the six remote conditions appear in the solution, where they constitute three distinct paths to the outcome. This is a *preliminary* solution that merely serves to establish the context conditions to be used in the second step. This is also why the low consistency of 0.656 is acceptable at this stage. For the second step of the analysis, Tomini and Wagemann (2018) create conditions for each of the three paths from table 8.5 and use them as conditions to complement the three proximate conditions.[6] The results of the second step are shown in table 8.6. We can see that the solution now reaches solid consistency and coverage scores. Effectively, the four paths occur under

Table 8.5   Two-Step QCA: Analysis of Remote Conditions

	Path		
Two-Step Analysis (First Step)	1	2	3
Remote conditions			
Economic development		⊗	●
Economic inequality	●		
Party system			
Duration of democracy			
Ethnolinguistic fractionalization		●	
External context			⊗
Consistency	0.77	0.65	0.77
Raw coverage	0.67	0.75	0.25
Unique coverage	0.10	0.23	0.02
Solution consistency		0.66	
Solution coverage		0.92	

Source: Tomini and Wagemann (2018).
Note: The black circles indicate the presence of a condition; the crossed-out circles indicate its absence.

Table 8.6   Two-Step QCA: Analysis of Remote and Proximate Conditions

Two-Step Analysis (Second Step)	Path			
	1	**2**	**3**	**4**
Remote conditions				
Economic development	⊗	⊗	⊗	
Economic inequality				●
Ethnolinguistic fractionalization	●	●	●	
Proximate conditions				
Concentration of executive power	●		●	●
Volatility of the party system	●	●		
Social instability		●	●	●
Consistency	0.88	0.86	0.82	0.88
Raw coverage	0.45	0.37	0.46	0.49
Unique coverage	0.14	0.05	0.06	0.13
Covered cases	BO2; BR; DO1; GM1; MR1; NG; PE; PH2; SE; VE2	BO1, 2; BR; DO1; EC2; ML2; PG1; PE	BO2; BR; CO2; DO1; IN1, 3; MW; PG2; PE; PH1; TH; VE1	AR2; BO2; BR; CO2; DO1; LS; MW; MX; PG2; TR
Solution consistency	0.83			
Solution coverage	0.79			

Source: Tomini and Wagemann (2018).
Note: The black circles indicate the presence of a condition; the crossed-out circles indicate its absence.

two different contexts (~DEVELO · ETHNOF for the first three paths and INEQUA for the last).

In sum, the two-step approach addresses the central problem of having too many conditions and logical remainders and thereby effectively "reduces complexity," as aimed for by Schneider and Wagemann (2006, 2012). A positive side effect is that the conceptual distinction between remote and proximate conditions resonates with various social science theories. Hence, many researchers should find it easy to translate their theoretical frameworks into two-step designs.

However, it should be noted that the two-step approach also entails downsides. Although the sequential analysis reduces the number of conditions that are used in a single truth table analysis, it also *increases* complexity because it leads to more truth tables and thus more solution terms, which poses a challenge for the substantive interpretation and the effective communication of QCA results. For example, if the first step yields three outcome-enabling contexts, this means that three additional truth table procedures must be run. If each of these also yields three solution paths, then a total of nine paths would need to be discussed and interpreted. For a journal publication, this is hardly feasible unless results are picked out selectively—which might provoke criticism due to the opacity of the process.

This point still applies, even when the solution paths from the first step are all inserted into a single truth table in the second step, as done by Tomini and Wagemann (2018) in the example discussed above. Moreover, though the concept of remote and proximate conditions has theoretical resonance, it appears that empirical applications do not always provide the necessary theoretical *reasoning* why some conditions are regarded as remote and others are seen as proximate. But without a well-grounded justification for this distinction, there will be many "moving parts" in a two-step study, because another setup and sequence in the conditions might yield different results. Here, the burden of proof is upon the researcher to justify that the distinction is plausible and required—as opposed to a more concise study with fewer conditions in a single truth table analysis (see chapter 2 on approaches to condition selection).

Recently, Schneider (2019) has reevaluated the two-step approach and, acknowledging weaknesses in the original procedure, has suggested a change in the analytical protocol to focus on *necessary conditions* during the first stage of the analysis. Essentially, the revised first step would be about finding "necessary contexts" for the sufficient terms to be identified in the second step (Schneider 2019, 1117). In a response to Schneider's suggestions for reformulating the two-step approach, Tim Haesebrouck (2019, 2766) has proposed an "alternative update" to improve the standard two-step protocol. Among others, this entails a new measure for "cumulative coverage." It remains to be seen whether users will adopt the suggested changes or continue using the original protocol for two-step QCA, but those interested in the two-step approach are advised to take these proposals into account when designing their QCA study.

FUZZY–SET IDEAL TYPE ANALYSIS

Fuzzy-set ideal type analysis was developed by Jon Kvist (1999, 2007), who applied it to compare Nordic welfare state regimes to preconceived ideal types. As the name indicates, the approach builds on fuzzy-set QCA (Ragin 2000, 2008b). However, unlike set-theoretic analysis, fuzzy-set ideal type analysis does not seek to identify necessary and/or sufficient conditions nor does it aim to develop an explanation for an outcome. Instead, fuzzy-set ideal type analysis is directed at *systematic empirical comparison* and *typological theorizing.*

The approach makes use of the fact that fuzzy sets describe an attribute space, where each case can be located in relation to preconceived ideal types. In empirical reality, most cases will not be "perfect" expressions of an ideal type (equated with a fuzzy score of 1), but they may come close to this ideal (fuzzy scores less than 1 but larger than 0.5). Fuzzy-set ideal type analysis can be particularly fruitful where a body of theory exists from which to derive distinct ideal types. For example, research on democracy and democratic subtypes (Lijphart 1968), organization research (Fiss 2011), or state behavior in international security (Elman 2005) would fit this description.

Although less well-known than some of the other QCA variants, fuzzy-set ideal type analysis has seen a range of applications in the study of welfare state regimes (Hudson and Kühner 2012; Vis 2007, 2010), and various dimensions of social policies (An and Peng 2016; Ciccia and Verloo 2012; Gran 2003), but there have also been applications in the areas of public health (Saltkjel et al. 2017) and communication (Büchel et al. 2016).[7]

AN EXAMPLE OF FUZZY-SET IDEAL TYPE ANALYSIS

Let us have a look at an example, to see how fuzzy-set ideal type analysis works in practice. As part of her analysis of welfare state reform in advanced democracies, Barbara Vis (2010) also conducted a fuzzy-set ideal type analysis, in addition to standard QCA analyses. Table 8.7 summarizes the five types of welfare regimes that Vis derived from the literature (Vis 2010, 60). We can see that the ideal types are defined along three conditions: *activation* (A), *benefit generosity* (G), and *employment protection* (P). It follows that there are eight different types of how these three conditions can be

Table 8.7 Fuzzy–Set Ideal Types

Ideal Type	Activation	Generosity	Protection
Social democratic welfare	●	●	●
Generous workfare	●	●	⊗
Conservative welfare	⊗	●	●
—	●	⊗	●
Lean workfare	●	⊗	⊗
—	⊗	⊗	●
—	⊗	●	⊗
Liberal welfare	⊗	⊗	⊗

Source: Vis (2010, 60).
Note: The black circles indicate the presence of a condition; the crossed-out circles indicate its absence.

Table 8.8 Membership in Fuzzy-Set Ideal Types

Ideal Type	A	G	P	France			Netherlands		
				1985	1995	2002	1985	1995	2002
Social democratic welfare	●	●	●	0.07	0.24	0.40	0.18	0.50	0.70
Generous workfare	●	●	⊗	0.07	0.05	0.05	0.09	0.30	0.30
Conservative welfare	⊗	●	●	0.75	0.76	0.60	0.82	0.50	0.00
Lean workfare	●	⊗	⊗	0.07	0.05	0.05	0.07	0.16	0.12
Liberal welfare	⊗	⊗	⊗	0.09	0.05	0.05	0.07	0.16	0.00

Source: Vis (2010: 65).
Note: The black circles indicate the presence of a condition; the crossed-out circles indicate its absence.

combined. For five of these, Vis assigned distinct labels because they match the definition of different welfare and workfare regimes that are discussed in the literature. For instance, *liberal welfare* is conceived as being represented by the configuration ~A · ~G · ~P, or the absence of all three conditions, whereas *social democratic welfare* is seen as being represented by the presence of all three, as in A · G · P. How many distinct labels are needed? Naturally, this will depend on the context of a given study, but it is rare that all logically possible configurations can be filled with theoretical ideal types. However, in order to make use of fuzzy-set ideal type analysis, there should be clearly distinguishable theoretical types that can be described as configurations. Otherwise, the approach would provide little additional value.

What to do with these ideal types? Table 8.8 displays partial results from the empirical analysis that Vis conducted in her study (the table only shows results for France and the Netherlands). As we can see, data were gathered for three different years (1985, 1995, and 2002), which allows the examination of trends over time. For instance, we can see that France stayed within the *conservative welfare* system, although its membership decreased between 1995 and 2002 and its membership score in *social democratic welfare* increased during the same time period. The Netherlands, by contrast, shifted from *conservative welfare* to *social democratic welfare* between 1985 and 2002, whereas in 1995 the country was right in between these two ideal types. At the same time, fuzzy-set ideal type analysis acknowledges nuance by showing that each case only approximates a certain ideal type and often contains traces of various types. We can imagine the ideal types as being situated in the corners of the *attribute space* (see figure 3.4) and the cases at various points inside this space. For instance, France in 2002 has a fuzzy-set membership score of 0.40 in *social democratic welfare*, which means it is outside the conceptualized ideal type, whereas the Netherlands in 1985 closely resemble the *conservative welfare* ideal type (fuzzy-set membership of 0.82), even though there are also traces of other types.

As the example illustrates, fuzzy-set ideal type analysis can be a fruitful tool for typological work. This resonates with methodologists' renewed interest in typologies (Collier, Laporte, and Seawright 2008; Elman 2005; George and Bennett 2005; Goertz 2020). What is required, however, are strong theoretical foundations to derive distinct ideal types, which are most often found in established research areas.

RELATED METHODS AND APPROACHES

This chapter has looked at multivalue QCA, temporal QCA, two-step QCA, and fuzzy-set ideal type analysis—as the most common variants and approaches under the big tent of set-theoretic methods. Although temporal QCA remains an area that is of particular methodological interest, but that has spawned few empirical applications, the other three variants have seen a healthy share of usage, even though crisp- and fuzzy-set studies still constitute the vast majority of published empirical work (mirrored in the survey results reviewed in chapter 2). That being said, several related methods and approaches should be mentioned to give a broader picture of the field, even though it is beyond the scope of this book to provide complete introductions.

The first of these is the *MDSO-MSDO* procedure, as formalized by Gisèle De Meur, Dirk Berg-Schlosser, and Alain Gottcheiner (Berg-Schlosser and De Meur 2009; De Meur and Gottcheiner 2009). MDSO stands for *most different cases, similar outcome*, while MSDO refers to *most similar cases, different outcome*. This is a technique for the pairwise Boolean comparison of cases and conditions. This can be used, for instance, to select a suitable number of conditions "that could be used with most success in explaining the phenomenon under study," as suggested by De Meur and Gottcheiner (2009, 215). As such, MDSO-MSDO can serve as a formalized way to filter out less relevant conditions from a larger pool of potential conditions, before the actual QCA analysis. This is the way how Haesebrouck (2017a) applies the technique, as a *preceding step* to his crisp-set QCA of UN peacekeeping contributions (see box 8.3).

Then there is *Necessary Condition Analysis* (NCA), as developed by Jan Dul. NCA encapsulates a distinct methodology for the identification of necessary conditions in data sets (Dul 2016; Dul, Van der Laan, and Kuik 2020). Rather than working with the metric of consistency, as QCA does, NCA employs different *levels* of conditions, as in *condition X is necessary for outcome Y at a certain level of X* (Dul 2016). From a QCA perspective, NCA can thus be seen as a complementary method to further assess identified necessary conditions with additional metrics, because NCA can make *degree statements* about necessity. It also appears that due to the more discriminate measures of fit, QCA tends to identify fewer necessary conditions than NCA. This means that studies with strong theoretical expectations of necessary conditions might be well advised to run NCA as a complementary step to their QCA analysis. A summary of NCA and its relation to QCA is provided by Vis and Dul (2018).[8]

Box 8.3 Using **MDSO-MSDO** and Crisp-Set **QCA** to Study **EU** Member States' Participation in Military Operations

Tim Haesebrouck, Ghent Institute for International Studies at Ghent University

Although the EU member states have similar interests, alliance ties, and domestic political systems, their patterns of military engagement differ significantly. In my article (Haesebrouck 2017a), I employed QCA to find out what combinations of conditions motivate or block EU member states' participation in military operations. I choose QCA because prior research suggests that participation in military missions results from a complex interplay between international- and domestic-level conditions. Therefore, QCA's ability to capture complex causal relations (multiple conjunctural causation) makes it especially suited for answering my research question. I examined EU member state contributions to five military operations: EUFOR Congo, EUFOR Chad, UNIFIL, the 2011 Libya intervention, and the air strikes against the self-proclaimed Islamic State. In line with the possibility principle, which suggests only including negative cases in which the outcome is possible, I only selected the member states that had the necessary military capabilities to participate in operations. This resulted in a total of 109 member state / operation dyads.

To find potential explanatory conditions, I conducted a review of the extensive academic literature on military intervention. This resulted in a total of 22 plausible explanatory conditions. Given that only 4 to 7 conditions should generally be included in QCA, I applied a less-known configurational method to select conditions: most similar different outcome / most different similar outcome (MSDO/MDSO). As its name suggests, this method allows us to find the similarities between the most different cases with a similar outcome and the differences between most similar cases with a different outcome. After the MDSO/MSDO analysis showed which conditions had most explanatory potential, I tested 12 alternative models that included between 3 and 7 conditions. I decided to focus on a model that included 4 conditions and was theoretically coherent, explained the largest share of the cases, and produced a truth table with few contradictory configurations.

Six of the 16 rows of the truth table corresponded to contradictory configurations. To code the outcome column of these rows, I took a look at the cases that deviated from the general pattern and noticed that many of these could be explained by case-specific, idiosyncratic, circumstances. Portugal, for example, did not participate in the 2011 Libya intervention, but was located in the same

(continued)

Box 8.3 (*continued*)

truth table row as 14 cases of military participation. However, given that the nonparticipation of Portugal could be explained by a political crisis, I decided to assign an outcome score of 1 to the truth table row. Moreover, I noticed that many deviant cases were nonparticipants in the air strikes against ISIS. Therefore, I decided to conduct a separate analysis for this operation, which included two conditions that were only relevant for this operation: constitutional restrictions and the presence of foreign fighters.

The resulting solutions for the presence and absence of military participation showed that the outcome in 3 out of 4 cases can be explained by 4 conditions, and more than 4 out of 5 cases if the air strikes against ISIS were analyzed separately. Combining MDSO/MSDO with QCA, thus, allowed me to arrive at a concise explanation for the pattern of military participation of the EU member states in five military operations.

Finally, there is Coincidence Analysis (CNA), a Boolean method developed by Michael Baumgartner that aims to identify complex causal structures with multiple outcomes on the basis of regularity theory (Baumgartner 2013a; Baumgartner and Ambühl 2020). In contrast to most of the approaches and techniques introduced so far in this chapter, CNA was explicitly designed as an *alternative* to QCA, with its own terminology and analytical protocol. Among other important differences, CNA does *not* use a truth table, as Baumgartner and Mathias Ambühl (2020, 533), explain: "Contrary to QCA, which transforms the data into an intermediate calculative device called a *truth table*, the CNA algorithm operates directly on the data" (emphasis in the original). Another difference is that because CNA seeks to establish *causal chains* between variables, it requires no prior determination of which condition is the outcome and what are the explanatory conditions.[9] Finally, contrary to QCA, CNA derives a single solution, which emphasizes parsimony (see chapter 9). In sum, CNA clearly contains several promising features and has been undergoing dynamic development in recent years. Yet, from a QCA perspective, the bottom line is that CNA entails an entirely different methodology, and users should be aware of these differences (Haesebrouck and Thomann, forthcoming). This applies particularly to some of the *case-oriented* aspects of QCA, because truth table analysis and the substantive, theory-grounded treatment of logical remainders are both not possible with CNA. Instead, CNA takes an "idealist" perspective that emphasizes formal logical coherence (Schneider 2018). Hence, interested users should weigh potential benefits and drawbacks before deciding whether their research aims are better served with QCA or the alternative proposed by CNA.

NOTES

Epigraph: Schneider and Wagemann (2012, 7).

1. As will be discussed, the set-theoretic status of multivalue QCA is contested, but the analytic procedure for mvQCA follows the same principles laid out for csQCA and fsQCA.

2. Multivalue QCA can be conducted with most software packages. The Tosmana software (Cronqvist 2019), including a QCA add-in for Excel, is available at www.tosmana.net.

3. As an alternative, condition values can also be written in subscript (e.g., *employment*$_0$, *employment*$_1$, *employment*$_2$).

4. Mannewitz (2011) provides a discussion of the two-step approach, combined with suggestions on how to integrate it in mvQCA and the analysis of necessary conditions.

5. See also the separate *infobox* by Maria Brockhaus and others (2017), where the authors share some insights on the larger research project behind their QCA studies (also see Korhonen-Kurki et al. 2014).

6. According to Schneider and Wagemann (2012, 254), "The second step consists of constructing truth tables for each outcome enabling context from step one and the proximate conditions," which would imply *multiple* truth table analyses in step two. However, it appears that Tomini and Wagemann (2018) ran a single truth table analysis during the second step, inserting all identified paths into the same analysis. This flexibility underscores that the two-step approach is a mere *guideline* to limit the number of conditions, which can be adapted depending on the research context of a given study.

7. Though not explicitly using fuzzy-set ideal type analysis, Ege (2017) conducts a similar "ideal-type" comparison on the autonomy of international public administrations.

8. See also the critical exchange on NCA between Thiem (2018) and Dul, Vis, and Goertz (2018).

9. Comparisons of QCA and CNA are provided, from various perspectives, by Duşa (2019b, 214–25), Baumgartner and Ambühl (2020), and Haesebrouck and Thomann, (forthcoming). Notably, Zhang (2017, 92) examines the minimization steps in CNA, finding that "there are situations in which the method's output apparently rules out the true causal structure."

9 • QCA and Its Critics

We agree with the critics . . . that case knowledge should play a central role in set-theoretic research; and that set calibration is both crucial and improvable. We disagree whenever matters of current QCA practice are confounded with the method's principles, and when statements about QCA's viability and quality are based on misunderstandings about its inner working.

—INGO ROHLFING AND CARSTEN Q. SCHNEIDER

In the three decades since *The Comparative Method* (Ragin 1987) was published, scholars and practitioners have recognized QCA as a valuable approach to comparative studies that helps to overcome the gulf between qualitative and quantitative research traditions. The considerable increase in the number of published studies and the dissemination across the social sciences—documented in chapter 1 of this book— speak to the fact that QCA has become an established method in the social-scientific toolbox (see also Marx, Rihoux, and Ragin 2014; Rihoux et al. 2013).

However, since its founding, the method has also spurred a diverse array of critiques. I argue that this is precisely because of the method's *hybrid* nature—bringing together qualitative and quantitative elements—which propels criticism from scholars trained in statistical methods, who usually work with hundreds or thousands of observations, as well as from those who conduct intensive studies on a handful of cases at most. Though not being limited to a certain number of observations, QCA typically operates with 20 to 50 cases, which means it is situated right in between these poles.[1]

Clearly, it is a sign of QCA's *maturity* as a social-scientific method that the approach is being scrutinized and critically evaluated by scholars with diverse expertise and backgrounds. This is a welcome development because it fosters improvement of the method and its analytical routines, and it will deepen the understanding of the method. In this spirit, early critiques of QCA have led to the introduction of fuzzy sets to overcome the dichotomization of data (Ragin 2000), measures of fit as numerical indicators to assess the strength of set-theoretic relationships (Ragin 2006b), standards of good practice for QCA applications (Schneider and Wagemann 2010), and many refinements of analytical procedures, as highlighted throughout this book, which relate both to the method's analytical protocol, including the treatment of logical remainders (Schneider and Wagemann 2013), and its implementation in various software solutions, particularly the R packages (Duşa 2019b; Oana and Schneider 2018; Oana, Schneider, and Thomann 2021), but also for other platforms and as stand-alone software (Cronqvist 2019; Drass and Ragin 1986; Longest and Vaisey 2008; Reichert and Rubinson 2014).[2] At the same time, QCA variants have been developed to address specific research needs (see chapter 8).

The downside is that critiques are sometimes taken out of context and are treated as matter of fact rather than as contributions to ongoing conversations. The scope of the methodological exchanges has exacerbated the problem, making it challenging for new users to attain a full view of the arguments.[3] In this chapter, I aim to provide a concise and up-to-date summary of existing critiques and responses, and to clarify recurring misunderstandings about QCA. With this in mind, emphasis is placed on the broad contours of the exchanges, rather than providing detailed accounts of every contribution made so far. I organize the discussion around four persistent themes in the methodological debates: (1) analytical robustness, (2) comparisons with other methods, (3) formalization and algorithms, and (4) causal analysis and solution terms. The chapter closes with a summary on the strengths and limitations of QCA.

ANALYTICAL ROBUSTNESS

Recently, a number of studies have run simulations with artificial data to assess the analytical robustness of QCA results, including its sensitivity to changes in the number of cases, the calibration of conditions, and the impact of potential measurement error on the analytical results (Arel-Bundock 2019; Hug 2013; Krogslund, Choi, and Poertner 2015; Krogslund and Michel 2014; Lucas and Szatrowski 2014; Seawright 2014). Although these studies differ in their research designs and the claims made, a common thread is that QCA is found to be prone to yield faulty conclusions because the findings are not stable when cases are removed from the analysis, when calibration thresholds are set differently, or when measurement error is taken into account.

Along these lines, Samuel Lucas and Alisa Szatrowski (2014, 67) conclude from their simulations, and from a reanalysis of empirical data on space shuttle launches that preceded the *Challenger* accident, that "our pre-*Challenger* launch data reanalysis suggests that QCA studies likely reach faulty conclusions." Vincent Arel-Bundock (2019, 16) infers from his Monte Carlo simulations "that crisp-set QCA algorithms can be very sensitive to measurement error," and, similarly, Chris Krogslund, Donghyun

Danny Choi, and Mathias Poertner (2015, 38–40) argue that QCA results "are questionably robust to even small changes in its calibration and reduction parameters"; hence they suggest that when calibrating conditions, QCA users should "first report results for a large number of different values of each calibration parameter" in order to help "convey the overall robustness of the results to the reader."

QCA proponents have responded to the simulation-based critiques in two ways. The first type of response has emphasized the importance of *case knowledge* and the roots of QCA as a *qualitative* method of inquiry—two characteristics that are essential to QCA but that tend to be overlooked when the method is treated solely as a data analysis technique (Olsen 2014; Ragin 2014a).[4] Based on this reasoning, simulations are inherently flawed because they lack the crucial component—case knowledge—without which it is not possible to make informed decisions throughout the design of a QCA study, including the conceptualization and selection of conditions and their calibration, the analysis of the truth table, the treatment of logical remainders, and the substantive interpretation of analytical findings. Wendy Olsen (2014, 102) puts it concisely: "Thus, the argument using artificial data . . . is poorly constructed. It does not refute QCA, because no background knowledge can be obtained: these data do not reflect reality."

The second type of response comes from QCA proponents who, in principle, see merit in simulations with artificial data but who take issue with the way in which simulations have been conducted and the claims that have been made by QCA critics on this basis (Fiss, Marx, and Rihoux 2014; Rohlfing 2015, 2016; Rohlfing and Schneider 2014; Thiem 2014; Vaisey 2014).

For instance, Ingo Rohlfing (2015) concludes from his assessment of the simulations done by Krogslund, Choi, and Poertner (2015) that, though some of their results are confirmed, "salient aspects of QCA are not adequately captured" and that "QCA is more robust than [Krogslund and colleagues'] simulations suggest" (Rohlfing 2015, 4). In a similar vein, Peer Fiss, Axel Marx, and Benoît Rihoux (2014, 98) examine the simulations done by Lucas and Szatrowski (2014) and arrive at the conclusion that "if based on a technically correct understanding of QCA, simulations confirm QCA's strength and analytical usefulness." Finally, Stephen Vaisey (2014, 108) also conducts a reanalysis of the research of Lucas and Szatrowski (2014) and finds that "my analysis using the same data and program has QCA get the right answer." Vaisey acknowledges that Lucas and Szatrowski (2014) identify problems of *naive* data analysis, which can lead to spurious results. However, he underlines that "straightforward workarounds" exist to mitigate such problems (Vaisey 2014, 110).

In sum, though critical studies express legitimate concerns about analytical robustness, their wholesale conclusions miss the mark. First, it must be noted that the criticism on analytical sensitivity *applies to many social scientific methods*, including statistics, where the data and coding decisions naturally affect the results. Surely, dropping a single case from a regression should not have an observable effect, but adding or excluding a country or region with several hundred observations will certainly have an impact on the findings. For example, a study of the conflict behavior of democracies will yield different results when using a threshold of 8, rather than 7 on the combined Polity IV autocracy–democracy scale. Likewise, the choice of conflict data and its coding will certainly affect the analysis and subsequent findings.

Second, the simulations also miss the *case-based nature* of QCA. As this book has emphasized, case selection is a crucial part of research design and criteria must be explicitly justified and made transparent (chapter 2). The processes of *casing* and case selection are essential to the research logic on which QCA is built (Ragin 1992; Ragin and Becker 1992). Good applications provide a thorough justification for their case selection. They should also discuss when the coding or interpretation of a particular case may be controversial, and hence they provide robustness tests by analyzing the data with and without the particular case. Rather than "anything goes," as some critics seem to imply, there will be a limited number of reasonable analytical options for decisions on the selection of cases, conditions, and their calibration. These decisions should be made explicit, so that others can scrutinize them and assess their plausibility. All this is good QCA practice (Schneider, Vis, and Koivu 2019; Schneider and Wagemann 2010, 2012; Wagemann and Schneider 2015).

That said, the above discussion should not be taken to imply that analytical robustness is of no concern for QCA studies. To the contrary, the method's relative sensitivity to changes in the research design—including the selection of cases, conditions, and calibration criteria—calls for theoretical and substantive justification, and the considerations that inform such decisions should always be made explicit. This mirrors the discussion of good research practice, as emphasized throughout this book, and specifically chapter 2 on research design and chapter 5 on calibration. Beyond that, researchers have also developed approaches to address sources of error and uncertainty (Maggetti and Levi-Faur 2013; Skaaning 2011), and specific tools to detect false positives (Braumoeller 2015) and false negatives in QCA results (Rohlfing 2018).[5]

The Data on the Space Shuttle Launch

As mentioned above, the critique by Lucas and Szatrowski (2014)—henceforth referred to as L&S—uses historical space shuttle launch data to conduct an empirical test with QCA. The background to this is the Space Shuttle *Challenger* accident of January 1986, after which a commission was charged with analyzing the accident and identifying its causes (Rogers et al. 1986). The Rogers Commission concluded that "failure was due to a faulty design unacceptably sensitive to a number of factors. These factors were the effects of temperature, physical dimensions, the character of the material, the effects of reusability, processing, and reaction of the joint to dynamic loading" (Rogers et al. 1986, 73). Moreover, it was found that "those who made that decision [to launch the space shuttle] were unaware . . . of the initial written recommendation of the contractor *advising against the launch at temperatures below 53 degrees Fahrenheit*" (emphasis added) (Rogers et al. 1986, 83). The bottom line is that low temperature was identified "as a cause of danger independent of field and nozzle pressure" (L&S 2014, 15).

Against this backdrop, L&S (2014, 15) used the Rogers data because it provided "a rare real-world data set of known causes [of O-ring erosion, as the identified cause of the accident], making them potentially useful for assessing QCA." These data comprise 23 space shuttle launches between 1981 and 1986, with information on field pressure, nozzle pressure, temperature, and O-ring erosion. For their QCA analysis, L&S report a parsimonious solution that is "the interaction of high nozzle pressure and low temperature," from which they surmise that "QCA finds that temperature *has no independent effect*, posing a danger only when low while field and nozzle pressure are high," which lets them conclude that "QCA *clearly fails* in real-world testing" (emphasis added) (L&S 2014, 15).

For his reply to L&S, Charles Ragin (2014a) reanalyzed the shuttle launch data with QCA. His analysis provided results that were in line with what is known about the accident's causes and that depart from those reported by L&S. Table 9.1 shows the raw data from Rogers and others (1986), the calibrated fuzzy-set conditions, and the crisp-set outcome, based on the calibration thresholds stated by L&S and Ragin (2014a). In my own reanalysis, I follow the calibration criteria of L&S (2014, 15) to create two pressure conditions, *high field pressure* and *high nozzle pressure* (fully out = 50, crossover = 125, and fully in = 200). However, as Ragin notes, in order to attain a meaningful set *low temperature*, the empirical anchors must be set differently than specified by L&S (fully out = 65 °F, crossover = 60 °F, and fully in = 45 °F). This is because the calibration criteria for low temperature stated in L&S (2014, 15) yield a truth table without any rows that meet the minimum consistency threshold of 0.75. Hence, for my reanalysis, I adopt Ragin's (2014a, 91) anchors for the low temperature condition.

As shown in table 9.2, the parsimonious solution *correctly* identifies low temperature as a sufficient condition for O-ring erosion—a cause that, ultimately, led to the space shuttle accident. The conservative solution further entails high field pressure as a contributing cause. This simply means that the data offer no empirical basis to rule out high field pressure as a potential cause, because there is no case with low temperature and low field pressure among the observed cases (Ragin 2014a, 91). Moreover, the low coverage values of the QCA solutions indicate that low temperature is but one of several pathways to O-ring erosion. As highlighted in the above quotation from the commission report (Rogers et al. 1986, 73), other factors were potentially exacerbating factors in the fatal launch. To put it differently, O-ring erosion also occurred in the *absence* of low temperature. In fact, 9 out of 12 cases of O-ring erosion happened under *not*-low temperatures (compare table 9.1). This is not discussed by L&S, but a case-oriented investigation would start from this observation to identify other relevant conditions and thus enhance the coverage of the QCA study, to eventually provide

Table 9.1 Space Shuttle Data, Raw and Calibrated

	Space Shuttle Flight	Raw Data			Calibrated Fuzzy Sets			Outcome
Case		Field Pressure	Nozzle Pressure	Temperature (°F)	High Field Pressure	High Nozzle Pressure	Low Temperature	O-Ring Erosion
1	STS-1	50	50	66	0.05	0.05	0.03	0
2	STS-2	50	50	70	0.05	0.05	0.00	1
3	STS-3	50	50	80	0.05	0.05	0.00	0
4	STS-5	50	50	68	0.05	0.05	0.01	0
5	STS-6	50	50	67	0.05	0.05	0.02	0
6	STS-7	50	50	72	0.05	0.05	0.00	0
7	STS-8	100	50	73	0.27	0.05	0.00	0
8	STS-9	100	100	70	0.27	0.27	0.00	0
9	STS-41-B	200	100	57	0.95	0.27	0.64	1
10	STS-41-C	200	100	63	0.95	0.27	0.15	1
11	STS-41-D	200	100	70	0.95	0.27	0.00	1
12	STS-41-G	200	100	67	0.95	0.27	0.02	0
13	STS-51-A	200	100	67	0.95	0.27	0.02	0
14	STS-51-C	200	100	53	0.95	0.27	0.80	1
15	STS-51-D	200	200	67	0.95	0.95	0.02	1
16	STS-51-B	200	100	75	0.95	0.27	0.00	1
17	STS-51-G	200	200	70	0.95	0.95	0.00	1
18	STS-51-F	200	200	81	0.95	0.95	0.00	0
19	STS-51-I	200	200	76	0.95	0.95	0.00	1
20	STS-51-J	200	200	79	0.95	0.95	0.00	0
21	STS-61-A	200	200	75	0.95	0.95	0.00	1
22	STS-61-B	200	200	76	0.95	0.95	0.00	1
23	STS-61-C	200	200	58	0.95	0.95	0.60	1

Source: Rogers et al. (1986, 130–31).

Table 9.2 Conservative and Parsimonious Solutions

Conservative solution:	Low temperature × high field pressure → O-ring erosion (Consistency = 0.961, coverage = 0.184)
Parsimonious solution:	Low temperature → O-ring erosion (Consistency = 0.961, coverage = 0.184)

a full account of the conditions under which O-ring erosion occurs in space shuttles. Remarkably, the regression analysis reported by Ragin shows no significant effect for *any* of the expected causes (Ragin 2014a, 92).

What this example demonstrates is that—contrary to the claims made by L&S—QCA *does* return meaningful analytical results when it is used appropriately. But this requires a sensible calibration and directionality of the target conditions and an analysis that is conducted in line with established standards of good research practice. When using the calibration criteria for low temperature as they are described by L&S (2014, 15), the analysis results in a truth table without rows that meet the consistency threshold of 0.75. Once this error in calibration is corrected, the analysis properly identifies the known cause of the shuttle failure, as described in the Rogers Commission report (Rogers et al. 1986). Moreover, the QCA analysis appropriately highlights *causal complexity*, rather than focusing solely on low temperature (which is one of *several* relevant factors examined and identified in the Rogers report). Hence, it is clear that *multiple pathways* in the Rogers data led to shuttle failure and that low temperature alone accounts for just a small part of the outcome. QCA researchers would take this as a starting point for developing a more complete explanation of the phenomenon.

COMPARISONS WITH OTHER METHODS

A recurrent theme in the methodological debates about QCA is its comparative assessment vis-à-vis other methods of inquiry. Most contributions have focused on comparing QCA with quantitative tools, such as regression analysis and related approaches (Clarke 2020; Lieberson 2004; Paine 2016a, 2016b; Seawright 2005a, 2005b; Tanner 2014), but there have also been comparisons with qualitative research methods such as process tracing and comparative case studies (George and Bennett 2005; Munck 2016), and a growing literature emphasizes the complementarity of QCA and process tracing (Beach, Pedersen, and Siewert 2019; Beach and Rohlfing 2018; Goertz 2017; Meegdenburg and Mello, forthcoming; Rohlfing and Schneider 2018; Schneider and Rohlfing 2019), as mentioned in the section on multimethod research in chapter 2.

Writing from a quantitative perspective, Jason Seawright (2005b, 24) sees QCA as a "major practical competitor" to statistical approaches for the purpose of cross-case inferences, but he concludes that, due to some of its more restrictive assumptions, "QCA is not an improvement over regression analysis." According to Seawright (2005a, 41), "scholars using QCA are reasonably close to employing a regression framework, and, in some respects, quite far from the case-study tradition." Hence, he argues that for QCA scholars, "embracing more elements of the regression tradition may therefore be compatible with what they are already doing" (Seawright 2005a, 41). A similar perspective is expressed by Stanley Lieberson (2004, 13), who focuses on what he regards as QCA's major limitation, namely, that it is a deterministic method without instruments to account for "chance and probabilistic processes."

In two more recent contributions, Jack Paine (2016a, 2016b) formulates views similar to those of Seawright and Lieberson, suggesting that set-theoretic methods "share common foundations with quantitative research" but that these are neither an improvement over regression analysis nor over qualitative methods like process tracing (Paine 2016a, 28–29). Therefore, he argues that the "qualitative methodology would be better served by focusing on tools such as process tracing that do possess distinctive advantages relative to quantitative methods" (Paine 2016b, 798). Likewise, Gerardo Munck (2016, 5) suggests in a short comment on the method that the integration of process tracing into set-theoretic methods might provide them with a comparative advantage over regression analysis, while also arguing that process tracing "clashes with the idea of causal relations and logical relations."

QCA scholars and those sympathetic to the method have engaged with these and related comments by lining out commonalities and differences as opposed to regression analysis, and by clarifying misconceptions about the principles of set-theoretic methods (Mahoney 2004; Ragin and Rihoux 2004a, 2004b; Rohlfing and Schneider 2014; Schneider 2016). In this vein, Ragin and Rihoux (2004b, 22) highlight that "analyzable truth tables are not the starting point of comparative research; rather, they are formed near the end of a long process of case-oriented comparative investigation." Some of the criticism has also been overtaken by methodological developments. For instance, the debate surrounding probability and determinism (see also chapter 2), as raised by Lieberson, has lost much of its relevance since the introduction of measures of fit to account for imperfect set relations (chapter 6). Hence, "QCA is not a deterministic method," as Carsten Schneider and Claudius Wagemann (2012, 316) underline (see also Goertz 2005).

As for the comparison between regression analysis and QCA, Ragin and Rihoux emphasize that these methods are based on *different assumptions* and that they are rarely "competing for the same turf" (2004b, 22). For Gary Goertz and James Mahoney (2012), set-theoretic methods and statistical analyses belong to different *cultures*, with their own, internally coherent scientific perspectives. Alrik Thiem, Michael

Baumgartner, and Damien Bol (2016) go a step further in delineating *fundamental differences* in the mathematical and conceptual roots of these methods. Irrespective of whether one agrees with these characterizations, there is a consensus among QCA scholars that set-theoretic methods *do not aim to replace* regression analysis or related approaches, contrary to what is insinuated in some contributions to the methodological debates. In fact, some work has made inroads into combining large-N QCA with regression analyses (Fiss, Sharapov, and Cronqvist 2013; Vis 2012). As Vis (2012, 192) argues, "adding a configurational approach to a regression analysis helps to uncover patterns in the empirical data that otherwise would have remained hidden." This rather speaks to the *complementarity* of the two methods, under the condition that certain requirements are met. For example, in their study on biological attributions of mental illness, Matthew Andersson and Sarah Harkness (2018) adopt a multimethod approach that combines QCA and regression analysis (see box 2.2), and Tobias Ide (2018) uses statistical techniques to derive a sample of cases before the QCA part of his study (see box 2.1).

As for process tracing, it is equally misleading to frame the debate in either/or terms. As discussed in chapter 4, the unique strength of process tracing is the identification of causal mechanisms through the intensive study of individual cases. Yet as a within-case method, process tracing lacks a cross-case perspective. This is where the connection with QCA can be especially fruitful. Though Munck (2016, 5) sees tension between process tracing and QCA, recent work highlights their common set-theoretic foundations (Beach, Pedersen, and Siewert 2019; Goertz 2017; Rohlfing and Schneider 2018; Schneider and Rohlfing 2013). This also resonates with the perspective expressed by George and Bennett (2005, 163), who suggested that QCA case comparisons should be complemented with process tracing.

FORMALIZATION AND ALGORITHMS

Another strand of critique has taken issue with QCA's use of algorithms and what is perceived as an increased formalization in the method's analytical protocol (Collier 2014a, 2014b; Munck 2016; Sartori 2014). From the commentators' perspective, it is the methods' evolution and refinement that have distanced QCA from the original goal of case-based comparative research. Moreover, the complexity of QCA solutions and the emphasis placed on formal logic are seen as undermining the method's value as an empirical research approach.

This view is expressed by David Collier (2014a, 2014b), who recommends that QCA "should set aside the algorithms," calling instead for a renewed emphasis on "case knowledge, process tracing, and the use of qualitative data" (2014b, 123–24). Moreover, Collier (2014b, 124–25) highlights that many "scholars now seek the most 'simple and intuitive' tools adequate to the task at hand," arguing that "case knowledge should not be an adjunct to the algorithms but rather the primary method of analysis." Likewise, Giovanni Sartori (2014), in a brief comment on *A Tale of Two Cultures* (Goertz and Mahoney 2012), cautions against an overreliance on technique: "Yet the intricate fuzzy set procedures cantilever out from these questions, posing dangers of technique that concern me. In some domains of social science we now see a growing skepticism about complex statistical techniques—and a turn to simpler tools. The elaborate procedures of fuzzy sets merit the same skepticism" (Sartori 2014, 15).

Munck (2016) seems to share this skepticism, particularly when it comes to arguments that are rooted exclusively in formal logic, such as the contrasting discussion of regression analysis and set-theoretic methods by Thiem, Baumgartner, and Bol (2016): "A key problem in Thiem et al.'s discussion is that they posit, as do other advocates of STCM [set-theoretic comparative methods], an analysis of causation *entirely in formal terms*. This is a basic oversight, because *a causal relation is not a logical relation* but, rather, a relation between events or, more precisely, between changes in the properties of things. But Thiem et al. have nothing to say about the semantics of empirical sciences" (emphasis added) (Munck 2016, 3).

These are reasonable points. In my view, Collier, Sartori, and Munck raise general concerns about research methods with which many QCA proponents would doubtless agree. To begin with, it should not be controversial to say that the minimization algorithm and the computation of measures of fit should *guide* the analysis, but they are not supposed to take the driver's seat. This is in line with the recommendation that QCA should never be applied mechanically, deprived of theoretical and substantive considerations—points that have been emphasized throughout this book. Yet, these concerns do not warrant the blanket conclusion to "set aside the algorithms," as Collier (2014b) proposes. Rather, more effort should be placed in clarifying what the computational routines in QCA effectively accomplish and where they depend on researcher input (see Duşa 2019b; and Oana, Schneider, and Thomann 2021).

As introduced in previous chapters, QCA's procedures for calibration and Boolean minimization are based on clear principles, and as such they can be manually reproduced. The solution terms are not the result of some impervious procedure but are based on the truth table and the treatment of logical remainders. Likewise, fuzzy sets and calibration draw on clear rules of mathematical transformation—there is no "magic ingredient" involved.

Surely, if one is not accustomed to calibrated data, then this requires some getting used to, but this applies even more to some advanced quantitative methods and formal modeling, both of which can appear impenetrable to the uninitiated. In this light, chapter 5 provides a guide to the mathematical transformation that is entailed in fuzzy-set calibration, whereas chapters 6 and 7 shed light on the calculation of measures of fit and the minimization algorithm that form the core of the analytical procedures for QCA (see also Duşa 2019b; Oana, Schneider, and Thomann 2021; Ragin 2008b; and Schneider and Wagemann 2012).

Finally, what is important to note is that we need to distinguish between QCA as a *method* and its *application* in empirical studies. As John Gerring (2012b, 350) rightly points out, "The *potential utility* of a method should be differentiated from its *actual employment*" (emphasis added). To put it bluntly, the existence of flawed statistical analyses or badly done case studies does not mean that either approach is invalidated. Just as there may be p-hacking in regression analyses and anecdotal evidence in case studies, there are QCA studies that do not fulfill criteria of good research practice. Such criteria have been formulated and will continue to evolve as QCA matures as a method (Oana, Schneider, and Thomann 2021; Rihoux and Ragin 2009; Rubinson et al. 2019; Schneider and Wagemann 2010, 2012). There have also been a variety of efforts to hold empirical applications against the developed standards concerning research design, calibration, and analytical routines (e.g., Mello 2013; Rohlfing 2020; Thiem 2016; Wagemann, Buche, and Siewert 2016).

CAUSAL ANALYSIS AND SOLUTION TERMS

In recent years, a debate has emerged about causal analysis and the contribution of the different QCA solution terms toward this aim (Baumgartner and Ambühl 2020; Baumgartner and Thiem 2020; Duşa 2019a; Haesebrouck and Thomann, forthcoming; Schneider 2018; Thiem 2019). Michael Baumgartner and Alrik Thiem (2020) argue on the basis of simulated data that only the parsimonious solution of QCA should be used for causal inference (see also Thiem 2019), while the conservative and intermediate solutions are both deemed incorrect due to their inclusion of redundant elements. By contrast, Adrian Duşa (2019a, 1) finds that an intermediate solution with directional expectations "emerges as the best hybrid that is suitable for causal analysis," which ties in with the long-standing recommendation to place emphasis on the intermediate solution (Ragin 2008b, 175; Schneider and Wagemann 2012, 279). This exchange has sparked exchanges about the accuracy of different solution types and the prerequisites of causal inference with set-theoretic methods (see also Haesebrouck and Thomann, forthcoming; and Schneider 2018).

It is beyond the scope of this book to develop each side's argument and evidence, but it should be noted that the simulations by Baumgartner and Thiem (2020, 24) were not run on approximations of "real-life" data with limited diversity and imperfect set relations, as the authors themselves acknowledge. There is also no mention of untenable assumptions, which can present a major problem for the parsimonious solution (see chapter 7).

In essence, the debate about the correctness of the solution types boils down to different understandings of methodological aims in social science research. The argument by Baumgartner and Thiem (2020) favoring the parsimonious solution appears consistent within a *formal perspective* on regularity theory and logic, driven by the impetus to find the last "difference maker" for an identified effect. From this perspective, any condition that is deemed "redundant" must be eliminated, even when this comes at the expense of context and background. This contrasts with a *case-based perspective* that acknowledges complex causation and aims at theory-guided analysis within specified boundaries. In fact, as Duşa (2019a, 19) shows, the intermediate solution *outperforms* the parsimonious solution once its directional expectations are correctly specified.

To put it differently, when *theory* is inserted into the picture, a purely logic-driven perspective becomes less persuasive. I contend that most social scientists who are interested in configurational comparative methods would prefer to inform their analysis with expectations derived from theory and their own knowledge of the field, rather than risk letting the algorithm include untenable assumptions in the computation of solution terms (as may happen with the parsimonious solution). This resonates with a position among methodologists on set-theoretic methods that substantive knowledge and research design should not be outweighed by the mechanical implementation of technical routines (Ragin 1987; Schneider and Wagemann 2010; Wagemann 2017).

Another way to look at the solution term debate is in terms of the *complexity–parsimony* continuum that characterizes the solution terms derived by QCA (see chapter 7). As is well known, due to the way Boolean minimization works, the solution terms stand in subset–superset relationships to each other, beginning with the complex solution, which is a subset of the intermediate solution, which in turn is a subset of the parsimonious solution. From this perspective, it would be nonsensical to claim that a complex solution was "incorrect" when its parsimonious superset was deemed "correct." The parsimonious solution would simply be the *most general claim*, whereas the complex solution constitutes a subset that makes a more *specific claim*.

For instance, the parsimonious solution may yield that smoking was a sufficient condition for cancer (among some observed groups of individuals), whereas the complex solution may suggest that the combination of smoking and obesity was sufficient for the outcome. If the parsimonious statement is deemed correct, then the complex statement must also be correct. As this example illustrates, the exchange may be less about the correctness or truth value of the specific solution terms but more about the weight assigned to parsimony as opposed to context-sensitivity. But focusing solely on difference makers may not suffice, as Rani Lill Anjum and Stephen Mumford (2018, 125) remind us: "There are some causes that are not difference makers; and there are some difference makers that are not causes." Moreover, John Mackie (1980, 34–36) acknowledged that research typically evolves within a "causal field" of context and background conditions. Distinguishing which of these should be considered a cause rather than a condition rests in no small part on the phrasing of the causal question at hand. Again, this points us back to the salience of theory and research design.

At this stage, one takeaway from this ongoing debate is what has long been considered *good practice* in applied QCA research—namely, that, depending on the research aims of a study, any of the three solutions can be emphasized (if untenable assumptions are taken care of), but that all three solution terms should be reported in publications, at least in a supplementary document (Rihoux and Ragin 2009; Schneider and Wagemann 2010).

In line with the discussion on theories of causation in chapter 4, I encourage a *pluralist* view on the matter of causal analysis, siding with the cautionary note by Anjum and Mumford (2018, 250) that "one should be open to evidence acquired through plural methods because causation has plural symptoms." Clearly, QCA is not tied to a single theory of causation, and different metatheoretical frameworks can be grafted onto set-theoretic research.

RECOGNIZING QCA'S STRENGTHS AND LIMITATIONS

To conclude this chapter, a sober look at QCA's strengths and limitations is warranted. In my view, the core strengths of QCA are threefold. To begin with, as outlined throughout this book, one of the distinctive features of the method is that it takes into account *causal complexity*, or "the combinatorial complexities of social causation," as noted by Ragin (1987, 170).[6] This is a conscious departure from "net effect" thinking on relations between individual variables (Mahoney 2010). Causal complexity acknowledges that social phenomena can often result from various configurations, recipes, or pathways (*equifinality*), each of which may entail several different conditions (*conjunctural causation*). Moreover, the relations between configurations and outcomes can usually not be mirrored symmetrically (*causal asymmetry*), as when the absence of a cause is assumed to also be the cause of the nonoutcome. Moreover, the concept of equifinality challenges the assumption that cases with similar outcomes must have common causes at their root (George and Bennett 2005, 161).

How to make the most of causal complexity when using QCA? Empirical applications stand to benefit when they are consciously modeled on set-theoretic relationships. This means that theory should be formulated in the language of necessary and sufficient conditions, including reference to INUS and SUIN conditions, where appropriate. This further entails thinking about specific combinations of conditions, rather than examining and justifying each condition individually. In this context, it can be helpful to *visualize* theoretical expectations, especially when these entail conjunctural causation and equifinality. Alternatively, the QCA solution terms can be visualized, which also helps enhance the understanding of causal complexity. In his discussion of causal mechanisms, Goertz (2017, chap. 2) covers helpful examples of graphic illustrations for relationships of causal complexity, and Rubinson (2019) addresses visualization in QCA research.

The second core strength of QCA is that the method allows for a *systematic comparison* across empirical cases and the incorporation of *counterfactual reasoning* on logically possible combinations of conditions that are not empirically substantiated. Both elements incorporate the truth table as analytic device. In this sense, QCA has a disciplining effect because it demands from researchers not just selective comparisons, as they often occur in small-N comparative studies, but instead requires systematic and exhaustive data generation and a consistent calibration for all cases entailed in the analysis. At the same time, the truth table will indicate the empirical distribution across the attribute space, and it will also show whether there are any empty configurations, information that can then be applied for the assessment of counterfactual cases. To profit from this strength, users should devote sufficient attention to the examination of the truth table, the distribution of empirical cases, and the consistency of the respective rows, and should also examine the nonsubstantiated configurations (logical remainders). As outlined in chapter 7, the latter provide an opportunity for counterfactual reasoning on whether cases with certain characteristics would show the outcome of interest if they existed. Such expectations can then be incorporated into the intermediate solution.

Finally, QCA gives researchers generous *flexibility* to adapt the approach to the context of their own research aims. Though QCA is often characterized as a medium-N method and the majority of applications work with a range of 20 to 30 cases (see the survey results in chapter 2), the method works equally well in large-N settings and, albeit some restrictions, it is also feasible to work with smaller numbers of cases. With small numbers, the main restriction is that the number of conditions should also be kept low, to maintain a ratio of at least four cases per condition (see table 2.2). Apart from the number of cases and conditions, QCA also allows for flexibility with regard to the kinds of data that are used for the analysis. The set-theoretic calibration can draw on all kinds of qualitative and quantitative information, and these can also be combined to create meaningful indicators for set-theoretic concepts. Moreover, given the diversity of QCA variants and analytical routines on offer, users can select the approach that best suits their research aims and the concepts they are working with (see chapter 8). The benefits of flexibility should be consciously utilized following a problem-driven approach. This means that there is no single "orthodox" way for how QCA must be done, but a menu of feasible options that users can choose from, in line with their own research aims. Yet it must be underlined that established standards of good practice apply equally to all QCA applications, irrespective of the chosen variant or approach (Rubinson et al. 2019; Schneider and Wagemann 2010).

Despite these strengths, QCA has limitations. There is no silver bullet method in the social sciences. First, as was acknowledged in the section on analytical robustness, the method is *sensitive* to changes in the selection of cases and conditions and the setting of calibration thresholds. On a practical level, this means that users should always provide theoretical and substantive reasons for the choices that inform their research design, while robustness tests can serve to increase the confidence in the analytical results. Having said this, it is important to keep in mind the *qualitative* core of QCA as a case-based method. This means that rather than conducting a battery of quantitative robustness tests, which might eventually mimic statistical approaches, there should be reasonable substantive arguments for why certain calibration thresholds were chosen, on which grounds the cases were selected, and which options existed for the researcher during the analytical procedure.

Second, as a comparative method, QCA simply requires a certain *number of cases* and *comparable data* to "get off the ground" and run reliably. This poses a research-pragmatic constraint for academic fields that are characterized by small-N and comparative case studies (Mello 2017). For applications in these areas, the first hurdle is collecting data on a sufficient number of cases and conditions to allow for a comparison of, say, at least 12 cases. Certainly, the number of observations can be increased by disaggregating cases into subunits, for example, when countries are separated into regions or municipalities, governments are examined rather than countries, or individuals are compared rather than groups or cohorts of people.

Table 9.3   Strengths, Limitations, and Strategies

Strengths	How to Make the Most of These
Accounts for causal complexity (conjunctural causation, equifinality, and causal asymmetry)	Focus on set-theoretic relationships, formulation of causally complex theoretical expectations, and visualization of causal complexity
Allows for systematic comparison across empirical cases and counterfactual reasoning on logical remainders	Emphasis on truth table, conscious treatment of logical remainders, and substantive interpretation of solution paths
Flexibility in adapting to specific research aims (cases, conditions, qualitative and quantitative data, analytical routines, and QCA variants)	Problem-driven use of most suitable research design, QCA variant, and analytical routine
Limitations	**How to Address These**
Sensitive to changes in calibration and case/condition selection	Thorough justification of analytical choices, conducting robustness tests
Requires a certain number of cases and comparable data	Adjustments in the case/condition ratio and calibration, disaggregation of cases
Comparison is inherently static, conditions are treated equally	Integration of time in conceptualization and research design, use of specific QCA variants, combination with other methods

Finally, as was mentioned in chapter 8 on QCA variants, there has not yet been a satisfying solution to the problem of *temporality*. At its core, QCA remains a static comparative approach where the conditions are treated in the same way in their relation to the outcome (Marx, Rihoux, and Ragin 2014). Yet the question of how to take into account time and sequence is pervasive in the social sciences (Büthe 2002), and as such it constitutes a limitation that applies to a large number of social science methods and is not restricted specifically to QCA. Apart from the recent introduction of "trajectory-based QCA" (Pagliarin and Gerrits 2020), which offers a promising approach to address temporality, feasible ways to address the issue through research design either (1) indirectly include timing and sequence in the concept formation for conditions, or (2) combine QCA with another method that is capable of acknowledging these features, such as process tracing (see chapter 2). Table 9.3 summarizes the strengths and limitations of QCA and strategies on how to make the most of the former and address the latter.

NOTES

Epigraph: Rohlfing and Schneider (2014, 32).

1. See the cross-disciplinary survey results at the end of chapter 2 for differences in the number of cases typically included in QCA studies in various academic fields.

2. At the time of writing, the COMPASSS community website lists 19 different software packages related to QCA and configurational methods; see https://compasss.org/software/.

3. Journal issues with a focus on QCA and set-theoretic methods include, in chronological order: *Sociological Methods & Research* 23, no. 1 (1994); *Field Methods* 15, no. 4 (2003); *Qualitative Methods* 2, no. 2 (2004); *Qualitative Methods* 3 (2005); *Studies in Comparative International Development* 40, no. 1 (2005); *International Sociology* 21, no. 5 (2006); *Political Analysis* 14, no. 3 (2006); *Political Research Quarterly* 66, no. 1 (2013); *Sociological Methodology* 44, no. 1 (2014); *Qualitative & Multi-Method Research* 12, no. 1 (2014); *Qualitative & Multi-Method Research* 12, no. 2 (2014); *Field Methods* 28, no. 3 (2016); *Comparative Political Studies* 49, no. 6 (2016); *Quality & Quantity* 51, no. 5 (2017); and *Quality & Quantity*, forthcoming.

4. For a concise articulation of the case-based perspective and its take on earlier critiques, see Rihoux (2003).

5. For an overview on robustness tests, see also Thomann and Maggetti (2020, 13–14).

6. A detailed discussion of causal complexity is given in chapter 4.

10 • Guiding Principles for QCA Research

Set-analytic social science is still in its infancy.
The Comparative Method was but a first step on
an important journey in social scientific inquiry.
There has been considerable progress along this path
since *The Comparative Method* was published, but
there is still much work to be done.

—CHARLES C. RAGIN

This book laid out the building blocks of Qualitative Comparative Analysis. In its outline, the chapters followed the stages of an ideal-typical research cycle (see figure 1.1). Beginning with matters of research design, subsequent chapters examined causation, causal complexity, and set theory. The core of the approach was contained in the chapters on calibrating sets, measures of fit, and set-theoretic analysis, whereas the chapters on QCA variants and critiques again widened the perspective.

With this foundation in place, I want to end with recommendations on *good research practice* when engaging with QCA. These are structured on the basis of three guiding principles, to serve as orientation marks for users when conducting their own research with QCA. In this sense, the principles do not introduce any new elements, but reflect the exposition of the method as it has been presented throughout the book. This is complemented by advice on how to effectively document and communicate QCA results. The chapter closes by pointing to online resources for users to take the next steps, and with a look at recent trends in QCA research.

GOOD RESEARCH PRACTICE

QCA's growing popularity across the social sciences has sparked various formulations of *best practices* for empirical applications (Emmenegger, Kvist, and Skaaning 2013;

Greckhamer et al. 2018; Kahwati and Kane 2020; Oana, Schneider, and Thomann 2021; Rihoux and Ragin 2009; Schneider, Vis, and Koivu 2019; Schneider and Wagemann 2010, 2012). Although this is an area of dynamic development, it has led to what can be considered a canon of agreed-upon standards to which published studies should adhere.[1]

However, even though a core of best practices exists, there remains a gap between the proscribed standards and actual research practice, as documented in published QCA applications (Emmenegger, Kvist, and Skaaning 2013; Mello 2013). This may also explain some of the criticism aimed at QCA, as discussed in chapter 9, which often does not differentiate between the method's potential and its actual application in published studies (Gerring 2012b, 350).

To be sure, when comparing publications, we must keep in mind that disciplinary standards vary in terms of manuscript length, level of methodological detail, referencing, and the usage of illustrations—to name just a few areas of divergence. Naturally, this also affects how QCA applications in different fields look. What is standard practice in one field may be unusual in another field. There are studies that report QCA results within 4,000-word articles and then there are studies of 12,000 words. Surely, the comprehensiveness of the documentation will differ when comparing such publications. That said, certain parts of the analysis should always be documented, irrespective of manuscript length. Moreover, there is always the option to provide additional documentation in online appendixes or supplementary documents.

The core elements of good research practice are adhering to the analytical procedures and sequences described in previous chapters. This includes the appropriate calibration of the raw data using the described techniques; defining conditions and an outcome that are directed towards a qualitative state; and a properly documented set-theoretic analysis that includes measures of fit, a discussion of how logical remainders were treated, which solution term was chosen for the substantive interpretation, and how the cases fit onto the identified solution paths.

Apart from these more or less technical points, I advocate three *guiding principles* that enhance good research practice with QCA: (1) suitability, (2) parsimony, and (3) transparency. These principles reflect the exposition of the method, as laid out throughout this book. *Suitability* means that even before designing a study, we should ask whether our research aim warrants a set-theoretic framework. If we expect causal complexity—as in conjunctural causation, equifinality, and causal asymmetry—then QCA will be a suitable choice. By contrast, if the research aims at identifying linear relationships between one or more independent variables and a dependent variable, then non-set-theoretic approaches will provide a better methodological fit. Suitability also means that the study should be designed in a way that builds on QCA's strengths, as outlined in chapter 9: theory should be formulated in set-theoretic language (which may require a translation of probabilistic statements), causal complexity should be addressed and incorporated in theoretical expectations, conditions and outcome should be calibrated toward meaningful qualitative states, and emphasis should be placed on cases and their configurations, also by returning to the cases after the set-theoretic analysis.

Parsimony means that research design and analysis should strive for simplicity by focusing on essential elements. With QCA, things can swiftly become *very* complex. Just imagine a solution term with six paths that contain seven conditions in various configurations, possibly even with further analyses of alternative outcomes. Such studies often do not succeed in verbalizing and making sense of their findings, especially within the scope of journal articles. The danger, then, is to limit oneself to a mere technical interpretation of the results, without relating the findings back to the academic literature on a topic or broader, more general patterns of social phenomena. I see this as a *crucial drawback* of QCA because overly complex solutions can undermine the broader dissemination of results, beyond a small group of scholars who are versed in set-theoretic methods (and even for these, it might be difficult to make sense of the analytical findings). This also reflects key points in the criticism discussed in the previous chapter, as voiced by David Collier (2014b) and Gerardo Munck (2016). Hence, it should be the aim to design a study and communicate its findings in a way that allows other researchers to grasp the results even without any prior knowledge of QCA.

For example, a focused study with just three or four conditions can provide sound inferential leverage and meaningful findings. Surely, this should not mean that studies with more than four conditions are unmanageable. But rather than increasing the number of conditions to cover all aspects of a topic (the misguided notion of adding "controls" for all potentially relevant factors; see chapter 2 on condition selection), the better strategy will be to *narrow the focus* and thereby limit the number of conditions (e.g., by reducing the analysis to institutional variables, public preferences, organizational features, or individual characteristics, rather than including all these different groups of explanations in the analysis). Parsimony also applies to calibration rules, which should be conceptualized in a straightforward way, to enhance the interpretability of the eventual findings (what it means to have a case that represents the corresponding set).

Finally, *transparency* is crucial when communicating QCA results in publications. This means that constitutive elements of the analysis and analytical decisions must be documented: the raw data, calibration thresholds, the truth table, the consistency and frequency thresholds, the solution term used for the substantive interpretation, measures of fit, and the treatment of logical remainders. Moreover, there should be an explicit discussion of how the cases were selected and whether other plausible cases could have been included but were not. Finally, there should also be a justification for the selection of conditions and, where applicable, alternative conditions that were not used for the analysis. All these considerations enhance the *analytical robustness* and *level of confidence* that one can have in the research findings (see chapter 9).

Transparency also extends to making the raw and calibrated data and R script available on a public repository or journal website, citing the R packages that were used (to enable others to reproduce the analysis with the same packages and to give credit to

Table 10.1   Guiding Principles for QCA Research

Guiding Principle	Implications
Suitability	(1) Research aims to explore set relations and causal complexity. (2) Conditions and outcome reflect directionality of a given set. (3) Theoretical expectations are formulated in set-theoretic terms.
Parsimony	(4) Research design aims for parsimony and conciseness. (5) The number of conditions is kept to the feasible minimum. (6) Calibration rules are made in a clear and concise manner.
Transparency	(7) All analytical decisions are made explicit. (8) All analytical steps are documented in publications. (9) Raw data, calibrated data, and R scripts are made available.

its developers), and highlighting subjective decisions throughout the analysis (e.g., the decision to drop a certain case because of unavailable or ambiguous data). Table 10.1 summarizes these guiding principles for QCA research.

DOCUMENTING AND COMMUNICATING QCA RESULTS

Two points raised in the previous section were the documentation and communication of analytical results. What should be included in the documentation, and how ought this to be done? Even more important, how to effectively communicate the findings from a QCA study? Beginning with *documentation*, there is a consensus that, for the sake of transparency and to enable others to comprehend what a study has done, QCA researchers should thoroughly document their data sources, raw and calibrated data, calibration criteria, and the analytical choices made throughout the analysis. Moreover, key elements like the truth table, solution terms, and case membership in individual solution paths should always be reported in publications (Schneider, Vis, and Koivu 2019; Schneider and Wagemann 2010). Ideally, these should be part of the main body of the text in a journal article or book chapter, but they can also be relegated to appendixes. Alternatively, some of these elements can be placed in supplementary documents that are made available online, as on a journal's website or a public repository. However, essentials like the truth table and solution should always be part of the main body of the text. To save space, one option is to omit logical remainders from the published truth table and to provide the complete truth table in an online appendix (in that case, there should be a footnote in the former to indicate that the truth table was abbreviated).

Beyond these points, it is considered good practice to provide other relevant information on the analysis in supplementary documents—including descriptive statistics on the conditions and the outcome, histograms on the distribution of set membership scores, X–Y plots of raw and calibrated data, and results of robustness tests that have been conducted. These help other researchers (and reviewers) in assessing, contextualizing, and reproducing the analytical results. Naturally, the content of such documents varies with the character of the respective study. Applications based on quantitative data and the direct method of calibration should provide descriptive statistics and, potentially, robustness tests with alternative calibration thresholds, whereas studies based on qualitative evidence can use supplementary documents to provide more detailed case narratives. There are numerous examples of such complementary documents, especially among more recent publications (Böller and Müller 2018; Johais, Bayer, and Lambach 2020; Kuehn et al. 2017; Mello 2020; Schneider and Maerz 2017; Vis, Woldendorp, and Keman 2013).

Finally, a central task for any QCA study is *communicating* its findings in an effective manner. This is where causal complexity *does* pose a challenge. How do you convey a clear message for readers (and reviewers) when there are multiple "moving parts," complex interrelationships between conditions, and imperfect set relations? Certainly, what should *not* be done is restricting the substantive interpretation to a mere technical description of the analytical results. Yet, undeniably, there are published studies that limit the discussion of their results and overall conclusions to such formalistic, technical accounts.

To enhance the communication of QCA results, I have three suggestions that tie in with the principles outlined in the previous section. First, a large part of this task occurs during the framing of the research problem and the development of theoretical expectations. When researchers make an *explicit connection* between their research aims and causal complexity, as the core methodological assumption of QCA, then the substantive interpretation of the analytical findings becomes a matter of contrasting theoretical expectations with the identified set relations.

Tying in with the previous point, one way to enhance the communication of QCA results is via *graphical representation*. This can be equally used to illustrate theoretical expectations and/or the analytical results. For instance, Claude Rubinson (2019) provides a useful compendium of different visualizations for QCA, including Venn and Euler diagrams, treemaps, star charts, radar charts, or branching diagrams. Users can draw from this menu of choices to identify the most suitable visualization for their own research context. More generally, Gary Goertz (2020) develops ways how to visualize complex concept structures—a discussion that resonates very well with QCA studies (see also Goertz 2017).

To provide an example for the graphical representation of causal complexity, figure 10.1 gives an abstract summary of hypothesized set-theoretic relationships of conjunctural causation and equifinality, involving four conditions and an outcome (based on Mello 2012). Essentially, the conditions are expected to combine in two distinct paths, both of which lead to the outcome. For each of these paths, the joint presence of

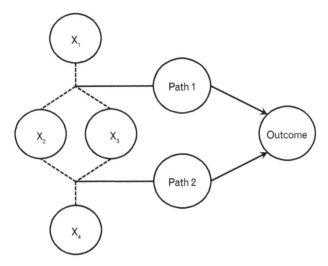

Figure 10.1   Visualizing Conjunctural Causation
and Equifinality

three conditions is required, as indicated by the dashed lines. Together, these conditions constitute the paths that bring about the outcome. In this manner, a variety of different set-theoretic expectations can be visualized. The advantage of graphical representation is that it enhances the understanding of larger patterns. For instance, in figure 10.1 conditions X_2 and X_3 are of central importance—also visually—because these conditions constitute elements in both of the theorized pathways, whereas conditions X_1 and X_4 are peripheral but make distinct contributions to the respective configurations.

Another way to use graphical representation is by visualizing the solution of the QCA analysis. For example, figure 10.2 shows the overall solution and the two solution paths for a fuzzy-set QCA study with 36 cases. Here, the common X–Y plot is enhanced with dashed lines to indicate the *qualitative* difference of whether cases are considered to be inside or outside the outcome and solution or respective solution path (Schneider and Rohlfing 2013).

The plot emphasizes three kinds of cases. The shaded area in the top right triangle highlights *typical cases* that hold membership in both the outcome and the solution, and consequently, also in at least one of the solution paths. Clearly, in an ideal QCA, most of the cases that show the outcome should appear in the top right corner. By contrast, the top left rectangle holds *unaccounted cases*. These are cases that show the outcome of interest but are outside the solution term. From a theoretical perspective, these cases are not in themselves problematic—because they do not share the features that are expected to lead to the outcome—but we would rather not have too many cases in this area, because this would mean that our explanation cannot account for a large part of the phenomenon we care about.

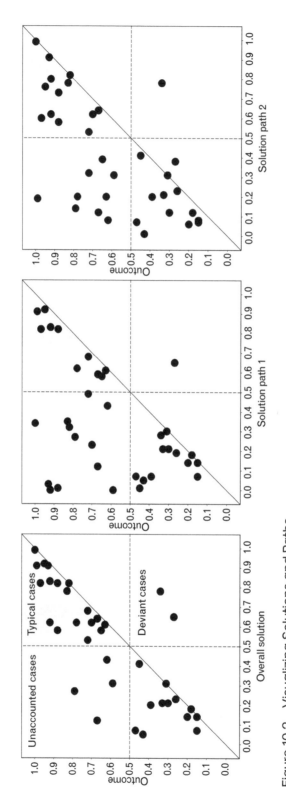

Figure 10.2   Visualizing Solutions and Paths

Then there are *deviant cases*, in the lower right rectangle of figure 10.2. These are problematic because they conflict with our expectations. Deviant cases hold membership in the QCA solution term, but their scores for the outcome are qualitatively lower than expected and suggested by the solution. In an ideal setting, there should be no deviant cases. Yet in empirical applications, researchers will occasionally identify deviant cases. What is important is that their number should remain small in relation to the number of typical cases. Researchers should also discuss plausible explanations as to why their deviant cases did not show the outcome. If there are too many deviant cases, then the research design and especially the selection of conditions and their conceptualization should be revisited.

The graphical representation given in figure 10.2 can be a useful starting point for the provision of *case narratives* for typical cases, deviant cases, and/or unexplained cases, depending on which cases appear in the respective study. This part could also emphasize pathway cases (see case selection, chapter 2), which are cases that are uniquely covered by one of the solution paths. These could also be highlighted separately in the X–Y plots for the solution paths. Clearly, the extent to which a QCA journal article can go into detail on specific cases is limited. But to do justice to the case-oriented nature of QCA, there should at least be illustrative examples of cases for each solution path, to illuminate the respective configurations and paths to the outcome. These can be complemented with additional information provided in appendixes. Table 10.2 summarizes the points on documenting and communicating QCA results.

Table 10.2 Documenting and Communicating QCA Results

Documentation	(1) Reporting all relevant analytical choices
	(2) Listing raw data, calibrated data, and calibration criteria
	(3) Showing the truth table with consistency/frequency thresholds, logical remainders, and discussion of their treatment
	(4) Including solution terms with measures of fit and case membership in solution paths
	(5) Identifying any typical cases, pathway cases, deviant cases, and unexplained cases
	(6) Providing descriptive statistics, histograms, X–Y plots of raw/calibrated data
Communication	(7) Making an explicit connection between research aims and QCA's methodological assumptions
	(8) Including a graphical representation of theoretic expectations and/or graphical representation of solution and solution paths
	(9) Providing case narratives on typical cases, pathway cases, deviant cases, and/or unexplained cases

QCA RESOURCES

Learning a new method requires not just a textbook but also *actual practice* to further this aim. In this light, the book's appendix refers to an online R Manual to conduct the analytical steps discussed in this book. This is complemented by online material available on my website, https://patrickmello.com. There you can find an R Script that mirrors the discussion from the analytical chapters in this book as well as sample data sets.

A helpful resource is the QCA community website of the COMPASSS network, www.compasss.org (the acronym stands for comparative methods for systematic cross-case analysis). On the COMPASSS website, you can find news entries on QCA-related topics, information about training opportunities, a newsletter that you can sign up for, working papers, and various other resources. The COMPASSS management team is headed by Benoît Rihoux and Claude Rubinson, whereas the methods network involves more than 60 QCA experts from around the globe.

A good way to learn QCA is by attending a dedicated course on it. By now, there are various different formats available, from short, one-day introductions and workshops to full courses that span over two weeks. Some courses are also offered in online formats. In the United States, a regular course on offer is entailed in the Institute for Qualitative and Multi-Method Research at Syracuse University. This covers a range of modules, including QCA and set-theoretic methods. There is also a dedicated QCA course at the ICPSR Summer Program in Quantitative Methods at the University of Michigan. In Europe, regular courses are held at the ECPR Summer School in Methods and Techniques, with a two-week introduction to QCA, and at the complementary ECPR Winter School, with a one-week format that aims at advanced users of QCA. Additionally, there are many other opportunities for summer schools and workshops, including an intensive, one-week QCA course at the FORS Swiss Summer School in Social Science Methods, co-organized by the University of Geneva and the Università della Svizzera Italiana in Lugano, where the course is hosted. A list of current training opportunities can be found on the COMPASSS website.

CURRENT DEVELOPMENTS

Originated over three decades ago, QCA continues to evolve and develop (Marx, Rihoux, and Ragin 2014). As shown in chapter 1, empirical applications now cover nearly all areas of the social sciences. At the same time, there is a great degree of *pluralism* under the broad tent of QCA, including not only an array of different variants and approaches, with more variants being developed, but also different ways in how the method is applied in diverse research settings, from qualitative case studies to large-N analyses. The examples used throughout this book and the contributions from other authors testify to this diversity of approaches.

Moreover, there has been *ontological differentiation*, as critical realism has been embraced by a number of QCA scholars, moving away from more positivist assumptions (e.g., Byrne and Ragin 2009; Gerrits and Pagliarin 2020; Gerrits and Verweij 2014; Olsen 2014; and Rutten 2019, 2020). At the same time, debates about causal claims and the conditions under which these could be substantiated with QCA have emerged, as touched upon in chapter 9 (Baumgartner and Thiem 2020; Duşa 2019a; Haesebrouck and Thomann, forthcoming; Rohlfing and Zuber 2019; Schneider 2018). These developments will certainly continue, leading to a further branching out and differentiation within the field of set-theoretic methods.

Where is QCA headed? As the previous sections have shown, the evolution of the method has served to clarify and refine the analytical procedures of QCA, to acknowledge its strengths, and to become aware of its limitations. Though QCA is conceived as a via media approach that combines advantages of qualitative and quantitative methods, there is no silver-bullet method for all research inquiries in the social sciences, and QCA should not be presented as such. However, the limitations of the method can be overcome when guidelines for good QCA research practice are followed and these also help to make the most out of the method's distinct strengths (see chapter 9).

Moreover, there is potential in combining QCA with other methods of inquiry. Indeed, multimethod research has become the gold standard in some areas of the social sciences. In particular, there are fruitful ways of combining set-theoretic comparative methods and within-case methods like process tracing. This remains a dynamic area of research, because scholars are trying to find appropriate ways to combine the research logics of these approaches (Beach and Rohlfing 2018; Goertz 2017; Meegdenburg and Mello, forthcoming; Schneider and Rohlfing 2013; 2019). Another vibrant area of research is software development, and particularly R packages, which have increased their functionality substantially over the past years (Duşa 2019b; Oana and Schneider 2018; Oana, Schneider, and Thomann 2021).[2] Because of R's open environment, this area should see plenty of future development.

THE WAY AHEAD

This book set out to provide a comprehensive guide to QCA and its successful empirical application. Moreover, the book has sought to give step-by-step guidance on how to turn a research project into an effective QCA study, and how to interpret and present set-theoretic analytical findings in publications. As stressed throughout these pages, I believe that *research design* is of central importance on these matters. This is why the book preceded the exposition of the analytical routines with chapters on research design, set theory, and causation and causal complexity. If there is one takeaway lesson, it is that rather than spending time on perfecting their set-theoretic measures of fit through analytical modifications, users should reconsider their research design and concepts. As a *case-oriented* approach with a decidedly *qualitative* bent, QCA is more than the technical exercise of minimizing configurations. It is my hope that the book conveys this holistic approach to QCA and that it proves useful to you—regardless of whether you are taking the first steps toward your own QCA study, have worked with it before and want to improve your application of the method, or want to try out new variants.

NOTES

Epigraph: Ragin (2014b, xxix).

1. This should not imply that the recommendations given are identical. The edited volume by Rihoux and Ragin (2009) contains 13 tables with guidelines on various aspects of QCA research. Similarly, the standards of good practice by Schneider and Wagemann (2010) contain 26 detailed points (see also Schneider and Wagemann 2012). Emmenegger, Kvist, and Skaaning (2013) derive several concrete recommendations from their review of welfare state research. Kahwati and Kane (2020) include many practice tips in their book on QCA in mixed-methods research.

2. A comprehensive listing of available software is maintained at http://compasss.org/software/. At the time of writing, 19 different software programs for various computer environments and research purposes were available.

Appendix • Link to the Online R Manual

The great (or perhaps infuriating) thing about
R is that there's always more to learn.
—ROBERT I. KABACOFF

This book is complemented by an R Manual that is made available online at https://
patrickmello.com/. This has the advantage that the contents of the manual can be
regularly updated to cover additional functions or to incorporate changes that were
made to the relevant R packages. The R Manual entails functions to prepare and analyze data and to conduct set-theoretic analyses, along the lines described in this book.
For this, we use the R software environment (R Core Team 2020) and the RStudio text
editor (2020), as well as the R packages QCA (Duşa 2019) and SetMethods (Oana and
Schneider 2018; Oana, Schneider, and Thomann 2021). The PDF file is complemented
by an R Script that contains all the code used in the R Manual.

As indicated in the above quotation from Robert Kabacoff, one is hardly ever done
learning R. Yet, for new users, the main hurdle is starting with R in the first place. With
this in mind, the R Manual aims to *get you started* toward conducting your own QCA
study and to reproduce the analytical steps introduced in this book. Unlike texts that
assume prior knowledge of R, the manual devotes adequate space to basic questions of
installing the software and working with the R editor, getting the data into shape, and
many of the issues that arise during the analysis.

That said, the R Manual cannot replace a comprehensive introduction to R and
its functionality. Nor can we cover all the potential ways of working with the QCA
packages. Hence, I recommend consulting at least one general introduction to R and
either of the volumes dedicated to the packages: Duşa 2019b; and Oana, Schneider, and Thomann 2021. As for general R introductions, there are plenty of textbooks available, and these are often tailored to usage in a specific research area (e.g.,
Field, Miles, and Field 2012; Gaubatz 2015; Imai 2017; Kabacoff 2015; Pollock and
Edwards 2018).

Another way of learning R is by using one of the many freely available online resources, for example, the "swirl" package.[1] There are also various online discussion forums, where you can find answers to all kinds of R-related questions.[2] When errors occur, it is often a good idea to start looking for a solution by copying the error message into a search engine. Most often, others experienced similar problems, and there may be an easy fix for the issue, especially when it is about common tasks like installing R and its packages, reading data, or working with data frames.

NOTES

Epigraph: Kabacoff (2015, 532).
  1. This can be reached at https://swirlstats.com/.
  2. One of these is https://stackoverflow.com/.

Glossary

This glossary provides definitions of key terms used throughout this book. The entries reflect conventional usage, as developed in book-length treatments of the method (Ragin 1987, 2000, 2008b), prior lexicons in QCA textbooks (Kahwati and Kane 2020; Rihoux and Ragin 2009; Schneider and Wagemann 2012), and general glossaries on research methods (Gerring 2012b; Seawright and Collier 2010). For contextual discussions, readers are referred to the respective pages highlighted in the index. Cross-references are given in italics.

asymmetry. See *causal complexity*.

attribute space. The multidimensional space, within which cases can be located. The attribute "space" has as many dimensions as the number of sets included in the truth table analysis. Also known as *property space*.

Boolean AND. Logical operator that refers to the *intersection* between two sets (also known as *conjunction* in the language of propositional logic). Case membership in the intersection between sets A and B equals the minimum membership score across the respective conditions.

Boolean minimization. Pairwise comparison of Boolean expressions to remove irrelevant elements and attain simpler expressions. Core of the *truth table algorithm*.

Boolean NOT. Logical operator that refers to the *negation* of a set (also known as *complement*, in set-theoretic language). Case membership in the negation of set A equals $1 - A$.

Boolean operations. QCA draws on three operators from Boolean algebra: *Boolean AND*, *Boolean OR*, and *Boolean NOT*. See the respective definitions.

Boolean OR. Logical operator that refers to the *union* between two sets (also known as *disjunction* in the language of propositional logic). Case membership in the union between sets A and B equals the maximum membership score across the respective conditions.

calibration. The transformation of qualitative and/or quantitative *raw data* (uncalibrated data) into membership scores in a target set. The *direct method* of calibration is a software-based transformation that requires the definition of three empirical anchors by the researcher. In the *manual approach*, the researcher directly assigns set-theoretic membership scores to cases. The less-often-used *indirect method* of calibration requires the assignment of preliminary scores to individual cases before a statistical estimation technique is applied to calculate predicted fuzzy values based on the raw data and the initially assigned scores. Each approach requires the prior definition of consistent criteria and close correspondence with the underlying social science concept.

case. Unit of analysis. In the truth table, cases are assigned to the *configuration* in which they hold the highest *set-membership score*.

case selection. The identification of cases for *set-theoretic analysis*. Case selection for QCA can be based on *purposeful selection*, *given populations*, or *scope conditions*, as the most common approaches, which also resonate with the qualitative research logic of QCA. Additionally, if certain requirements are met, it may be viable to use *sampling* techniques, such as random or stratified sampling, to conduct the case selection. As a general principle, case selection should include only *relevant cases*.

causal asymmetry. See *causal complexity*.

causal complexity. An umbrella concept that entails three methodological assumptions that QCA rests on: (1) *conjunctural causation* describes a setting where single conditions do not individually suffice to generate the phenomenon of interest but where specific combinations of conditions are jointly sufficient for the outcome. (2) *Equifinality* relates to a setting where multiple paths made up of individual conditions or combinations of conditions independently lead to the same outcome. Finally, (3) *causal asymmetry* means that a recipe for the outcome can usually not be mirrored symmetrically to explain the nonoutcome but instead requires a separate analysis.

causal mechanism. Generative process where several elements interact to bring about an outcome. Closely related to the within-case method of process tracing, which aims at the identification of a causal link between a condition and an outcome. See also *multimethod research*.

causation. The relation between a cause and its effect. The main theories of causation emphasize regularity, probability, counterfactuals, or mechanisms (see chapter 4).

complement. See *negation*.

complex solution. See *conservative solution*.

complexity. See *causal complexity*.

condition. An attribute, characteristic, or feature of a *case* that is used to describe and/or explain an *outcome*. In each condition, cases have set-theoretic *membership scores* that result from calibration. The term corresponds to what are described as *variables* in statistical usage. A key difference between variables and conditions is that the latter result from calibration, whereas the former can also be uncalibrated measures.

configuration. A combination of conditions represented in a row of the *truth table*.

conjunction. A combination of two or more conditions. See *Boolean AND*.

conjunctural causation. See *causal complexity*.

conservative solution (also: *complex solution*). One of three QCA solution types. The conservative solution results from the Boolean minimization of the truth table rows that are associated with the outcome and that meet the consistency and frequency thresholds specified by the researcher. This solution is termed conservative, because it works solely with empirical cases and does not incorporate logical remainders to achieve further simplification. See also *parsimonious solution* and *intermediate solution*.

consistency. Metric that helps to assess the fit of the empirical evidence with a set-theoretic relationship of necessity or sufficiency. Consistency is calculated separately for necessary and sufficient conditions.

contradiction. Truth table row that entails cases with qualitatively different outcome values (crisp-set membership scores of 1 and 0, or fuzzy-set membership scores above and below 0.5). Also referred to as *contradictory configuration*.

contradictory assumptions. Logical remainders that are assumed to be sufficient for both the outcome and the nonoutcome, which occurs when the same logical remainders are used for both analyses. Also referred to as *contradictory simplifying assumptions* and *incoherent counterfactuals*.

contradictory configuration. See *contradiction*.

counterfactual. Reasoning about a case that did not occur. *Logical remainders* are potential counterfactual cases. That is, they are combinations of conditions without empirical instances for which the plausibility of the outcome can be evaluated by the researcher.

counterfactual theories of causation. Perspectives on causation where a potential cause is a difference maker without which the outcome would not have occurred.

coverage. Metric that helps to assess the empirical relevance of necessary and/or sufficient conditions. For set relations of sufficiency, this shows how much of the empirical evidence is accounted for by a condition or conjunction. For set relations of necessity, this helps to distinguish relevant from trivial necessary conditions. See also *relevance of necessity*.

crisp-set QCA. Analysis solely conducted with *crisp sets*, where set-membership scores in all conditions and the outcome take on binary values.

crossover. Empirical anchor for the set-theoretic *calibration*, which specifies the qualitative point between membership and nonmembership in a set. Also known as *point of maximum ambiguity*.

csQCA. See *crisp-set QCA*.

dependent variable. See *outcome*.

deviant case. Case that holds membership in the *solution* but not in the *outcome*. For fuzzy sets, this means that membership scores in the solution exceed 0.5 and membership scores in the outcome are below 0.5.

difficult counterfactuals. Logical remainders that are simplifying (and that thus contribute to a less complex solution), but for which theoretical and substantive knowledge do not suggest the presence of the outcome. Difficult counterfactuals should be excluded from the *intermediate solution*.

direct method of calibration. See *calibration*.

directional expectation. Expectation derived from theoretical or substantive knowledge of whether the presence or absence of a condition should be associated with the outcome of the analysis. The *intermediate solution* allows for the specification of directional expectations for any number of conditions.

disjunction. See *Boolean OR*.

easy counterfactuals. Logical remainders that are simplifying (and that thus contribute to a less complex solution) and for which theoretical and substantive knowledge suggests the presence of the outcome.

empirical anchors. Also known as *qualitative anchors*. See *calibration*.

Enhanced Standard Analysis (ESA). Analytical refinement of the *standard analysis* (Ragin 2008b), which excludes logical remainders that rest on *untenable assumptions* (Schneider and Wagemann 2013).

epistemology. Perspective on the constitution and origins of knowledge ("what can be known").

equifinality. See *causal complexity*.

Euler diagram. Visual representation of existing intersections between crisp sets (binary values), whereas a *Venn diagram* shows all logically possible intersections.

explanatory condition. See *condition*.

external standards. Criteria used for set-theoretic *calibration*, with particular importance for the definition of the empirical anchors for the direct method of calibration.

fsQCA. See *fuzzy-set QCA*.

fuzzy sets. Sets that allow for graded membership with scores ranging from 0 to 1. Fuzzy sets express qualitative and quantitative differences, distinguishing between being inside a set (scores above 0.5) and being outside a set (scores below 0.5), as well as gradations of imperfect set membership.

fuzzy-set ideal type analysis. QCA variant that employs fuzzy sets for systematic empirical comparison and typological theorizing but that does not aim to explain or account for an outcome (Kvist 2007). The *attribute space* that is circumscribed by the truth table represents the number of ideal types in a given analysis.

fuzzy-set QCA. Analysis conducted with *fuzzy sets*, where set-membership scores in the conditions and/or the outcome take on values from 0 to 1.

general causation. Perspective on causation where individual observations are seen as representations of classes of phenomena. See also *singular causation*.

given population. A predefined population of cases circumscribed by social facts (e.g., member states in an international organization, voters in an electoral district, or companies in a stock index).

good counterfactuals. Counterfactuals that do not rest on *untenable assumptions* and that may or may not contribute to parsimony (Schneider and Wagemann 2012). See also *plausible counterfactuals*.

ideal type. See *fuzzy-set ideal type analysis*.

implausible counterfactuals. Logical remainders that are not plausible as counterfactuals because they meet at least one of the following criteria: (1) theoretical and substantive knowledge does not suggest the presence of the outcome, (2) the respective configuration is contradictory, (3) it is empirically impossible, or (4) it conflicts with a statement of necessity. Antonym: *plausible counterfactuals*.

impossible cases. Cases where the outcome or the nonoutcome is deemed impossible by what is known about the world. As a general principle, only *relevant cases* should be included where the outcome could possibly happen, and which are substantively important. See also *irrelevant cases*.

impossible counterfactuals. Logical remainders that entail a conjunction of conditions that is not possible in logical terms or by what is known about the world.

incoherent counterfactuals. Logical remainders that conflict with a previously identified necessary condition.

indirect method of calibration. See *calibration*.

intermediate solution. One of three solution types. The intermediate solution results from the *Boolean minimization* of the truth table rows that are associated with the outcome and that meet the consistency and frequency thresholds specified by the researcher. To derive a less complex solution, the procedure for the intermediate solution is further allowed to consider certain logical remainders in the pairwise Boolean minimization. This can be done via specifying *directional expectations* for each condition or by excluding *implausible counterfactuals*. As such, the intermediate solution is positioned between the *conservative solution* and the *parsimonious solution*.

intersection. A combination of two or more *conditions*. See *Boolean AND*.

INUS condition. Insufficient but necessary part of a condition that is itself unnecessary but sufficient for the result (Mackie 1965).

irrelevant cases. Cases where either (1) the outcome or the nonoutcome is deemed impossible by what is known about the world, or that are (2) substantively unimportant in light of a study's research aims. As a general principle, only *relevant cases* should be included for case selection. Antonym *relevant cases*. See also *impossible cases*.

limited diversity. A phenomenon that occurs when the number of logically possible configurations exceeds the number of empirical cases. Hence, the extent to which there is limited diversity in a given analysis can be seen from the number of *logical remainder* rows in the *truth table*.

logical remainder. A truth table row that is not associated with any empirical case.

MDSO-MSDO. Technique for pairwise Boolean comparison of cases and conditions. MDSO stands for *most different cases, similar outcome*, whereas MSDO refers to *most similar cases, different outcome* (De Meur and Gottcheiner 2009).

measurement. See *calibration*.

measures of fit. Metrics to assess set-theoretic relationships in empirical data. The primary measures of fit for QCA are *consistency* and *coverage*, which are calculated independently for set-theoretic relations of necessity and sufficiency.

mechanistic theories of causation. Perspectives on causation that identify the *causal mechanism* that links a causal condition to an outcome.

membership score (synonym: *membership value*). Numerical representation of case membership in a given set. Crisp-set membership can assume scores of 1 and 0, while fuzzy-set membership can also take on decimal scores in between these values.

Mill's methods. Methods of scientific inquiry developed by John Stuart Mill in *A System of Logic* (1843). Mill's methods include the method of agreement and method of difference, as well as the lesser-known method of residues and method of concomitant variations, and the joint method of agreement and difference. QCA builds on a systematic application of the joint method. However, it is important to note that QCA goes well beyond Mill's methods. These include the consideration of *causal complexity*, *limited diversity*, *measures of fit*, and *Boolean minimization* for a systematic comparative procedure and inferential analysis.

minimization. See *Boolean minimization*.

model. Term used for the entirety of conditions used in a truth table analysis.

model ambiguity. The phenomenon that, depending on the structure of the truth table and the assumptions made, several logically equivalent solution terms may be derived from the same empirical data (Baumgartner and Thiem 2017).

multimethod research. The combination of two or more research methods to gain inferential leverage. In the set-theoretic context, multimethod research designs typically entail the combination of QCA, as a method for cross-case analysis, with process tracing to conduct within-case analysis, and specifically, for the identification of causal mechanisms. This does not preclude the combination of QCA with other qualitative and/or quantitative methods.

multivalue QCA. Variant of QCA that incorporates multivalue conditions (Cronqvist and Berg-Schlosser 2009).

mvQCA. See *multivalue QCA*.

Necessary Condition Analysis (NCA). A distinct methodology for the identification of necessary conditions in data sets. Rather than working with the metric of consistency, as QCA does, NCA employs different levels of conditions, as in "level X is necessary for level Y" (Dul 2016; Vis and Dul 2018).

necessary condition. A necessary condition means that a factor is always present when the outcome of interest occurs. Put differently, the outcome does occur without the presence of the necessary condition. From a theory perspective, we can say that necessary conditions explain failure because they are a prerequisite for a phenomenon to occur.

negation. See *Boolean NOT*.

negative case. Case that does not hold membership in the *outcome*.

neopositivism. Social scientific perspective that regards social phenomena as governed by observable regularities that can be objectively assessed by researchers.

notation. QCA draws on different notational systems. Depending on a subfield's custom, it may be preferred to use symbols and terms from Boolean algebra, propositional logic, and/or set theory.

ontology. Perspective on social and physical reality ("what the world is made of"). Ontological assumptions have epistemological and methodological implications, but by definition they cannot be proven.

outcome. The phenomenon to be accounted for in the set-theoretic analysis. Similar (but not identical) to the *dependent variable* in statistical approaches.

parsimonious solution. One of three solution types. The parsimonious solution results from the *Boolean minimization* of the truth table rows that are associated with the outcome and that meet the consistency and frequency thresholds specified by the researcher. To derive a less complex solution, the procedure for the parsimonious solution is further allowed to consider all logical remainders in the pairwise minimization. Those logical remainders that are used are referred to as *simplifying assumptions*, because they simplify the resultant solution and rest on assumptions about counterfactual cases. Notably, the parsimonious solution may rest on *untenable assumptions*. See also *conservative solution* and *intermediate solution*.

path. One configuration in a solution (which typically includes several paths).

pathway case. Case that is uniquely covered by one solution path. See also *typical case*.

plausible counterfactuals. Logical remainders that meet all these criteria: (1) theoretical and substantive knowledge suggests the presence of the outcome, (2) the respective configuration is not contradictory, (3) it is empirically possible, and (4) it does not conflict with a statement of necessity. Antonym: *implausible counterfactuals*.

point of maximum ambiguity. See *crossover*.

population. See *case selection*.

positive case. Case that holds membership in the *outcome*.

positivism. See *neopositivism*.

Proportional Reduction in Inconsistency (PRI). PRI is a measure to identify *simultaneous subset relations* in the analysis of sufficient conditions.

prime implicants. Boolean expressions that result from the minimization of truth table rows that are associated with the outcome (*primitive expressions*). Prime implicants are supersets of the primitive expressions they are derived from. The prime implicant chart helps to determine whether any prime implicants are redundant because the entailed information is already covered by other prime implicants. In such a situation, a simpler solution term can be derived by eliminating the redundant prime implicants.

primitive expression. Expression that represents a truth table row associated with the outcome. See also *prime implicants*.

probability theories of causation. Perspectives on causation where a potential cause is seen as a probability raiser for the occurrence of its effect.

property space. See *attribute space*.

purposeful selection. See *case selection*.

qualitative anchors. Also known as *empirical anchors*. See *calibration*.

Qualitative Comparative Analysis (QCA). A comparative method that regards cases as combinations of conditions and that aims for the identification of conditions that are necessary and/or sufficient for an outcome.

Quine-McCluskey algorithm. See *truth table algorithm*.

random selection. See *case selection*.

raw coverage. Metric to assess how much of the empirical evidence is accounted for by a given solution path. See also *solution coverage* and *unique coverage*.

raw data. See *calibration*.

recipe. A *configuration* that is sufficient for the outcome. In this sense, the term is used interchangeably with *path* and *pathway*. But recipe is also used to denote entire *solutions*.

regularity theories of causation. Perspectives on causation where a potential cause appears repeatedly and in a regular fashion.

Relevance of Necessity (RoN). Metric to assess whether a condition that fulfills the formal criteria for necessity may be a trivial necessary condition (Schneider and Wagemann 2012).

relevant cases. Cases where (1) the outcome and the nonoutcome are deemed possible by what is known about the world, (2) and which are substantively important in light of a study's research aims. As a general principle, only relevant cases should be included for case selection. Antonym: *irrelevant cases*. See also *impossible cases*.

remainders. See *logical remainders*.

research cycle. Ideal-typical conception of the social-scientific research process, which starts with the definition of the research problem and research question and moves on to include the formulation of theoretical expectations, the selection of cases and conditions, data gathering, calibration, and set-theoretic analysis, before closing with substantive interpretation, which in turn may give rise to revisiting the initial stages of the research cycle.

research design. Strategy of scientific inquiry that aims to identify appropriate solutions to scientific problems.

robustness tests. Procedures to establish the extent to which the results of the set-theoretic analysis are conditional upon specific analytical choices, such as case selection criteria, calibration thresholds, or decisions made throughout the analysis, including consistency and frequency levels, and the treatment of logical remainders.

sampling. See *case selection*.

scope condition. Criterion that confines the selection of cases on the basis of theoretical or substantive considerations.

set operations. See *Boolean operations*.

set relations. QCA evolves around set relations of necessity and sufficiency. See *necessary condition* and *sufficient condition*.

set-theoretic analysis. Analysis of set-theoretic relationships of necessity and/or sufficiency. See also *truth table analysis*.

set theory. Unifying theory of mathematics. QCA draws on set theory to analyze social phenomena and the set relations between them.

set. A group of elements that share certain characteristics.

simplifying assumptions. *Logical remainders* that are treated as if they were sufficient for the outcome when deriving the parsimonious and/or intermediate solution.

simultaneous subset relations. Phenomenon that may occur with fuzzy-set data when a configuration is both a subset of the outcome and a subset of the nonoutcome. This would be a logical contradiction. However, based solely on the measures of *consistency* and *coverage*, it would be difficult to determine whether a configuration should be treated as sufficient for the outcome or the nonoutcome. To identify such situations, the PRI metric was introduced; see *proportional reduction in inconsistency*.

singular causation. Perspective where causal claims are derived from singular cases, without assuming a larger, more general pattern. See also *general causation*.

solutions. QCA entails three different solution types. These result from the *Boolean minimization* procedure and the treatment of *logical remainders*. See *complex solution*, *parsimonious solution*, and *intermediate solution*.

solution coverage. Metric that helps to assess how much of the empirical evidence is accounted for by all paths in a given solution. See also *raw coverage* and *unique coverage*.

standard analysis. Term used to describe the analytical procedure of deriving a complex solution, parsimonious solution, and intermediate solution (Ragin 2008b). See also *enhanced standard analysis*.

sufficient condition. This means that whenever a factor is present, the outcome is also present. Hence, we can say that sufficient conditions serve to explain success, as they always lead to the outcome.

SUIN Condition. A sufficient but unnecessary part of a factor that is insufficient but necessary for an outcome (Mahoney, Kimball, and Koivu 2009).

token-level explanation. See *singular causation*.

Tosmana. Software initially developed for crisp-set and multivalue QCA, but its functionality has been expanded to also cover fuzzy-set QCA (Cronqvist 2019).

trivialness. A condition or configuration that fulfills the criteria for set relations of necessity and/or sufficiency but that constitutes a trivial finding. See also *relevance of necessity*.

truth table. The truth table shows the number of possible combinations of conditions and the empirical distribution of cases across those configurations. The number of possible rows equals 2^k, where k is the number of conditions included in a given study. The truth table further indicates how consistent the set-theoretic relationship of sufficiency is for each row.

truth table algorithm. The algorithm used for the Boolean minimization and the construction of QCA solution terms. The standard remains the Quine-McCluskey (QMC) algorithm, but this has been complemented by an enhanced version (eQMC) and the Consistency Cubes algorithm (Duşa 2018).

truth table analysis. Analytical procedure that involves the *Boolean minimization* of configurations that are sufficient for the outcome, based on consistency and frequency thresholds specified by the researcher. The truth table analysis yields different *solution terms*, depending on the treatment of logical remainders.

two-step approach. QCA variant that splits up the analysis into separate truth table procedures based on the distinction between remote and proximate conditions (Schneider and Wagemann 2006).

type-level causation. See *general causation*.

typical case. Case that holds membership in the solution and the outcome and where set-membership scores in the latter exceed those in the former. See also *pathway case*.

typological reasoning. See *fuzzy-set ideal-type analysis*.

union. See *Boolean OR*.

unique coverage. Metric that helps to assess how much of the empirical evidence is accounted for by a given solution path. See also *solution coverage* and *raw coverage*.

untenable assumptions. Umbrella category that contains *incoherent counterfactuals* and *impossible counterfactuals* (Schneider and Wagemann 2012).

Venn diagram. Visual representation of all logically possible intersections between crisp sets (binary values), whereas a *Euler diagram* only shows existing intersections.

X–Y Plot. Visual representation of set relations between fuzzy sets (degrees of membership).

References

Adcock, Robert. 2007. "Who's Afraid of Determinism? The Ambivalence of Macro-Historical Inquiry." *Journal of Philosophy of History* 1, no. 3: 346–64.

Ahmed, Amel, and Rudra Sil. 2009. "Is Multi-Method Research Really 'Better'?" *Qualitative & Multi-Method Research* 7, no. 2: 2–6.

Ahn, Sang-Hoon, and Sophia Seung-yoon Lee. 2012. "Explaining Korean Welfare State Development with New Empirical Data and Methods." *Asian Social Work and Policy Review* 6, no. 2: 67–85.

Allen, Myles R., Opha Pauline Dube, and William Solecki. 2018. "Framing and Context." In *Global Warming of 1.5°C: An IPCC Special Report*, edited by Masson-Delmotte, Valérie, Panmao Zhai, and Hans-Otto Pörtner. Geneva: Intergovernmental Panel on Climate Change.

Amenta, Edwin, and Jane D. Poulsen. 1994. "Where to Begin: A Survey of Five Approaches to Selecting Independent Variables for Qualitative Comparative Analysis." *Sociological Methods & Research* 23, no. 1: 22–53.

An, Mi Young, and Ito Peng. 2016. "Diverging Paths? A Comparative Look at Childcare Policies in Japan, South Korea, and Taiwan." *Social Policy and Administration* 50, no. 5: 540–58.

Andersson, Matthew A., and Sarah K. Harkness. 2018. "When Do Biological Attributions of Mental Illness Reduce Stigma? Using Qualitative Comparative Analysis to Contextualize Attributions." *Society and Mental Health* 8, no. 3: 175–94.

Anjum, Rani Lill, and Stephen Mumford. 2018. *Causation in Science*. New York: Oxford University Press.

Arel-Bundock, Vincent. 2019. "The Double Bind of Qualitative Comparative Analysis." *Sociological Methods & Research*, November 7. doi:10.1177/0049124119882460.

Avdagic, Sabina. 2010. "When Are Concerted Reforms Feasible? Explaining the Emergence of Social Pacts in Western Europe." *Comparative Political Studies* 43, no. 5: 628–57.

Bakker, René M., Bart Cambré, Leonique Korlaar, and Joerg Raab. 2011. "Managing the Project Learning Paradox: A Set-Theoretic Approach toward Project Knowledge Transfer." *International Journal of Project Management* 29, no. 5: 494–503.

Basedau, Matthias, and Thomas Richter. 2014. "Why Do Some Oil Exporters Experience Civil War But Others Do Not? Investigating the Conditional Effects of Oil." *European Political Science Review* 6, no. 4: 549–74.

Baumgartner, Michael. 2008. "Regularity Theories Reassessed." *Philosophia* 36: 327–54.

——. 2009. "Inferring Causal Complexity." *Sociological Methods & Research* 38, no. 1: 71–101.

——. 2013a. "Detecting Causal Chains in Small-*n* Data." *Field Methods* 25, no. 1: 3–24.

——. 2013b. "A Regularity Theoretic Approach to Actual Causation." *Erkenntnis* 78: 85–109.

——. 2015. "Parsimony and Causality." *Quality & Quantity* 49, no. 2: 839–56.

Baumgartner, Michael, and Mathias Ambühl. 2020. "Causal Modeling with Multi-Value and Fuzzy-Set Coincidence Analysis." *Political Science Research and Methods* 8, no. 3: 526–42.

Baumgartner, Michael, and Alrik Thiem. 2017. "Model Ambiguities in Configurational Comparative Research." *Sociological Methods & Research* 46, no. 4: 954–87.

——. 2020. "Often Trusted but Never (Properly) Tested: Evaluating Qualitative Comparative Analysis." *Sociological Methods & Research* 49, no. 2: 279–311.

Beach, Derek. 2018. "Achieving Metholodogical Alignment When Combining QCA and Process Tracing in Practice." *Sociological Methods & Research* 47, no. 1: 64–99.

——. 2020. "Multi-Method Research in the Social Sciences: A Review of Recent Frameworks and a Way Forward." *Government and Opposition* 55, no. 1: 163–82.

Beach, Derek, and Rasmus Brun Pedersen. 2013. *Process-Tracing Methods: Foundations and Guidelines*, 1st ed. Ann Arbor: University of Michigan Press.

——. 2016. *Causal Case Study Methods: Foundations and Guidelines for Comparing, Matching, and Tracing.* Ann Arbor: University of Michigan Press.

——. 2019. *Process-Tracing Methods: Foundations and Guidelines*, 2nd ed. Ann Arbor: University of Michigan Press.

Beach, Derek, Rasmus Brun Pedersen, and Markus B. Siewert. 2019. "Case Selection and Nesting of Process-Tracing Case Studies." In *Process-Tracing Methods: Foundations and Guidelines*, edited by Derek Beach and Rasmus Brun Pedersen, 89–154. Ann Arbor: University of Michigan Press.

Beach, Derek, and Ingo Rohlfing. 2018. "Integrating Cross-Case Analyses and Process Tracing in Set-Theoretic Research: Strategies and Parameters of Debate." *Sociological Methods & Research* 47, no. 1: 3–36.

Beebee, Helen, Christopher Hitchcock, and Peter Menzies, eds. 2009. *The Oxford Handbook of Causation*. Oxford: Oxford University Press.

Bennett, Andrew. 2008. "Process Tracing: A Bayesian Perspective." In *The Oxford Handbook of Political Methodology*, edited by Janet M. Box-Steffensmeier, Henry E. Brady, and David Collier, 702–21. Oxford: Oxford University Press.

——. 2013. "The Mother of All Isms: Causal Mechanisms and Structured Pluralism in International Relations Theory." *European Journal of International Relations* 19, no. 3: 459–81.

Bennett, Andrew, and Jeffrey T. Checkel, eds. 2015. *Process Tracing: From Metaphor to Analytic Tool.* Cambridge: Cambridge University Press.

Berg-Schlosser, Dirk, and Gisèle De Meur. 2009. "Comparative Research Design: Case and Variable Selection." In *Configurational Comparative Methods*, edited by Benoît Rihoux and Charles C. Ragin, 19–32. Thousand Oaks, CA: Sage.

Berg-Schlosser, Dirk, Gisèle De Meur, Benoît Rihoux, and Charles C. Ragin. 2009. "Qualitative Comparative Analysis (QCA) as an Approach." In *Configurational Comparative Methods*, edited by Benoît Rihoux and Charles C. Ragin, 1–18. Thousand Oaks, CA: Sage.

Berger, Elisabeth S. C., Matthias Wenzel, and Veit Wohlgemuth. 2018. "Imitation-Related Performance Outcomes in Social Trading: A Configurational Approach." *Journal of Business Research* 89 (August): 322–27.

Bevir, Mark, and Jason Blakely. 2018. *Interpretive Social Science: An Anti-Naturalist Approach.* Oxford: Oxford University Press.

Bhaskar, Roy. 2008. *A Realist Theory of Science*, 3rd ed. London: Verso.

Binder, Martin. 2015. "Paths to Intervention: What Explains the UN's Selective Response to Humanitarian Crises?" *Journal of Peace Research* 52, no. 6: 712–26.

Birkland, Thomas A. 2006. *Lessons of Disaster: Policy Change after Catastrophic Events.* Washington, DC: Georgetown University Press.

Blatter, Joachim, and Markus Haverland. 2012. *Designing Case Studies: Explanatory Approaches in Small-n Research.* Basingstoke, UK: Palgrave Macmillan.

Bol, Damien, and Francesca Luppi. 2013. "Confronting Theories Based on Necessary Relations: Making the Best of QCA Possibilities." *Political Research Quarterly* 66, no. 1: 205–10.

Böller, Florian, and Marcus Müller. 2018. "Unleashing the Watchdogs: Explaining Congressional Assertiveness in the Politics of US Military Interventions." *European Political Science Review* 10, no. 4: 637–62.

Boogaerts, Andreas. 2018. "Beyond Norms: A Configurational Analysis of the EU's Arab Spring Sanctions." *Foreign Policy Analysis* 14, no. 3: 408–28.

Boogaerts, Andreas, and Edith Drieskens. 2020. "Lessons from the MENA Region: A Configurational Explanation of the (In)Effectiveness of UN Security Council Sanctions between 1991 and 2014." *Mediterranean Politics* 25, no. 1: 71–95.

Boole, George. 1854. *An Investigation of the Laws of Thought on Which Are Founded the Mathematical Theories of Logic and Probabilities.* Urbana, IL: Project Gutenberg.

Boudet, Hilary, Leanne Giordono, Chad Zanocco, Hannah Satein, and Hannah Whitley. 2019. "Event Attribution and Partisanship Shape Local Discussion of Climate Change After Extreme Weather." *Nature Climate Change* 10: 69–76.

Brady, Henry E. 2008. "Causation and Explanation in Social Science." In *The Oxford Handbook of Political Methodology*, edited by Janet M. Box-Steffensmeier, Henry E. Brady, and David Collier, 217–70. Oxford: Oxford University Press.

Brady, Henry E., and David Collier, eds. 2004. *Rethinking Social Inquiry: Diverse Tools, Shared Standards.* Lanham, 1st ed. MD: Rowman & Littlefield.

———, eds. 2010. *Rethinking Social Inquiry: Diverse Tools, Shared Standards*, 2nd ed. Lanham, MD: Rowman & Littlefield.

Braumoeller, Bear F. 2015. "Guarding Against False Positives in Qualitative Comparative Analysis." *Political Analysis* 23, no. 4: 471–87.

Braumoeller, Bear F., and Gary Goertz. 2000. "The Methodology of Necessary Conditions." *American Journal of Political Science* 44, no. 4: 844–58.

Brockhaus, Maria, Kaisa Korhonen-Kurki, Jenniver Sehring, Monica Di Gregorio, Samuel Assembe-Mvondo, Hermann Kambire, Felicien Kengoum, Demetrius Kweka, Mary Menton, Moira Moeliono, Naya Sharma Paudel, Thuy Thu Pham, Ida Aju Pradnja Resosudarmo, Almeida Sitoe, Sven Wunder, and Mathurin Zida. 2017. "REDD+, Transformational Change and the Promise of Performance-Based Payments: A Qualitative Comparative Analysis." *Climate Policy* 17, no. 6: 708–30.

Brown, Michael E., Steven E. Miller, and Sean M. Lynn-Jones, eds. 1996. *Debating the Democratic Peace*. Cambridge, MA: MIT Press.

Buche, Jonas, and Markus B. Siewert. 2015. "Qualitative Comparative Analysis (QCA) in der Soziologie: Perspektiven, Potentiale, und Anwendungsbereiche." *Zeitschrift für Soziologie* 44, no. 6: 386–406.

Büchel, Florin, Edda Humprecht, Laia Castro-Herrero, Sven Engesser, and Michael Brüggemann. 2016. "Building Empirical Typologies with QCA: Toward a Classification of Media Systems." *International Journal of Press/Politics* 21, no. 2: 209–32.

Büthe, Tim. 2002. "Taking Temporality Seriously: Modeling History and the Use of Narratives as Evidence." *American Journal of Political Science* 54, no. 3: 667–85.

Büthe, Tim, and Alan M. Jacobs. 2015. "Introduction to the Symposium: Transparency in Qualitative and Multi-Method Research." *Qualitative & Multi-Method Research* 13, no. 1: 2–8.

Buzogány, Aron, and Jens R. Häsing. 2018. "Explaining Subnational Parliamentary Scrutiny Powers: A Fuzzy-Set Analysis of German Landtage." *Regional & Federal Studies* 28, no. 5: 547–74.

Byrne, David. 2009. "Complex Realist and Configurational Approaches to Cases: A Radical Synthesis." In *The Sage Handbook of Case-Based Methods*, edited by David Byrne and Charles C. Ragin, 101–11. Los Angeles: Sage.

Byrne, David, and Charles C. Ragin, eds. 2009. *The Sage Handbook of Case-Based Methods*. Los Angeles: Sage.

Cacciatore, Federica, Alessandro Natalini, and Claudius Wagemann. 2015. "Clustered Europeanization and National Reform Programmes: A Qualitative Comparative Analysis." *Journal of European Public Policy* 22, no. 8: 1186–211.

Caporaso, James A. 1995. "Research Design, Falsification, and the Qualitative-Quantitative Divide." *American Political Science Review* 89, no. 2: 457–60.

Caren, Neal, and Aaron Panofsky. 2005. "TQCA: A Technique for Adding Temporality to Qualitative Comparative Analysis." *Sociological Methods & Research* 34, no. 2: 147–72.

Cartwright, Nancy. 1979. "Causal Effects and Effective Strategies." *Noûs* 13, no. 4: 419–37.

Castillo Ortiz, Pablo José. 2017. "Councils of the Judiciary and Judges' Perceptions of Respect to Their Independence in Europe." *Hague Journal on the Rule of Law* 9, no. 2: 315–36.

Ciccia, Rosella, and Mieke Verloo. 2012. "Parental Leave Regulations and the Persistence of the Male Breadwinner Model: Using Fuzzy-Set Ideal Type Analysis to Assess Gender Equality in an Enlarged Europe." *Journal of European Social Policy* 22, no. 5: 507–28.

Clarke, Kevin A. 2020. "Logical Constraints: The Limitations of QCA in Social Science Research." *Political Analysis*, April 20. doi:10.1017/pan.2020.7.

Collier, David. 2011. "Understanding Process Tracing." *Political Science & Politics* 44, no. 4: 823–30.

———. 2014a. "Problematic Tools: Introduction to a Symposium on Set Theory in Social Science." *Qualitative & Multi-Method Research* 12, no. 1: 2–9.

———. 2014b. "QCA Should Set Aside the Algorithms." *Sociological Methodology* 44, no. 1: 122–26.

Collier, David, Henry E. Brady, and Jason Seawright. 2010a. "Critiques, Responses, and Trade-Offs: Drawing Together the Debate." In *Rethinking Social Inquiry*, edited by Henry E. Brady and David Collier, 125–59. Lanham, MD: Rowman & Littlefield.

——. 2010b. "Sources of Leverage in Causal Inference: Toward an Alternative View of Methodology." In *Rethinking Social Inquiry*, edited by Henry E. Brady and David Collier, 161–99. Lanham, MD: Rowman & Littlefield.

Collier, David, Jody Laporte, and Jason Seawright. 2008. "Typologies: Forming Concepts and Creating Categorical Variables." In *The Oxford Handbook of Political Methodology*, edited by Janet M. Box-Steffensmeier, Henry E. Brady, and David Collier, 152–73. Oxford: Oxford University Press.

Cooper, Barry, and Judith Glaesser. 2016. "Qualitative Comparative Analysis, Necessary Conditions, and Limited Diversity: Some Problematic Consequences of Schneider and Wagemann's Enhanced Standard Analysis." *Field Methods* 28, no. 3: 300–315.

Cooper, Barry, Judith Glaesser, Roger Gomm, and Martyn Hammersley. 2012. *Challenging the Qualitative-Quantitative Divide: Explorations in Case-Focused Causal Analysis*. London: Continuum.

Coppedge, Michael. 2009. "Speedbumps on the Road to Multi-Method Consensus in Comparative Politics." *Qualitative & Multi-Method Research* 7, no. 2: 15–17.

Cronqvist, Lasse. 2004. "Presentation of Tosmana: Adding Multi-Value Variables and Visual Aids to QCA." COMPASSS Working Paper 20.

——. 2019. *Tosmana [Version 1.61]*. University of Trier.

Cronqvist, Lasse, and Dirk Berg-Schlosser. 2009. "Multi-Value QCA (mvQCA)." In *Configurational Comparative Methods: Qualitative Comparative Analysis (QCA) and Related Techniques*, edited by Benoît Rihoux and Charles C. Ragin, 69–86. Los Angeles: Sage.

Culpepper, Pepper D. 2014. "The Political Economy of Unmediated Democracy: Italian Austerity under Mario Monti." *West European Politics* 37, no. 6: 1264–81.

Cunningham, Daniel W. 2016. *Set Theory: A First Course*. New York: Cambridge University Press.

Damonte, Alessia. 2018. "Gauging the Import and Essentiality of Single Conditions in Standard Configurational Solutions." *Sociological Methods & Research*, September 11. doi:10.1177/0049124118794678.

De Block, Debora, and Barbara Vis. 2019. "Addressing the Challenges Related to Transforming Qualitative into Quantitative Data in Qualitative Comparative Analysis." *Journal of Mixed Methods Research* 13, no. 4: 503–35.

De Meur, Gisèle, and Alain Gottcheiner. 2009. "The Logic and Assumptions of MDSO-MSDO Designs." In *The Sage Handbook of Case-Based Methods*, edited by David Byrne and Charles C. Ragin, 208–21. Los Angeles: Sage.

De Meur, Gisèle, Benoît Rihoux, and Sakura Yamasaki. 2009. "Addressing the Critiques of QCA." In *Configurational Comparative Methods*, edited by Benoît Rihoux and Charles C. Ragin, 147–65. Thousand Oaks, CA: Sage.

Drass, Kriss A., and Charles C. Ragin. 1986. "QCA: A Microcomputer Package for Qualitative Comparative Analysis of Social Data." Center for Urban Affairs and Policy Research, Northwestern University.

Dul, Jan. 2016. "Necessary Condition Analysis (NCA): Logic and Methodology of 'Necessary but Not Sufficent' Causality." *Organization Studies* 19, no. 1: 10–52.

Dul, Jan, Erwin Van der Laan, and Roelof Kuik. 2020. "A Statistical Significance Test for Necessary Condition Analysis." *Organizational Research Methods* 32, no. 2: 385–95.

Dul, Jan, Barbara Vis, and Gary Goertz. 2018. "Necessary Condition Analysis (NCA) Does Exactly What It Should Do When Applied Properly: A Reply to a Comment on NCA." *Sociological Methods & Research*, October 7. doi:10.1177/0049124118799383.

Durán Mogollón, Lía, Olga Eisele, and Maria Paschou. 2020. "Applied Solidarity in Time of Crisis: Exploring the Contexts of Civil Society Activities in Greece and Germany." *Acta Politica*, March 24. doi:10.1057/s41269-020-00154-8.

Duşa, Adrian. 2018. "Consistency Cubes: A Fast, Efficient Method for Exact Boolean Minimization." *R Journal* 10, no. 2: 357–70.

———. 2019a. "Critical Tension: Sufficiency and Parsimony in QCA." *Sociological Methods & Research*, November 18. doi:10.1177/0049124119882456.

———. 2019b. *QCA with R: A Comprehensive Resource*. Cham, UK: Springer.

Duverger, Maurice. 1954. *Political Parties: Their Organization and Activity in the Modern State*. London: Methuen.

Eckstein, Harry. 1975. "Case Study and Theory in Political Science." In *Handbook of Political Science*, edited by Fred I. Greenstein and Nelson W. Polsby, 79–137. Reading, UK: Addison-Wesley.

Ege, Jörn. 2017. "Comparing the Autonomy of International Public Administrations: An Ideal-Type Approach." *Public Administration* 95, no. 3: 555–70.

Eliason, Scott R., and Robin Stryker. 2009. "Goodness-of-Fit Tests and Descriptive Measures in Fuzzy-Set Analysis." *Sociological Methods & Research* 38, no. 1: 102–46.

Elman, Colin. 2005. "Explanatory Typologies in Qualitative Studies of International Politics." *International Organization* 59: 293–326.

Elster, John. 2015. *Explaining Social Behavior: More Nuts and Bolts for the Social Sciences*. New York: Cambridge University Press.

Emmenegger, Patrick. 2011. "How Good Are Your Counterfactuals? Assessing Quantitative Macro-Comparative Welfare State Research with Qualitative Criteria." *Journal of European Social Policy* 21, no. 4: 365–80.

Emmenegger, Patrick, Jon Kvist, and Svend-Erik Skaaning. 2013. "Making the Most of Configurational Comparative Analysis: An Assessment of QCA Applications in Comparative Welfare State Research." *Political Research Quarterly* 66, no. 1: 185–90.

Engeli, Isabelle, and Christine Rothmayr Allison. 2013. "Diverging Against All Odds? Regulatory Paths in Embryonic Stem Cell Research across Western Europe." *Journal of European Public Policy* 20, no. 3: 407–24.

European Parliamentary Research Service. 2019. "The Fight against Unemployment." Briefing, PE 630.274.

Eurostat. 2020. "Euro Area Unemployment at 7.4%, EU at 6.6%." Eurostat News Release, April 30.

Ewert, Christian, Céline Kaufmann, and Martino Maggetti. 2020. "Linking Democratic Anchorage and Regulatory Authority: The Case of Internet Regulators." *Regulation & Governance* 14, no. 2: 184–202.

Fagerholm, Andreas. 2014. "Social Democratic Parties and the Rise of Ecologism: A Comparative Analysis of Western Europe." *Comparative European Politics* 14, no. 5: 1–25.

Falleti, Tulia G., and Julia F. Lynch. 2009. "Context and Causal Mechanisms in Political Analysis." *Comparative Political Studies* 42, no. 9: 1143–66.

Fearon, James D. 1991. "Counterfactuals and Hypothesis Testing in Political Science." *World Politics* 43, no. 2: 169–95.

Fernández-García, Belén, and Óscar G. Luengo. 2019. "Electoral Scenarios of Success for Anti-Establishment Political Parties in Western Europe: A Fuzzy-Set Qualitative Comparative Analysis." *Journal of Contemporary Europan Studies* 27, no. 1: 77–95.

Field, Andy, Jeremy Miles, and Zoë Field. 2012. *Discovering Statistics Using R.* Los Angeles: Sage.

Fischer, Manuel, and Martino Maggetti. 2017. "Qualitative Comparative Analysis and the Study of Policy Processes." *Journal of Comparative Policy Analysis: Research and Practice* 19, no. 4: 345–61.

Fiss, Peer C. 2011. "Building Better Causal Theories: A Fuzzy Set Approach to Typologies in Organization Research." *Academy of Management Journal* 54, no. 2: 393–420.

Fiss, Peer C., Axel Marx, and Benoît Rihoux. 2014. "Comment: Getting QCA Right." *Sociological Methodology* 44, no. 1: 95–100.

Fiss, Peer C., Dmitry Sharapov, and Lasse Cronqvist. 2013. "Opposites Attact? Opportunities and Challenges for Integrating Large-*N* QCA and Econometric Analysis." *Political Research Quarterly* 66, no. 1: 191–98.

Frankfort-Nachmias, Chava, and David Nachmias. 2008. *Research Methods in the Social Sciences*, 7th ed. New York: Worth.

Gallie, William B. 1956. "Essentially Contested Concepts." *Proceedings of the Aristotelian Society* 56: 167–98.

Ganghof, Steffen. 2005. "Kausale Perspektiven in der vergleichenden Politikwissenschaft: X-zentrierte und Y-zentrierte Forschungsdesigns." In *Vergleichen in der Politikwissenschaft*, edited by Sabine Kropp and Michael Minkenberg, 76–93. Wiesbaden: VS Verlag.

Gansemans, Annelien, Deborah Martens, Marijke D'Haese, and Jan Orbie. 2017. "Do Labour Rights Matter for Export? A Qualitative Comparative Analysis of Pineapple Trade to the EU." *Politics and Governance* 5, no. 4: 93–105.

García-Castro, Roberto, Ruth V. Aguilera, and Miguel A. Ariño. 2013. "Bundles of Firm Corporate Governance Practices: A Fuzzy Set Analysis." *Corporate Governance: An International Review* 21, no. 4: 390–407.

García-Castro, Roberto, and Miguel A. Ariño. 2016. "A General Approach to Panel Data Set-Theoretic Research." *Journal of Advances in Management Sciences & Information Systems* 2: 63–76.

Gaubatz, Kurt Taylor. 2015. *A Survivor's Guide to R: An Introduction for the Uninitiated and the Unnerved.* Los Angeles: Sage.

Geddes, Barbara. 2007. *Paradigms and Sand Castles: Theory Building and Research Design in Comparative Politics.* Ann Arbor: University of Michigan Press.

George, Alexander L., and Andrew Bennett. 2005. *Case Studies and Theory Development in the Social Sciences.* Cambridge, MA: MIT Press.

Gerring, John. 2004. "What Is a Case Study and What Is It Good for?" *American Political Science Review* 98, no. 2: 341–54.

———. 2005. "Causation: A Unified Framework for the Social Sciences." *Journal of Theoretical Politics* 17, no. 2: 163–98.

———. 2007a. *Case Study Research: Principles and Practices.* Cambridge: Cambridge University Press.

———. 2007b. "Review Article: The Mechanismic Worldview—Thinking Inside the Box." *British Journal of Political Science* 37: 1–19.

———. 2010. "Causal Mechanisms: Yes, But..." *Comparative Political Studies* 43, no. 11: 1499–526.

———. 2012a. "Mere Description." *British Journal of Political Science* 42: 721–46.

———. 2012b. *Social Science Methodology: A Unified Framework*, 2nd ed. Cambridge: Cambridge University Press.

Gerring, John, Sebastian Karcher, and Brendan Apfeld. 2020. "Impact Metrics." In *The Production of Knowledge: Enhancing Progress in Social Science*, edited by Colin Elman, John Gerring, and James Mahoney, 371–99. Cambridge: Cambridge University Press.

Gerrits, Lasse, and Sofia Pagliarin. 2020. "Social and Causal Complexity in Qualitative Comparative Analysis (QCA): Strategies to Account for Emergence." *International Journal of Social Research Methodology*, August 4. doi:10.1080/13645579.2020.1799636.

Gerrits, Lasse, and Stefan Verweij. 2014. "Critical Realism as a Meta-Framework for Understanding the Relationships between Complexity and Qualitative Comparative Analysis." *Journal of Critical Realism* 12, no. 2: 166–82.

Giordono, Leanne, Hilary Boudet, and Alexander Gard-Murray. 2020. "Local Adaptation Policy Responses to Extreme Weather Events." *Policy Sciences* 53, no. 4: 609–36.

Gleditsch, Nils Petter. 1995. "Democracy and the Future of European Peace." *European Journal of International Relations* 1, no. 4: 539–71.

Glennan, Stuart. 2009. "Mechanisms." In *The Oxford Handbook of Causation*, edited by Helen Beebee, Christopher Hitchcock, and Peter Menzies, 315–25. Oxford: Oxford University Press.

Goanta, Catalina, and Mathias Siems. 2019. "What Determines National Convergence of EU Law? Measuring the Implementation of Consumer Sales Law." *Legal Studies* 39: 714–34.

Goertz, Gary. 2003a. "Cause, Correlation, and Necessary Conditions." In *Necessary Conditions*, edited by Gary Goertz and Harvey Starr, 47–64. Lanham, MD: Rowman & Littlefield.

———. 2003b. "The Substantive Importance of Necessary Condition Hypotheses." In *Necessary Conditions*, edited by Gary Goertz and Harvey Starr, 65–94. Lanham, MD: Rowman & Littlefield.

———. 2005. "Necessary Condition Hypotheses as Deterministic or Probabilistic: Does It Matter?" *Qualitative Methods* 3, no. 1: 22–26.

———. 2006. "Assessing the Trivialness, Relevance, and Relative Importance of Necessary or Sufficient Conditions in Social Science." *Studies in Comparative and International Development* 41, no. 2: 88–109.

———. 2017. *Multimethod Research, Causal Mechanisms, and Case Studies*. Princeton, NJ: Princeton University Press.

———. 2020. *Social Science Concepts and Measurement*. Princeton, NJ: Princeton University Press.

Goertz, Gary, and Jack S. Levy, eds. 2007. *Explaining War and Peace: Case Studies and Necessary Condition Counterfactuals*. Abingdon, UK: Routledge.

Goertz, Gary, and James Mahoney. 2006. "Negative Case Selection: The Possibility Principle." In *Social Science Concepts*, edited by Gary Goertz, 177–210. Princeton, NJ: Princeton University Press.

———. 2012. *A Tale of Two Cultures: Qualitative and Quantitative Research in the Social Sciences.* Princeton, NJ: Princeton University Press.

Goertz, Gary, and Harvey Starr. 2003a. "Introduction: Necessary Condition Logics, Research Design, and Theory." In *Necessary Conditions*, edited by Gary Goertz and Harvey Starr, 1–23. Lanham, MD: Rowman & Littlefield.

———, eds. 2003b. *Necessary Conditions: Theory, Methodology, and Applications.* Lanham, MD: Rowman & Littlefield.

Gran, Brian. 2003. "Charitable Choice Policy and Abused Children: The Benefits and Harms of Going Beyond the Public-Private Dichotomy." *International Journal of Sociology and Social Policy* 23, no. 11: 80–125.

Grauvogel, Julia, and Christian von Soest. 2014. "Claims to Legitimacy Count: Why Sanctions Fail to Instigate Democratisation in Authoritarian Regimes." *European Journal of Political Research* 53, no. 4: 635–53.

Greckhamer, Thomas. 2011. "Cross-Cultural Differences in Compensation Level and Inequality across Occupations: A Set-Theoretic Analysis." *Organization Studies* 32, no. 1: 85–115.

Greckhamer, Thomas, Santi Furnari, Peer C. Fiss, and Ruth V. Aguilera. 2018. "Studying Configurations with Qualitative Comparative Analysis: Best Practices in Strategy and Organization Research." *Strategic Organization* 16, no. 4: 482–95.

Gromes, Thorsten. 2019. "Does Peacekeeping Only Work in Easy Environments? An Analysis of Conflict Characteristics, Mission Profiles, and Civil War Recurrence." *Contemporary Security Policy* 40, no. 4: 459–80.

Gschwend, Thomas, and Frank Schimmelfennig, eds. 2007. *Research Design in Political Science.* Basingstoke, UK: Palgrave Macmillan.

Guimarães, Feliciano de Sá, and Maria Hermínia Tavares de Almeida. 2017. "From Middle Powers to Entrepreneurial Powers in World Politics: Brazil's Successes and Failures in International Crises." *Latin American Politics and Society* 59, no. 4: 26–46.

Guzzini, Stefano. 2017. "Power and Cause." *Journal of International Relations and Development* 20, no. 4: 737–59.

Hackett, Ursula. 2015. "But Not Both: The Exclusive Disjunction In Qualitative Comparative Analysis (QCA)." *Quality & Quantity* 49, no. 1: 75–92.

———. 2016. "The Goldilocks Principle: Applying the Exclusive Disjunction to Fuzzy Sets." *International Journal of Social Research Methodology* 19, no. 5: 551–74.

Haesebrouck, Tim. 2015a. "Democratic Contributions to UN Peacekeeping Operations. A Two-Step Fuzzy Set QCA of Unifil II." *Romanian Journal of Political Science* 15, no. 1: 4–51.

———. 2015b. "Pitfalls in QCA's Consistency Measure." *Journal of Comparative Politics*, no. 2: 65–80.

———. 2016. "The Added Value of Multi-Value Qualitative Comparative Analysis." *Forum Qualitative Sozialforschung / Forum Qualitative Research* 17: 1–29.

———. 2017a. "EU Member State Participation in Military Operations: A Configurational Comparative Analysis." *Cambridge Review of International Affairs* 30, nos. 2–3: 137–59.

———. 2017b. "NATO Burden Sharing in Libya: A Fuzzy Set Qualitative Comparative Analysis." *Journal of Conflict Resolution* 61, no. 10: 2235–61.

———. 2018. "Democratic Participation in the Air Strikes Against Islamic State: A Qualitative Comparative Analysis." *Foreign Policy Analysis* 14, no. 2: 254–75.

———. 2019. "An Alternative Update of the Two-Step QCA Procedure." *Quality & Quantity* 53, no. 6: 2765–80.

Haesebrouck, Tim, and Eva Thomann. Forthcoming. "Introduction: Causation, Correctness, and Solution Types in Configurational Comparative Methods." *Quality & Quantity*.

Haig, Brian D. 2018. *The Philosophy of Quantitative Methods*. New York: Oxford University Press.

Hall, Peter A. 2003. "Aligning Ontology and Methodology in Comparative Politics." In *Comparative Historical Analysis in the Social Sciences*, edited by James Mahoney and Dietrich Rueschemeyer, 373–404. New York: Cambridge University Press.

Harvey, David L. 2009. "Complexity and Case." In *The Sage Handbook of Case-Based Methods*, edited by David Byrne and Charles C. Ragin, 15–38. Los Angeles: Sage.

Harvey, Frank P. 2012. *Explaining the Iraq War: Counterfactual Theory, Logic, and Evidence*. New York: Cambridge University Press.

Hedström, Peter. 2008. "Studying Mechanisms to Strengthen Causal Inference in Quantitative Research." In *The Oxford Handbook of Political Methodology*, edited by Janet M. Box-Steffensmeier, Henry E. Brady, and David Collier, 319–35. Oxford: Oxford University Press.

Hedström, Peter, and Richard Swedberg, eds. 1998. *Social Mechanisms: An Analytical Approach to Social Theory*. Cambridge: Cambridge University Press.

Held, Tobias, and Lasse Gerrits. 2019. "One the Road to Electrification: A Qualitative Comparative Analysis of Urban E-Mobility Policies in 15 European Cities." *Transport Policy* 81: 12–23.

Hempel, Carl G., and Paul Oppenheim. 1948. "Studies in the Logic of Explanation." *Philosophy of Science* 15, no. 2: 135–75.

Hicks, Alexander, Joya Misra, and Tang Nah Ng. 1995. "The Programmatic Emergence of the Social Security State." *American Sociological Review* 60, no. 3: 329–49.

Hino, Airo. 2009. "Time-Series QCA: Studying Temporal Change through Boolean Analysis." *Sociological Theory and Methods* 24, no. 2: 247–65.

Holland, Paul W. 1986. "Statistics and Causal Inference." *Journal of the American Statistical Association* 81, no. 396: 945–60.

Hörisch, Felix. 2013. "Fiscal Policy in Hard Times: A Fuzzy-Set QCA of Fiscal Policy Reactions to the Financial Crisis." *Zeitschrift für Vergleichende Politikwissenschaft* 7: 117–41.

Hörisch, Felix, and Stefan Wurster. 2019. "The Policies of the First Green-Red Government in the German Federal State of Baden-Württemberg, 2011–2016." *Politische Vierteljahresschrift* 60, no. 3: 513–38.

Hudson, John, and Stefan Kühner. 2012. "Analyzing the Productive and Protective Dimensions of Welfare: Looking Beyond the OECD." *Social Policy and Administration* 46, no. 1: 35–60.

———. 2013. "Qualitative Comparative Analysis and Applied Public Policy Analysis: New Applications of Innovative Methods." *Policy and Society* 32, no. 4: 279–87.

Hug, Simon. 2013. "Qualitative Comparative Analysis: How Inductive Use and Measurement Error Lead to Problematic Inference." *Political Analysis* 21, no. 2: 252–65.

Hume, David. 2010 *An Enquiry Concerning Human Understanding*. Oxford: Oxford University Press. Orig. pub. 1772.

Ide, Tobias. 2015. "Why Do Conflicts over Scarce Renewable Resources Turn Violent? A Qualitative Comparative Analysis." *Global Environmental Change* 33: 61–70.

———. 2018. "Does Environmental Peacemaking between States Work? Insights on Coopera-tive Environmental Agreements and Reconciliation in International Rivalries." *Journal of Peace Research* 55, no. 3: 351–65.

Ide, Tobias, Miguel Rodriguez Lopez, Christiane Fröhlich, and Jürgen Scheffran. 2020. "Path-ways to Water Conflict during Drought in the MENA Region." *Journal of Peace Research*, July 2. doi:10.1177/0022343320910777.

Illari, Phyllis, and Federica Russo. 2014. *Causality: Philosophical Theory Meets Scientific Prac-tice*. Oxford: Oxford University Press.

Imai, Kosuke. 2017. *Quantitative Social Science: An Introduction*. Princeton, NJ: Princeton Uni-versity Press.

Inguanzo, Isabel. 2020. "Asian Women's Paths to Office: A Qualitative Comparative Analysis Approach." *Contemporary Politics* 26, no. 2: 186–205.

Jackson, Patrick Thaddeus. 2011. *The Conduct of Inquiry in International Relations: Philosophy of Science and Its Implications for the Study of World Politics*. London: Routledge.

Jackson, Patrick Thaddeus, and Daniel H. Nexon. 2013. "International Theory in a Post-Paradigmatic Era: From Substantive Wagers to Scientific Ontologies." *European Journal of International Relations* 19, no. 3: 543–65.

Jacobs, Alan M. 2016. "Introduction: Mechanisms and Process Tracing." *Qualitative & Multi-Method Research* 14, nos. 1–2: 13–15.

Jervis, Robert. 1996. "Counterfactuals, Causation, and Complexity." In *Counterfactual Thought Experiments in World Politics: Logical, Methodological, and Psychological Perspectives*, ed-ited by Philip E. Tetlock and Aaron Belkin, 309–16. Princeton, NJ: Princeton University Press.

Johais, Eva, Markus Bayer, and Daniel Lambach. 2020. "How Do States Collapse? Towards a Model of Causal Mechanisms." *Global Change, Peace & Security* 32, no. 2: 179–97.

Kabacoff, Robert I. 2015. *R in Action: Data Analysis and Graphics with R*. Shelter Island, NY: Manning.

Kahwati, Leila C., and Heather L. Kane. 2020. *Qualitative Comparative Analysis in Mixed Meth-ods Research and Evaluation*. Los Angeles: Sage.

Kane, Heather , Laurie Hinnant, Kristine Day, Mary Council, Janice Tzeng, Robin Soler, Megan Chambard, Amy Roussel, and Wendy Heirandt. 2016. "Pathways to Program Success: A Qualitative Comparative Analysis (QCA) of Communities Putting Prevention to Work Case Study Programs." *Journal of Public Health Management and Practice* 23, no. 2: 1–8.

Karlas, Jan. 2012. "National Parliamentary Control of EU Affairs: Institutional Design after Enlargement." *West European Politics* 35, no. 5: 1095–113.

Kim, Yushim, and Stefan Verweij. 2016. "Two Effective Causal Paths that Explain the Adoption of US State Environmental Justice Policy." *Policy Sciences* 49: 505–23.

King, Gary, Robert O. Keohane, and Sidney Verba. 1994. *Designing Social Inquiry: Scientific Inference in Qualitative Research*. Princeton, NJ: Princeton University Press.

King, Gary, and Langche Zeng. 2007. "When Can History Be Our Guide? The Pitfalls of Counter-factual Inference." *International Studies Quarterly* 51, no. 1: 183–210.

Kirchherr, Julian, Mats-Philip Ahrenshop, and Katrina Charles. 2019. "Resettlement Lies: Sug-gestive Evidence from 29 Large Dam Projects." *World Development* 114: 208–19.

Kirchherr, Julian, Katrina J. Charles, and Matthew J. Walton. 2016. "Multi-Causal Pathways of Public Opposition to Dam Projects in Asia: A Fuzzy Set Qualitative Comparative Analysis (fsQCA)." *Global Environmental Change* 41: 33–45.

Klingemann, Hans-Dieter, Andrea Volkens, Judith Bara, Ian Budge, and Michael McDonald, eds. 2006. *Mapping Policy Preferences II: Estimates for Parties, Electors, and Governments in Eastern Europe, European Union and OECD 1990–2003*. Oxford: Oxford University Press.

Koivu, Kendra L., and Erin Kimball Damman. 2015. "Qualitative Variations: The Sources of Divergent Qualitative Methodological Approaches." *Quality & Quantity* 49: 2617–32.

Korhonen-Kurki, Kaisa, Jenniver Sehring, Maria Brockhaus, and Monica Di Gregorio. 2014. "Enabling Factors for Establishing REDD+ in a Context of Weak Governance." *Climate Policy* 14, no. 2: 167–86.

Kraus, Sascha, Domingo Ribeiro-Soriano, and Miriam Schüssler. 2018. "Fuzzy-Set Qualitative Comparative Analysis (fsQCA) in Entrepreneurship and Innovation Research: The Rise of a Method." *International Entrepreneurship and Management Journal* 14, no. 1: 15–33.

Kröger, Markus. 2021. *Studying Complex Interactions and Outcomes Through Qualitative Comparative Analysis: A Practical Guide to Comparative Case Studies and Ethnographic Data Analysis*. London: Routledge.

Krogslund, Chris, Donghyun Danny Choi, and Mathias Poertner. 2015. "Fuzzy Sets on Shaky Ground: Parameter Sensitivity and Confirmation Bias in fsQCA." *Political Analysis* 23, no. 1: 21–41.

Krogslund, Chris, and Katherine Michel. 2014. "A Large-*N*, Fewer Variables Problem? The Counterintuitive Sensitivity of QCA." *Qualitative & Multi-Method Research* 12, no. 1: 25–33.

Kuehn, David, Aurel Croissant, Jil Kamerling, Hans Lueders, and André Strecker. 2017. "Conditions of Civilian Control in New Democracies: An Empirical Analysis of 28 'Third Wave' Democracies." *European Political Science Review* 9, no. 3: 425–47.

Kuehn, David, and Ingo Rohlfing. 2009. "Does It, Really? Measurement Error and Omitted Variables in Multi-Method Research." *Qualitative & Multi-Method Research* 7, no. 2: 18–22.

Kurki, Milja. 2007. "Critical Realism and Causal Analysis in International Relations." *Millennium: Journal of International Studies* 35, no. 2: 361–78.

———. 2008. *Causation in International Relations: Reclaiming Causal Analysis*. Cambridge: Cambridge University Press.

Kvist, Jon. 1999. "Welfare Reform in the Nordic Countries in the 1990s: Using Fuzzy-Set Theory to Assess Conformity to Ideal Types." *Journal of European Social Policy* 9, no. 3: 231–52.

———. 2007. "Fuzzy Set Ideal Type Analysis." *Journal of Business Research* 60, no. 5: 474–81.

Lakoff, George. 1973. "Hedges: A Study in Meaning Criteria and the Logic of Fuzzy Concepts." *Journal of Philosophical Logic* 2, no. 4: 458–508.

Lakoff, George, and Rafael E. Núñez. 2000. *Where Mathematics Comes From: How the Embodied Mind Brings Mathematics into Being*. New York: Basic Books.

Laux, Thomas. 2016. "Institutionalizing Equal Pay Laws. A Comparative Analysis of OECD Countries." *Zeitschrift für Soziologie* 45, no. 6: 393–409.

Lazarsfeld, Paul. 1937. "Some Remarks on the Typological Procedures in Social Research." *Zeitschrift für Sozialforschung* 6, no. 1: 119–39.

Lebow, Richard Ned. 2000. "What's So Different About A Counterfactual?" *World Politics* 52, no. 4: 550–85.

——. 2014. *Constructing Cause in International Relations*. New York: Cambridge University Press.

Levy, Jack S. 2008a. "Case Studies: Types, Designs, and Logics of Inference." *Conflict Management and Peace Science* 25, no. 1: 1–18.

——. 2008b. "Counterfactuals and Case Studies." In *The Oxford Handbook of Political Methodology*, edited by Janet M. Box-Steffensmeier, Henry E. Brady, and David Collier, 627–44. Oxford: Oxford University Press.

Lewis, David. 1973. *Counterfactuals*. Cambridge, MA: Harvard University Press.

Lieberman, Evan S. 2005. "Nested Analysis as a Mixed-Method Strategy for Comparative Research." *American Political Science Review* 99, no. 3: 435–52.

——. 2015. "Nested Analysis: Toward the Integration of Comparative-Historical Analysis with other Social Science Methods." In *Advances in Comparative-Historical Analysis*, edited by James Mahoney and Kathleen Thelen, 240–63. Cambridge: Cambridge University Press.

Lieberson, Stanley. 1985. *Making It Count: The Improvement of Social Research and Theory*. Berkeley: University of California Press.

——. 1991. "Small *N*s and Big Conclusions: An Examination of the Reasoning in Comparative Studies Based on a Small Number of Cases." *Social Forces* 70, no. 2: 307–20.

——. 2004. "Comments on the Use and Utility of QCA." *Qualitative Methods* 2, no. 2: 13–14.

Lieshout, Robert H. 2007. "A Note on Causality and Causal Mechanisms." *Qualitative & Multi-Method Research* 5, no. 2: 18–21.

Lijphart, Arend. 1968. "Typologies of Democratic Systems." *Comparative Political Studies* 1, no. 3: 3–44.

——. 1971. "Comparative Politics and the Comparative Method." *American Political Science Review* 65, no. 3: 682–93.

Lilliefeldt, Emelie. 2012. "Party and Gender in Western Europe Revisited: A Fuzzy-Set Qualitative Comparative Analysis of Gender-Balanced Parliamentary Parties." *Party Politics* 18, no. 2: 193–214.

Lindemann, Stefan, and Andreas Wimmer. 2018. "Repression and Refuge: Why Only Some Politically Excluded Ethnic Groups Rebel." *Journal of Peace Research* 55, no. 3: 305–19.

Longest, Kyle C., and Stephen Vaisey. 2008. "Fuzzy: A Program for Performing Qualitative Comparative Analyses (QCA) in Stata." *Stata Journal* 8, no. 1: 79–104.

Lucas, Samuel R., and Alisa Szatrowski. 2014. "Qualitative Comparative Analysis in Critical Perspective." *Sociological Methodology* 44, no. 1: 1–79.

Maat, Eelco van der. 2011. "Sleeping Hegemons: Third-Party Intervention Following Territorial Integrity Transgressions." *Journal of Peace Research* 48, no. 2: 201–15.

Machamer, Peter, Lindley Darden, and Carl F. Craver. 2000. "Thinking About Mechanisms." *Philosophy of Science* 67: 1–25.

Mackie, John L. 1965. "Causes and Conditions." *American Philosophical Quarterly* 2, no. 4: 245–64.

——. 1980. *The Cement of the Universe: A Study of Causation*. New York: Oxford University Press.

Maggetti, Martino. 2009. "The Role of Independent Regulatory Agencies in Policy-Making: A Comparative Analysis." *Journal of European Public Policy* 16, no. 3: 450–70.

Maggetti, Martino, and David Levi-Faur. 2013. "Dealing with Errors in QCA." *Political Research Quarterly* 66, no. 1: 198–204.

Mahoney, James. 2003. "Strategies of Causal Assessment in Comparative Historical Analysis." In *Comparative Historical Analysis in the Social Sciences*, edited by James Mahoney and Dietrich Rueschemeyer, 337–72. New York: Cambridge University Press.

———. 2004. "Reflections on Fuzzy-Set/QCA." *Qualitative Methods* 2, no. 2: 17–21.

———. 2008. "Toward a Unified Theory of Causality." *Comparative Political Studies* 41, nos. 4–5: 412–36.

———. 2010. "After KKV: The New Methodology of Qualitative Research." *World Politics* 62, no. 1: 120–47.

Mahoney, James, and Gary Goertz. 2004. "The Possibility Principle: Choosing Negative Cases in Comparative Research." *American Political Science Review* 98, no. 4: 653–69.

Mahoney, James, Erin Kimball, and Kendra L. Koivu. 2009. "The Logic of Historical Explanation in the Social Sciences." *Comparative Political Studies* 42, no. 1: 114–46.

Mahoney, James, and Rachel Sweet Vanderpoel. 2015. "Set Diagrams and Qualitative Research." *Comparative Political Studies* 48, no. 1: 65–100.

Mannewitz, Tom. 2011. "Two-Level Theories in QCA: A Discussion of Schneider and Wagemann's Two-Step Approach." COMPASSS Working Paper

Mantilla, Luis Felipe. 2012. "Mobilizing Religion for Democracy: Explaining Catholic Church Support for Democratization in South America." *Politics and Religion* 3, no. 3: 553–79.

Mariani, Giulia. 2020. "Failed and Successful Attempts at Institutional Change: The Battle for Marriage Equality in the United States." *European Political Science Review* 12, no. 2: 255–70.

Marshall, Monty G., Ted Robert Gurr, and Keith Jaggers. 2019. "Polity IV Project: Dataset User's Manual." Vienna, VA: Center for Systemic Peace.

Marx, Axel. 2006. "Towards More Robust Model Specification in QCA: Results from a Methodological Experiment." COMPASSS Working Paper, 1–25.

Marx, Axel, and Adrian Duşa. 2011. "Crisp-Set Qualitative Comparative Analysis (csQCA), Contradictions and Consistency Benchmarks for Model Specification." *Methodological Innovations Online* 6, no. 2: 102–48.

Marx, Axel, Benoît Rihoux, and Charles C. Ragin. 2014. "The Origins, Development, and Application of Qualitative Comparative Analysis: The First 25 Years." *European Political Science Review* 6, no. 1: 115–42.

Massie, Justin. 2016. "Why Democratic Allies Defect Prematurely: Canadian and Dutch Unilateral Pullouts from the War in Afghanistan." *Democracy and Security* 12, no. 2: 85–113.

McCawley, James D. 1993. *Everything That Linguists Have Always Wanted to Know about Logic but Were Ashamed to Ask*. Chicago: University of Chicago Press.

McNeill, Daniel, and Paul Freiberger. 1993. *Fuzzy Logic*. New York: Touchstone.

Meegdenburg, Hilde van, and Patrick A. Mello. Forthcoming. *Case-Based Methods: Combining Process Tracing and Qualitative Comparative Analysis*. London: Palgrave Macmillan.

Melendez-Torres, G. J., Katy Sutcliffe, Helen E. D. Burchett, Rebecca Rees, Michelle Richardson, and James Thomas. 2018. "Weight Management Programmes: Re-Analysis of a Systematic Review to Identify Pathways to Effectiveness." *Health Expectations* 21, no. 3: 574–84.

Mello, Patrick A. 2012. "Parliamentary Peace or Partisan Politics? Democracies' Participation in the Iraq War." *Journal of International Relations and Development* 15, no. 3: 420–53.

———. 2013. "From Prospect to Practice: A Critical Review of Applications in Fuzzy-Set Qualitative Comparative Analysis." Paper presented at Eighth Pan-European Conference on International Relations, Warsaw, September 18–21.

———. 2014. *Democratic Participation in Armed Conflict: Military Involvement in Kosovo, Afghanistan, and Iraq*. Basingstoke, UK: Palgrave Macmillan.

———. 2017. "Qualitative Comparative Analysis and the Study of Non-State Actors." In *Researching Non-State Actors in International Security: Theory & Practice*, edited by Andreas Kruck and Andrea Schneiker, 123–42. Oxford: Routledge.

———. 2020. "Paths towards Coalition Defection: Democracies and Withdrawal from the Iraq War." *European Journal of International Security* 5, no. 1: 45–76.

Mendel, Jerry M., and Charles C. Ragin. 2011. "fsQCA: Dialog Between Jerry M. Mendel and Charles C. Ragin." USC-SIPI Report 411.

Merton, Robert K. 1958. *Social Theory and Social Structure*. New York: Free Press.

Meuer, Johannes, and Christian Rupietta. 2017. "A Review of Integrated QCA and Statistical Analyses." *Quality & Quantity* 51, no. 5: 2063–83.

Mill, John Stuart. 2006. *Collected Works of John Stuart Mill: Volume VII*. Indianapolis: Liberty Fund.

Møller, Jørgen, and Svend-Erik Skaaning. 2019. "Set-Theoretic Methods in Democratization Research: An Evolution of their Uses and Contributions." *Democratization* 26, no. 1: 78–96.

Moore, Will H., and David A. Siegel. 2013. *A Mathematics Course for Political and Social Research*. Princeton, NJ: Princeton University Press.

Morgan, Stephen L., and Christopher Winship. 2007. *Counterfactuals and Causal Inference: Methods and Principles for Social Research*. New York: Cambridge University Press.

Moses, Jonathon W., and Torbjørn L. Knutsen. 2019. *Ways of Knowing: Competing Methodologies in Social and Political Research*, 3rd ed. Basingstoke, UK: Red Globe Press.

Mross, Karina. 2019. "Democracy Support and Peaceful Democratization after Civil War: A Disaggregate Analysis." PhD thesis, University of St. Gallen.

Mumford, Stephen, and Rani Lill Anjum. 2013. *Causation: A Very Short Introduction*. New York: Oxford University Press.

Munck, Gerardo L. 2016. "Assessing Set-Theoretic Comparative Methods: A Tool for Qualitative Comparativists?" *Comparative Political Studies* 49, no. 6: 775–80.

Nelson, Jennifer M. 2017. "Pathways to Green(er) Pastures: Reward Bundles, Human Capital, and Turnover Decisions in a Semi-Profession." *Qualitative Sociology* 40, no. 1: 23–57.

North, Douglass C. 1984. "Government and the Cost of Exchange." *Journal of Economic History* 44, no. 2: 255–64.

Oana, Ioana-Elena, and Carsten Q. Schneider. 2018. "SetMethods: An Add-on R Package for Advanced QCA." *R Journal* 10, no. 1: 507–33.

Oana, Ioana-Elena, Carsten Q. Schneider, and Eva Thomann. 2021. *Qualitative Comparative Analysis Using R: A Beginner's Guide*. New York: Cambridge University Press.

Olsen, Wendy. 2014. "The Usefulness of QCA under Realist Assumptions." *Sociological Methodology* 44, no. 1: 101–7.

———, ed. 2010. *Realist Methodology*. Los Angeles: Sage.

Olson, James M., Neal J. Roese, and Ronald J. Deibert. 1996. "Psychological Biases in Counterfactual Thought Experiments." In *Counterfactual Thought Experiments in World Politics: Logical, Methodological, and Psychological Perspectives*, edited by Philip E. Tetlock and Aaron Belkin, 296–300. Princeton, NJ: Princeton University Press.

Oppermann, Kai, and Klaus Brummer. 2020. "Who Gets What in Foreign Affairs? Explaining the Allocation of Foreign Ministries in Coalition Governments." *Government and Opposition* 55, no. 2: 241–59.

Pagliarin, Sofia, and Lasse Gerrits. 2020. "Trajectory-Based Qualitative Comparative Analysis: Accounting for Case-Based Time Dynamics." *Methodological Innovations*, September 27. doi:10.1177%2F2059799120959170.

Pagliarin, Sofia, Anna M. Hersperger, and Benoît Rihoux. 2020. "Implementation Pathways of Large-Scale Urban Development Projects (lsUDPs) in Western Europe: A Qualitative Comparative Analysis (QCA)." *European Planning Studies* 28, no. 6: 1242–63.

Paine, Jack. 2016a. "Set-Theoretic Comparative Methods: Less Distinctive Than Claimed." *Comparative Political Science* 49, no. 6: 703–41.

———. 2016b. "Still Searching for the Value-Added: Persistent Concerns About Set-Theoretic Comparative Methods." *Comparative Political Studies* 49, no. 6: 793–800.

Palinkas, Lawrence A., Sapna J. Mendson, and Alison B. Hamilton. 2019. "Innovations in Mixed Methods Research." *Annual Review of Public Health* 40: 423–42.

Pattyn, Valérie, Priscilla Álamos-Concha, Bart Cambré, Benoît Rihoux, and Benjamin Schalembier. 2020. "Policy Effectiveness through Configurational and Mechanistic Lenses: Lessons for Concept Development." *Journal of Comparative Policy Analysis: Research and Practice*, June 26. doi:10.1080/13876988.2020.1773263.

Paul, L. A. 2009. "Counterfactual Theories." In *The Oxford Handbook of Causation*, edited by Helen Beebee, Christopher Hitchcock, and Peter Menzies, 158–84. Oxford: Oxford University Press.

Paul, L. A., and Ned Hall. 2013. *Causation: A User's Guide*. New York: Oxford University Press.

Pearl, Judea. 2009. *Causality: Models, Reasoning, and Inference*, 2nd ed. New York: Cambridge University Press.

Pearl, Judea, Madelyn Glymour, and Nicholas P. Jewell. 2016. *Causal Inference in Statistics: A Primer*. Chichester, UK: Wiley.

Pearl, Judea, and Dana Mackenzie. 2018. *The Book of Why: The New Science of Cause and Effect*. New York: Basic Books.

Peters, B. Guy. 2020. "Can We Be Casual about Being Causal?" *Journal of Comparative Policy Analysis: Research and Practice*, August 10. doi:10.1080/13876988.2020.1793327.

Pilster, Ulrich, Tobias Böhmelt, and Atsushi Tago. 2013. "Political Leadership Changes and the Withdrawal from Military Coalition Operations, 1946–2001." *International Studies Perspectives* 16, no. 4: 463–83.

Pinfari, Marco. 2011. "Time to Agree: Is Time Pressure Good for Peace Negotiations?" *Journal of Conflict Resolution* 55, no. 5: 683–709.

Pollock, Philip H., and Barry C. Edwards. 2018. *An R Companion to Political Analysis*. Thousand Oaks, CA: Sage.

Potter, Michael. 2004. *Set Theory and Its Philosophy: A Critical Introduction*. New York: Oxford University Press.

Przeworski, Adam, and Henry Teune. 1970. *The Logic of Comparative Social Inquiry*. New York: Wiley-Interscience.

Psillos, Stathis. 2009. "Regularity Theories." In *The Oxford Handbook of Causation*, edited by Helen Beebee, Christopher Hitchcock, and Peter Menzies, 131–57. Oxford: Oxford University Press.

Pullum, Amanda. 2016. "Social Movements, Strategic Choice, and Recourse to the Polls." *Mobilization: An International Journal* 21, no. 2: 177–92.

Putnam, Robert. 1988. "Diplomacy and Domestic Politics: The Logic of Two-Level Games." *International Organization* 42, no. 3: 427–60.

Quine, Willard Van Orman. 1969. *Set Theory and Its Logic*. Cambridge, MA: Harvard University Press.

———. 1982. *Methods of Logic*, 4th ed. Cambridge, MA: Harvard University Press.

R Core Team. 2020. "R: A Language and Environment for Statistical Computing [Computer Software]." Vienna: R Foundation for Statistical Computing. Available at www.R-project.org.

Radaelli, Claudio M., and Claudius Wagemann. 2019. "What Did I Leave Out? Omitted Variables in Regression and Qualitative Comparative Analysis." *European Political Science* 18, no. 2: 275–90.

Ragin, Charles C. 1987. *The Comparative Method: Moving Beyond Qualitative and Quantitative Strategies*. Berkeley: University of California Press.

———. 1992. "'Casing' and the Process of Social Inquiry." In *What Is A Case? Exploring the Foundations of Social Inquiry*, edited by Charles C. Ragin and Howard S. Becker, 217–26. New York: Cambridge University Press.

———. 2000. *Fuzzy-Set Social Science*. Chicago: University of Chicago Press.

———. 2003a. "Fuzzy-Set Analysis of Necessary Conditions." In *Necessary Conditions*, edited by Gary Goertz and Harvey Starr, 179–96. Lanham, MD: Rowman & Littlefield.

———. 2003b. "Recent Advances in Fuzzy-Set Methods and Their Application to Policy Questions." COMPASSS Working Paper.

———. 2006a. "How to Lure Analytic Social Science Out of the Doldrums: Some Lessons from Comparative Research." *International Sociology* 21, no. 5: 633–46.

———. 2006b. "Set Relations in Social Research: Evaluating Their Consistency and Coverage." *Political Analysis* 14, no. 3: 291–310.

———. 2006c. *User's Guide to Fuzzy-Set / Qualitative Comparative Analysis*. Irvine: University of California.

———. 2008a. "Measurement versus Calibration: A Set-Theoretic Approach." In *The Oxford Handbook of Political Methodology*, edited by Janet M. Box-Steffensmeier, Henry E. Brady, and David Collier, 174–98. Oxford: Oxford University Press.

———. 2008b. *Redesigning Social Inquiry: Fuzzy Sets and Beyond*. Chicago: University of Chicago Press.

———. 2009a. "Qualitative Comparative Analysis Using Fuzzy Sets (fsQCA)." In *Configurational Comparative Methods*, edited by Benoît Rihoux and Charles C. Ragin, 87–121. Thousand Oaks. CA: Sage.

———. 2009b. "Reflections on Casing and Case-Oriented Research." In *The Sage Handbook of Case-Based Methods*, edited by David Byrne and Charles C. Ragin, 522–34. Los Angeles: Sage.

———. 2011. "PRI Consistency ('PRE' in fsQCA's Truth Table Spreadsheet)." Syracuse: Institute for Qualitative and Multi-Method Research.

———. 2014a. "Comment: Lucas and Szatrowski in Critical Perspective." *Sociological Methodology* 44, no. 1: 80–94.

———. 2014b. *The Comparative Method: Moving Beyond Qualitative and Quantitative Strategies*, 2nd ed. Berkeley: University of California Press.

Ragin, Charles C., and Howard S. Becker, eds. 1992. *What Is a Case? Exploring the Foundations of Social Inquiry.* New York: Cambridge University Press.

Ragin, Charles C., and Peer C. Fiss. 2008. "Net Effects Versus Configurations: An Empirical Demonstration." In *Redesigning Social Inquiry: Fuzzy Sets and Beyond*, edited by Charles C. Ragin, 190–212. Chicago: University of Chicago Press.

———. 2017. *Intersectional Inequality: Race, Class, Test Scores, and Poverty*. Chicago: University of Chicago Press.

Ragin, Charles C., Susan E. Mayer, and Kriss A. Drass. 1984. "Assessing Discrimination: A Boolean Approach." *American Sociological Review* 49, no. 2: 221–34.

Ragin, Charles C., and Benoît Rihoux. 2004a. "Qualitative Comparative Analysis (QCA): State of the Art and Prospects." *Qualitative Methods* 2, no. 2: 3–13.

———. 2004b. "Replies to Commentators: Reassurances and Rebuttals." *Qualitative Methods* 2, no. 2: 22–24.

Ragin, Charles C., and John Sonnett. 2005. "Between Complexity and Parsimony: Limited Diversity, Counterfactual Cases, and Comparative Analysis." In *Vergleichen in der Politikwissenschaft*, edited by Sabine Kropp and Michael Minkenberg, 180–97. Wiesbaden: Verlag für Sozialwissenschaften.

Ragin, Charles C., and Sarah I. Strand. 2008. "Using Qualitative Comparative Analysis to Study Causal Order: Comment on Caren and Panofsky (2005)." *Sociological Methods & Research* 36, no. 4: 431–41.

Ragin, Charles, and Sean Davey. 2017. *fs/QCA [Version 3.0]*. Irvine: University of California.

Ray, James Lee. 2000. "Democracy: On the Level(s), Does Democracy Correlate with Peace?" In *What Do We Know about War?* edited by John A. Vasquez, 299–316. Lanham, MD: Rowman & Littlefield.

Reichert, Christopher, and Claude Rubinson. 2014. *Kirq*. Houston: University of Houston–Downtown.

Rihoux, Benoît. 2003. "Bridging the Gap between the Qualitative and Quantitative Worlds? A Retrospective and Prospective View on Qualitative Comparative Analysis." *Field Methods* 15, no. 4: 351–65.

Rihoux, Benoît, Priscilla Álamos-Concha, Damien Bol, Axel Marx, and Ilona Rezsöhazy. 2013. "From Niche to Mainstream Method? A Comprehensive Mapping of QCA Applications in Journal Articles from 1984 to 2011." *Political Research Quarterly* 66, no. 1: 175–84.

Rihoux, Benoît, Priscilla Álamos-Concha, and Bojana Lobe. 2021. "Qualitative Comparative Analysis (QCA): An Integrative Approach Suited for Diverse Mixed Method and Multi-method Research Strategies." In *The Routledge Reviewer's Guide to Mixed Methods Analysis*, edited by Anthony J. Onwuegbuzie and R. Burke Johnson. London: Routledge.

Rihoux, Benoît, and Gisèle De Meur. 2009. "Crisp-Set Qualitative Comparative Analysis (csQCA)." In *Configurational Comparative Methods: Qualitative Comparative Analysis (QCA) and Related Techniques*, edited by Benoît Rihoux and Charles C. Ragin, 33–68. Thousand Oaks, CA: Sage.

Rihoux, Benoît, and Heike Grimm, eds. 2006. *Innovative Comparative Methods for Policy Analysis: Beyond the Quantitative-Qualitative Divide*. Boston: Springer.

Rihoux, Benoît, and Bojana Lobe. 2009. "The Case for Qualitative Comparative Analysis (QCA): Adding Leverage for Thick Cross-Case Comparison." In *The Sage Handbook of Case-Based Methods*, edited by David Byrne and Charles C. Ragin, 222–42. Los Angeles: Sage.

Rihoux, Benoît, and Charles C. Ragin, eds. 2009. *Configurational Comparative Methods: Qualitative Comparative Analysis (QCA) and Related Techniques*. Thousand Oaks, CA: Sage.

Rihoux, Benoît, Charles C. Ragin, Sakura Yamasaki, and Damien Bol. 2009. "Conclusions: The Way(s) Ahead." In *Configurational Comparative Methods*, edited by Benoît Rihoux and Charles C. Ragin, 167–77. Thousand Oaks, CA: Sage.

Rihoux, Benoît, Ilona Rezsöhazy, and Damien Bol. 2011. "Qualitative Comparative Analysis (QCA) in Public Policy Analysis: an Extensive Review." *German Policy Studies* 7, no. 3: 9–82.

Rogers, William P., Neil A. Armstrong, David C. Acheson, Eugene E. Covert, Richard P. Feynman, Donald J. Kutnya, Sally K. Ride, Robert W. Rummel, Joseph F. Sutter, Arthur B. C. Walker Jr., Albert D. Wheelen, and Charles E. Yeager. 1986. *Report of the Presidential Commission on the Space Shuttle Challenger Accident*. Washington, DC: US Government Printing Office.

Rohlfing, Ingo. 2012. *Case Studies and Causal Inference: An Integrative Framework*. Basingstoke. UK: Palgrave Macmillan.

——. 2015. "Mind the Gap: A Review of Simulation Designs for Qualitative Comparative Analysis." *Research & Politics* 2, no. 4: 1–4.

——. 2016. "Why Simulations Are Appropriate for Evaluating Qualitative Comparative Analysis." *Quality & Quantity* 50, no. 5: 2073–84.

——. 2018. "Power and False Negatives in Qualitative Comparative Analysis: Foundations, Simulation and Estimation for Empirical Studies." *Political Analysis* 26, no. 1: 72–89.

——. 2020. "The Choice between Crisp and Fuzzy Sets in Qualitative Comparative Analysis and the Ambiguous Consequences for Finding Consistent Set Relations." *Field Methods* 32, no. 1: 75–88.

Rohlfing, Ingo, and Carsten Q. Schneider. 2014. "Clarifying Misunderstandings, Moving Forward: Towards Standards and Tools for Set-Theoretic Methods." *Qualitative & Multi-Method Research* 12, no. 2: 27–34.

——. 2018. "A Unifying Framework for Causal Analysis in Set-Theoretic Multimethod Research." *Sociological Methods & Research* 47, no. 1: 37–63.

Rohlfing, Ingo, and Christina Isabel Zuber. 2019. "Check Your Truth Conditions! Clarifying the Relationship between Theories of Causation and Social Science Methods for Causal Inference." *Sociological Methods & Research*, February 26. doi:10.1177/0049124119826156.

Rosato, Sebastian. 2003. "The Flawed Logic of Democratic Peace Theory." *American Political Science Review* 97, no. 4: 585–602.

——. 2005. "Explaining the Democratic Peace." *American Political Science Review* 99, no. 3: 467–72.

Rosenberg, Andrew S., Austin J. Knuppe, and Bear F. Braumoeller. 2017. "Unifying the Study of Asymmetric Hypotheses." *Political Analysis* 25, no. 3: 381–401.

RStudio. 2020. *RStudio: Integrated Development Environment for R [Computer Software]*. Boston: RStudio. Available at www.rstudio.com.

Rubinson, Claude. 2013. "Contradictions in fsQCA." *Quality & Quantity* 47: 2847–67.

———. 2019. "Presenting Qualitative Comparative Analysis: Notation, Tabular Layout, and Visualization." *Methodological Innovations*, July 18. doi:10.1177/2059799119862110.

Rubinson, Claude, Lasse Gerrits, Roel Rutten, and Thomas Greckhamer. 2019. "Avoiding Common Errors in QCA: A Short Guide for New Practitioners." COMPASSS Research Network.

Russett, Bruce, and John R. Oneal. 2001. *Triangulating Peace: Democracy, Interdependence, and International Organizations*. New York: W. W. Norton.

Rutten, Roel. 2019. *Critical Realism and Complex Causality: On the Assumptions You Buy In To When You Are Making Causal Claims*. Oisterwijk: Wolf Publishers.

———. 2020. "Applying and Assessing Large-*N* QCA: Causality and Robustness from a Critical-Realist Perspective." *Sociological Methods & Research*, April 26. doi:10.1177/0049124120914955.

Saltkjel, Therese, Mari Holm Ingelsrud, Espen Dahl, and Knut Halvorsen. 2017. "A Fuzzy Set Approach to Economic Crisis, Austerity and Public Health, Part I: European Countries' Conformity to Ideal Types during the Economic Downturn." *Scandinavian Journal of Public Health* 45, no. 18: 41–47.

Sartori, Giovanni. 2014. "Logic and Set Theory: A Note of Dissent." *Qualitative & Multi-Method Research* 12, no. 1: 14–15.

Schimmelfennig, Frank. 2001. "The Community Trap: Liberal Norms, Rhetorical Action, and the Eastern Enlargement of the European Union." *International Organization* 55, no. 1: 47–80.

———. 2005. "The International Promotion of Political Norms in Eastern Europe: A Qualitative Comparative Analysis." Cambridge, MA: Harvard University, Center for European Studies.

Schmitt, Olivier. 2018. *Allies That Count: Junior Partners in Coalition Warfare*. Washington, DC: Georgetown University Press.

Schmitter, Philippe C. 2008. "The Design of Social and Political Research." In *Approaches and Methodologies in the Social Sciences*, edited by Donatella Della Porta and Michael Keating, 263–95. Cambridge: Cambridge University Press.

Schneider, Carsten Q. 2016. "Real Differences and Overlooked Similarities: Set-Methods in Comparative Perspective." *Comparative Political Studies* 49, no. 6: 781–92.

———. 2018. "Realists and Idealists in QCA." *Political Analysis* 26, no. 2: 246–54.

———. 2019. "Two-Step QCA Revisited: The Necessity of Context Conditions." *Quality & Quantity* 53, no. 3: 1109–26.

Schneider, Carsten Q., and Seraphine F. Maerz. 2017. "Legitimation, Cooptation, and Repression and the Survival of Electoral Autocracies." *Zeitschrift für Vergleichende Politikwissenschaft* 11, no. 2: 213–35.

Schneider, Carsten Q., and Kristin Makszin. 2014. "Forms of Welfare Capitalism and Education-Based Participatory Inequality." *Socio-Economic Review* 12, no. 2: 437–62.

Schneider, Carsten Q., and Ingo Rohlfing. 2013. "Combining QCA and Process Tracing in Set-Theoretic Multi-Method Research." *Sociological Methods & Research* 42, no. 4: 559–97.

———. 2019. "Set-Theoretic Multimethod Research: The Role of Test Corridors and Conjunctions for Case Selection." *Swiss Political Science Review* 25, no. 3: 253–75.

Schneider, Carsten Q., Barbara Vis, and Kendra Koivu. 2019. "Set-Analytic Approaches, Especially Qualitative Comparative Analysis (QCA)." APSA Section for Qualitative and Multi-Method Research, Final Report of the Qualitative Transparency Deliberations Working Group III.4.

Schneider, Carsten Q., and Claudius Wagemann. 2006. "Reducing Complexity in Qualitative Comparative Analysis (QCA): Remote and Proximate Factors and the Consolidation of Democracy." *European Journal of Political Research* 45, no. 5: 751–86.

———. 2010. "Standards of Good Practice in Qualitative Comparative Analysis (QCA) and Fuzzy-Sets." *Comparative Sociology* 9, no. 3: 397–418.

———. 2012. *Set-Theoretic Methods for the Social Sciences: A Guide to Qualitative Comparative Analysis.* New York: Cambridge University Press.

———. 2013. "Doing Justice to Logical Remainders in QCA: Moving Beyond the Standard Analysis." *Political Research Quarterly* 66, no. 1: 211–20.

———. 2016. "Assessing ESA on What It Is Designed for: A Reply to Cooper and Glaesser." *Field Methods* 28, no. 3: 316–21.

Schoeller, Magnus, Mattia Guidi, and Yannis Karagiannis. 2017. "Explaining Informal Policy-Making Patterns in the Eurozone Crisis: Decentralized Bargaining and the Theory of EU Institutions." *Public Administration* 40, no. 14: 1211–22.

Seawright, Jason. 2005a. "Assumptions, Causal Inference, and the Goals of QCA." *Studies in Comparative and International Development* 40, no. 1: 39–42.

———. 2005b. "Qualitative Comparative Analysis vis-à-vis Regression." *Studies in Comparative and International Development* 40, no. 1: 3–26.

———. 2014. "Comment: Limited Diversity and the Unreliability of QCA." *Sociological Methodology* 44, no. 1: 118–21.

———. 2016. *Multi-Method Social Science: Combining Qualitative and Quantitative Tools.* Cambridge: Cambridge University Press.

Seawright, Jason, and David Collier. 2010. "Glossary." In *Rethinking Social Inquiry*, edited by Henry E. Brady and David Collier, 313–59. Lanham, MD: Rowman & Littlefield.

Seawright, Jason, and John Gerring. 2008. "Case Selection Techniques in Case Study Research: A Menu of Qualitative and Quantitative Options." *Political Research Quarterly* 61, no. 2: 294–308.

Sekhon, Jasjeet S. 2008. "The Neyman-Rubin Model of Causal Inference and Estimation via Matching Methods." In *The Oxford Handbook of Political Methodology*, edited by Janet M. Box-Steffensmeier, Henry E. Brady, and David Collier, 271–99. Oxford: Oxford University Press.

Selvin, Steve. 2019. *The Joy of Statistics: A Treasury of Elementary Statistical Tools and their Application.* New York: Oxford University Press.

Sessions, Roger. 1950. "How A 'Difficult' Composer Gets That Way." *New York Times*, January 8.

Sewell, William H. 1996. "Three Temporalities: Toward an Eventful Sociology." In *The Historic Turn in the Human Sciences*, edited by Terrance J. McDonald, 245–80. Ann Arbor: University of Michigan Press.

Shin, Sun-Joo. 1994. *The Logical Status of Diagrams.* New York: Cambridge University Press.

Sil, Rudra, and Peter J. Katzenstein. 2010. *Beyond Paradigms: Analytic Eclecticism in the Study of World Politics.* Basingstoke, UK: Palgrave Macmillan.

Skaaning, Svend-Erik. 2011. "Assessing the Robustness of Crisp-Set and Fuzzy-Set QCA Results." *Sociological Methods & Research* 40, no. 2: 391–408.

Skocpol, Theda. 1979. *States and Social Revolutions: A Comparative Analysis of France, Russia, and China.* Cambridge: Cambridge University Press.

Slantchev, Branislav L., Anna Alexandrova, and Erik Gartzke. 2005. "Probabilistic Causality, Selection Bias, and the Logic of the Democratic Peace." *American Political Science Review* 99, no. 3: 459–62.

Smithson, Michael, and Jay Verkuilen. 2006. *Fuzzy Set Theory: Applications in the Social Sciences.* Thousand Oaks. CA: Sage.

Stevens, Alex. 2020. "Critical Realism and the 'Ontological Politics of Drug Policy.'" *International Journal of Drug Policy*, 84: 1–24.

Stoklasa, Jan, Pasi Luukka, and Tomáš Talášek. 2017. "Set-Theoretic Methodology Using Fuzzy Sets in Rule Extraction and Validation: Consistency and Coverage Revisited." *Information Sciences.* Volumes 412–413: 154–73.

Swinkels, Marij. 2020a. "Beliefs of Political Leaders: Conditions for Change in the Eurozone Crisis." *West European Politics* 43, no. 5: 1163–86.

———. 2020b. "How Ideas Matter in Public Policy: A Review of Concepts, Mechanisms, and Methods." *International Review of Public Policy* 2, no. 3: 281–316.

Tanner, Sean. 2014. "QCA Is of Questionable Value for Policy Research." *Policy and Society* 33, no. 3: 287–98.

Tarrow, Sidney. 1995. "Bridging the Quantitative-Qualitative Divide in Political Science." *American Political Science Review* 89, no. 2: 471–74.

Tetlock, Philip E., and Aaron Belkin, eds. 1996. *Counterfactual Thought Experiments in World Politics: Logical, Methodological, and Psychological Perspectives.* Princeton, NJ: Princeton University Press.

Thiem, Alrik. 2013. "Clearly Crisp, and Not Fuzzy: A Reassessment of the (Putative) Pitfalls of Multi-Value QCA." *Field Methods* 25, no. 2: 197–207.

———. 2014. "Mill's Methods, Induction, and Case Sensitivity in Qualitative Comparative Analysis: A Comment on Hug (2013)." *Qualitative & Multi-Method Research* 12, no. 2: 19–24.

———. 2016. "Standards of Good Practice and the Methodology of Necessary Conditions in Qualitative Comparative Analysis." *Political Analysis* 24, no. 4: 478–84.

———. 2018. "The Logic and Methodology of "Necessary but Not Sufficient Causality": A Comment on Necessary Condition Analysis (NCA)." *Sociological Methods & Research*, July 15. doi:10.1177/0049124118782548.

———. 2019. "Beyond the Facts: Limited Empirical Diversity and Causal Inference in Qualitative Comparative Analysis." *Sociological Methods & Research*, November 13. doi:10.1177/0049124119882463.

Thiem, Alrik, Michael Baumgartner, and Damien Bol. 2016. "Still Lost in Translation! A Correction of Three Misunderstandings Between Configurational Comparativists and Regressional Analysts." *Comparative Political Studies* 49, no. 6: 742–74.

Thomann, Eva, and Jörn Ege. 2020. "Qualitative Comparative Analysis (QCA) in Public Administration." In *The Oxford Encyclopedia of Public Administration*, edited by B. Guy Peters and Ian Thynne. Oxford: Oxford University Press.

Thomann, Eva, Peter Hupe, and Fritz Sager. 2018. "Serving Many Masters: Public Accountability in Private Policy Implementation." *Governance* 31, no. 2: 299–319.

Thomann, Eva, and Martino Maggetti. 2020. "Designing Research with Qualitative Comparative Analysis (QCA): Approaches, Challenges, and Tools." *Sociological Methods & Research* 49, no. 2: 356–86.

Tomassi, Paul. 1999. *Logic*. Oxford: Routledge.

Tomini, Luca, and Claudius Wagemann. 2018. "Varieties of Contemporary Democratic Breakdown and Regression: A Comparative Analysis." *European Journal of Political Research* 57, no. 3: 687–716.

Toshkov, Dimiter. 2016. *Research Design in Political Science*. Basingstoke, UK: Palgrave Macmillan.

United Nations. 2018. *Human Development Indices and Indicators*. New York: United Nations Development Program.

Vaisey, Stephen. 2014. "Comment: QCA Works: When Used with Care." *Sociological Methodology* 44, no. 1: 108–12.

Van Esch, Femke A.W.J. 2014. "Exploring the Keynesian–Ordoliberal Divide. Flexibility and Convergence in French and German Leaders' Economic Ideas during the Euro-Crisis." *Journal of Contemporary European Studies* 22, no. 3: 288–302.

Van Esch, Femke A.W.J., Sebastiaan Steenmann, Rik Joosen, Lieke Brand, and Jeroen Snellens 2018. "Final Report for WP3: Making Meaning of the Euro-Crisis." Utrecht University.

Van Evera, Stephen. 1997. *Guide to Methods for Students of Political Science*. Ithaca, NY: Cornell University Press.

Veri, Francesco. 2018. "Coverage in Fuzzy Set Qualitative Comparative Analysis (fsQCA): A New Fuzzy Proposition for Describing Empirical Relevance." *Comparative Sociology* 17, no. 2: 133–58.

———. 2019. "Aggregation Bias and Ambivalent Cases: A New Parameter of Consistency to Understand the Significance of Set-Theoretic Sufficiency in fsQCA." *Comparative Sociology* 18, no. 2: 229–55.

Verweij, Stefan, and Elen-Maarja Trell. 2019. "Qualitative Comparative Analysis (QCA) in Spatial Planning Research and Related Disciplines: A Systematic Literature Review of Applications." *Journal of Planning Literature* 34, no. 3: 300–317.

Vink, Maarten P., and Olaf van Vliet. 2009. "Not Quite Crisp, Not Yet Fuzzy? Assessing the Potentials and Pitfalls of Multi-Value QCA." *Field Methods* 21, no. 3: 265–89.

———. 2013. "Potentials and Pitfalls of Multi-Value QCA: Response to Thiem." *Field Methods* 25, no. 2: 208–13.

Vis, Barbara. 2007. "States of Welfare or States of Workfare? Welfare State Restructuring in 16 Capitalist Democracies, 1985–2002." *Policy & Politics* 35, no. 1: 105–22.

———. 2010. *Politics of Risk-Taking: Welfare State Reform in Advanced Democracies*. Amsterdam: Amsterdam University Press.

———. 2011. "Under Which Conditions Does Spending on Active Labor Market Policies Increase? An fsQCA Analysis of 53 Governments between 1985 and 2003." *European Political Science Review* 3, no. 2: 229–52.

———. 2012. "The Comparative Advantages of fsQCA and Regression Analysis for Moderately Large-*N* Analyses." *Sociological Methods & Research* 41, no. 1: 168–98.

Vis, Barbara, and Jan Dul. 2018. "Analyzing Relationships of Necessity Not Just in Kind but Also in Degree: Complementing fsQCA with NCA." *Sociological Methods & Research* 47, no. 4: 872–99.

Vis, Barbara, Jaap Woldendorp, and Hans Keman. 2013. "Examining Variation in Economic Performance Using Fuzzy-Sets." *Quality & Quantity* 47, no. 4: 1971–89.

Volkens, Andrea, Judith Bara, Ian Budge, and Michael D. McDonald, eds. 2013. *Mapping Policy Preferences from Texts III: Statistical Solutions for Manifesto Analysts*. Oxford: Oxford University Press.

Wagemann, Claudius. 2017. "Qualitative Comparative Analysis (QCA) and Set Theory." In *Oxford Research Encylopedia of Politics*, edited by William R. Thompson, 1–36. Oxford: Oxford University Press.

Wagemann, Claudius, Jonas Buche, and Markus B. Siewert. 2016. "QCA and Business Research: Work in Progress or a Consolidated Agenda?" *Journal of Business Research* 49, no. 7: 2531–10.

Wagemann, Claudius, and Carsten Q. Schneider. 2010. "Qualitative Comparative Analysis (QCA) and Fuzzy-Sets: Agenda for a Research Approach and a Data Analysis Technique." *Comparative Sociology* 9, no. 3: 397–418.

———. 2015. "Transparency Standards in Qualitative Comparative Analysis." *Qualitative & Multi-Method Research* 13, no. 1: 38–42.

Weber, Max. 1922. *Gesammelte Aufsätze zur Wissenschaftslehre*. Tübingen: Mohr.

Whitesitt, J. Eldon. 2010. *Boolean Algebra and Its Applications*. Mineola, NY: Dover.

Wight, Colin. 2007. "A Manifesto for Scientific Realism in IR: Assuming the Can-Opener Won't Work!" *Millennium: Journal of International Studies* 35, no. 2: 379–98.

Williams, Robert L., Cirila Estela Vasquez, Christina M. Getrich, Miria Kano, Blake Boursaw, Crystal Krabbenhoft, and Andrew L. Sussman. 2018. "Racial/Gender Biases in Student Clinical Decision-Making: A Mixed-Method Study of Medical School Attributes Associated with Lower Incidence of Biases." *Journal of General Internal Medicine* 33, no. 12: 2056–64.

Williamson, Jon. 2009. "Probabilistic Theories." In *The Oxford Handbook of Causation*, edited by Helen Beebee, Christopher Hitchcock, and Peter Menzies, 185–212. Oxford: Oxford University Press.

Woodward, James L. 2009. "Agency and Interventionist Theories." In *The Oxford Handbook of Causation*, edited by Helen Beebee, Christopher Hitchcock, and Peter Menzies, 234–62. Oxford: Oxford University Press.

Wurster, Stefan, and Christian Hagemann. 2018. "Two Ways to Success: Expansion of Renewable Energies in Comparison between Germany's Federal States." *Energy Policy* 119: 610–19.

Yamasaki, Sakura, and Benoît Rihoux. 2009. "A Commented Review of Applications." In *Configurational Comparative Methods*, edited by Benoît Rihoux and Charles C. Ragin, 123–45. Thousand Oaks, CA: Sage.

Zadeh, Lotfi A. 1965. "Fuzzy Sets." *Information and Control* 8, no. 1: 338–53.

Zhang, Jiji. 2017. "On the Minimization Principle in the Boolean Approach to Causal Discovery." In *Philosophical Logic: Current Trends in Asia*, edited by Syraya Chin-Mu Yang, Kok Yong Lee, and Hiroakira Ono, 79–94. Singapore: Springer Nature.

Index

Italicized page numbers denote illustrations (*t* for table, *f* for figure).

About the Author

Patrick A. Mello is a visiting scholar at the Willy Brandt School of Public Policy at the University of Erfurt, where he formerly served as the interim Franz Haniel Professor for Public Policy. He is also a *privatdozent* at the TUM School of Governance of the Technical University of Munich. He received a PhD in political science from Humboldt University of Berlin and a habilitation in political science from the Technical University of Munich. His research focuses on the domestic politics of international security and comparative research methods. He is the author of *Democratic Participation in Armed Conflict*, which won the 2015 Dissertation Award from the German Political Science Association. He has taught QCA courses at various institutions, including the European Consortium for Political Research (ECPR) Summer School in Methods and Techniques and the FORS Swiss Summer School in Social Science Methods.